THE AUTHOR (IN HAMMOCK) AND HIS CARRIERS.

THE AUTHOR (AND NATIVE SERVANT) AT HIS BUNGALOW
NEAR WATERLOO (SIERRA LEONE).
The Paw-paw tree (and fruit) in background.

Frontispiece.

SIERRA LEONE:
Its People, Products, and Secret Societies

A journey by Canoe, Rail, and Hammock, through
a land of Kernels, Coconuts, and Cacao, with
Instructions for Planting and Development

BY

H. OSMAN NEWLAND, F.R.Hist.S., F.I.D.

ILLUSTRATED BY 19 PLATES

NEGRO UNIVERSITIES PRESS
NEW YORK

Originally published in 1916
by John Bale, Sons & Danielsson, London

Reprinted 1969 by
Negro Universities Press
A Division of Greenwood Publishing Corp.
New York

SBN 8371-1471-3

PRINTED IN UNITED STATES OF AMERICA

DEDICATED TO

THE RIGHT HONOURABLE LEWIS HARCOURT, M.P.,

IN RECOGNITION OF
HIS INTEREST IN AND WORK FOR WEST AFRICA,
PARTICULARLY WHILE IN OFFICE AS HIS MAJESTY'S
SECRETARY OF STATE FOR THE COLONIES

PREFACE.

SIERRA LEONE has not yet received the attention it deserves. Is it because information has, hitherto, emanated entirely from officials, active or retired? Or is it because, as a recent traveller says, "No one goes to West Africa for pleasure, and of those who gain their livelihood from the country three-fourths regard themselves as martyrs and heroes, counting the days till the steamer shall take them home again"?

Officialdom, martyrdom, heroics attracted me not. For pleasure I sought Sierra Leone, and I found pleasure. Other objects also I had in view. I desired to satisfy myself and some friends at home regarding certain information about which there was ubiquitous uncertainty and considerable contradiction. I wished also to study the life and habits of the West African natives. And I wanted, or believed I wanted, rest; and where else could one better seek rest than in the "White Man's Grave"? But I was not obliged to go.

Once there I was loath to leave. I had accomplished more than I anticipated or intended. The railway carried me within a few miles of Liberia. Canoe, hammock, enthusiasm, and a good constitution did the rest, and enabled me to penetrate into parts of Sierra Leone seldom visited and less frequently described by Europeans. The goodwill and hospitality of the natives procured me knowledge and admission to their inner life, dances, ceremonies, and ideas.

I had settled a boundary dispute, overcome a labour difficulty, reorganized a plantation, and planned out a model native village under European supervision; visited or met European and Creole officials, native chiefs, missionaries, and traders; slept on a native boat, in the bush, in a comfortable European bungalow, and in an equally comfortable native palace.

I had seen Sierra Leone in its "dries" and in its "wets," its swamps, its savannahs, its forests, and its fetishes. I had sampled its fruits, met representatives of its various races, and enjoyed its entertainments. And while thus, I had every reason to like Sierra Leone, I was more fortunate in the fact that Sierra Leone and its people seemed to like me. Not only was I never for a moment indisposed, but I actually felt fitter for the experience. The sun scorched, but never incapacitated. The mosquito and the tsetse-fly left me unmolested. The beasts of the forest manifested no desire to add me to their menu. And, although the crocodile and the snake occasionally cast longing glances in my direction, something else always diverted their attention at the right moment.

Of the people, Creoles and aborigines alike, I have only happy memories. True, one of the chiefs with whom I sojourned has, since my return, been exiled for participation in secret societies—some of which are herein described—and for murders and poisonings said to have taken place within his chiefdom; but tributes to the fallen and disgraced are few, and I am sure my readers will appreciate my story none the less because I record the personal kindness and help which I received from that chief and his people.

One thing alone eluded me. I failed to find rest. Not that I suffered from sleeplessness. But before I left Sierra Leone I discovered that I had never really wanted the rest I fancied I needed; and that had I found it and yielded to it, as so many do, with a temperature of 90° F. to 98° F. in the shade, I should not have returned without a moment's malaria. In such a country rest often brings retribution rather than resurrection. There, as elsewhere, the man who has much to do and loves his work has no time to feel ill. While indulgence in inglorious ease may at home at times be rich in results, there it invites illness.

There is no grave in Sierra Leone, or anywhere in West Africa, save for him who digs one for himself.

That there are, however, vast possibilities in Sierra Leone, and West Africa generally, my readers will gather from the following pages.

This book was originally written for no particular purpose, save for general information and the record of a very happy time; but, as a historian and sociologist, I have naturally given particular attention to the ethnology, customs, and pursuits of the people. After the manuscript was prepared, however, the great World War broke out. This event, while retarding publication of the volume, directed new attention, as the result of Britain's campaign and conquests in West Africa, to this part of our Empire, which has been too long neglected. Great commercial enterprises in Great Britain are seeking not only to capture the German trade there, which was enormous, but also to command or control the sources of the raw material so essential to our oil, food, and rubber industries. Hence, I have revised the MS. to render it up to date and incorporated special chapters dealing with the principal natural products, especially palm kernels, oils, cacao, and rubber, in order that the volume may serve as a general reference book to planters and commercial houses and stimulate investment and enterprise in the Colony.

In describing the different districts of Sierra Leone, I have naturally devoted most space to those parts in which I sojourned longest, and which, while impressing me most, have received less attention from others. In the nomenclature of the various tribes, trees, and territories I have adopted, generally, the spelling used by the Government. For permission to reprint or refer to portions of articles previously written by me I have to acknowledge the courtesy of the Editors of the *Financial Times, Empire Review, Rubber World, Literary Guide,* and the *Colony and Provincial Reporter* of Sierra Leone. To Mr. W. H. Seymour—formerly manager to Messrs. Lever Brothers in Sierra Leone, and recently brought into prominence by his litigation with Liptons, Ltd., in connection with Sierra Leone

concessions—I am also indebted for some of the photographs; and to Mr. Lane Poole, of the Sierra Leone
Forestry Department, for many references on the forest
and agricultural products.

Finally, I have to thank Mr. Hamel Smith, Editor
of *Tropical Life*, for the chatty articles he has contributed (pp. 194-238) for the benefit of those who,
having read what I had to say of Sierra Leone and its
products, may wish to know more practical details concerning the laying out of estates and the raising of
crops which the Colony can produce.

H. O. NEWLAND.

The Authors' Club,
  Whitehall Court, S.W.

CONTENTS.

ILLUSTRATIONS.

SIERRA LEONE :

Its People, Products, and Secret Societies.

CHAPTER I.

ON BOARD THE " MONKEY-BOAT."

THOSE who believe in Fate might say that the author was destined for West Africa. Always interested from early boyhood in African ethnology and in stories and incidents concerning native life, I had, nevertheless, at an early age, let slip two opportunities to work in the Gold Coast and Nigeria, when suddenly circumstances arose which caused me to take a new, peculiar, and preponderating interest in West Africa generally, and in Sierra Leone in particular.

Within a short time this interest became so absorbing that, when one day I was casually asked if I would go to West Africa within two or three weeks, I instantly accepted.

The period of the year at which I left for the Coast was not, perhaps, the best from the health point of view. I should arrive in Sierra Leone during the hottest months of the year and leave it during the " wet " season, passing through plantation and forest, associated in the lay mind with dampness, darkness, and rubber atrocities. But from a sociological standpoint, these were advantages, enabling me to see the country and its people under both climatic conditions. As for malaria, it haunted me not; while the stories

I

of rubber horrors I discounted as I should any missionary tales. And so one spring morn found me on board an African liner, jotting down impressions of what promised to be an eventful and enjoyable tour.

* * * *

To board a West African mail steamer is not now regarded as a mark of heroism. Too many, given up as lost, have returned like the Prodigal Son; and nearness to the White Man's Grave has not converted sinners to saints. The day of the old Coaster has indeed departed, but his sins live after him; and there are still followers in his wake. You see them congregating at that end of the deck where smoke and alcohol reign supreme. Cards, sweepstakes, and cocktails occupy them till they reach the Coast, when any indisposition they may feel is attributed to the damnable climate. Next year, if not before, they will return, and after haunting Liverpool, London, or Manchester for several months with dubious concessions, hoping, like Micawber, for something to turn up, they will re-embark on the "monkey-boat"—but not for the same firm. A few more years and they will have waxed wealthy by impositions on the innocent, or "blackwater" will have claimed them for its own. Yet without them the West African boat would miss one of its best sources of income, as well as some of its characteristic charm.

Then there is the supercilious dapper crowd which forms into quite a separate clique, but leads the sport and tries to lead the fashion and "play the deuce don't-cher-know." These are young subalterns and civilians with certain connections, who are either returning to or joining for the first time their respective regiments or colonial appointments in West Africa. The military element is usually predominant, because among the District Commissioners and their assistants are many ex-subalterns—a useful factor in times of war or tribal dissensions.

Of course, there are exceptions to the supercilious

type. Here and there you can detect the true manly
ring, the official who is neither boastful nor patroniz-
ing—the silent, sympathetic and modest greatness conscious of itself, and that dexterity in difficulty which
no University education or system of examination can
evolve, but which is inherent in a natural leader or
administrator.

These are the kind of men which West Africa wants.
Most of this type appeared to have come direct from
the public schools without going through the University. A good proportion is certainly to be found in
Sierra Leone. But the West African boat would be
poorer without their supercilious brethren; and, after
all, a little hardship and a few tribal wars bring out
the better qualities even of these, while the recent
conquests of Togoland and the Cameroons show how
advantageous it is to have civilian officers who can
be turned into soldiers at short notice.

Of the remaining passengers on board, the adventurer, the educated African, the expert, the missionary,
and the boy traders are the most interesting.

No boat is complete without the man who lives on
his wits, or, perhaps, one should say, on the lack of
wits in others. Every business man and traveller
knows this type. He is always talking in millions and
borrowing half-a-crown, always giving presents—to
inspire confidence, as he thinks—presents which he
has never paid for and never will; always going to
float a prosperous company and never does; always
borrowing and never worth suing. On board the boat
he tips extravagantly, dresses dashingly, and when he
is not playing or drinking in the smoke-room, tries to
frequent the rooms of the captain or chief officer. The
young freshman—trader or D.C.—the missionary, and
even the expert, are frequently duped in one way or
another by this type, but perhaps he is less dangerous
at sea than on land.

The missionary and the expert need no special
comment. Both are out for love of their work alone.

True, the one may save souls and the other rescue companies; the one may reap reward in trading and planting around his mission-house, and the other in discovering a gold mine or a new oil. But the chances of both are probably more remote than those of any others who go to West Africa, unless, indeed, the expert be going out as residential planter or manager.

But the two most neglected types of passengers on board are decidedly the African and the boy trader. The first is travelling home after taking his English degree in arts, law, or medicine, to practise upon his brethren on the Coast. He wants to fraternize with the European on board as he has done in the Inns of Court, in the hotels or the playing fields of England. But the European has left Britain behind. He is *en route* for Africa, and the native of that continent must be kept in his place. Only the missionary or expert will, as a rule, have anything to do with him; the former because he sees a possible convert, the latter to secure possible information, or possibly, perhaps, by virtue of his wider outlook or greater tolerance, strengthened by the fact that he is not living in Africa in any authoritative position for any length of time.

The administrator pays the African too little attention, the missionary too much. Meanwhile the boy traders are worse neglected. These lads—for many are only between 17 and 20, and a few even younger— are going out for the big Liverpool and Manchester firms trading on the West Coast. They start first as store book-keepers on a two or three years' agreement at about £80 a year with food and lodging. Later, they travel up country by rail or river with experienced traders, and, if they survive, ultimately become traders and managers themselves. Some go as book-keepers to plantations or to the mines, and become planters or prospectors. Usually they come from an inferior class to the other passengers except perhaps some of the missionaries on board; and they would be far happier in the second than the first-class saloon. Their

employers usually take first-class passages for them to
keep up the reputation of the firm ; but I am sure most
of them would prefer the difference between the fares
in their pockets.

For the enterprising and healthy youngster there are
great scope and possibilities if he ignore the old
Coaster's habits ; but the ways of the transgressor are
easy and pleasant on the surface, and times have
changed since Pope wrote :—

> " Vice is a creature of such fearful mien
> That to be hated needs but to be seen."

Much incipient disaster is courted on the journey
to and from West Africa; on the other hand, the
voyage itself, with the excellent menu and arrangements of the steamship company, is more conducive
than anything to prepare one for the tropical climate
and recuperate from any of its ill-effects.

Speaking of the boat and its arrangements, one must
not forget the officers. You may travel on many liners
but upon none will there be found such pleasant,
capable, and obliging officers and crew. Messrs. Elder
Dempster's officers are all young, but they are
thoroughly experienced. They are full of life and
vigour, and they are gentlemen. On the first outward
journey on the *Elmina* the author was seated at the
officers' table in the dining saloon, and therefore had
special opportunities of judging. On the ill-fated
Falaba also—upon which I travelled along a portion
of the West Coast—the officers were just the same, and
I should like to take this opportunity to record my
appreciation of those who have departed into the deep
over which they had once so successfully pioneered
others.

*   *   *   *

There is but one halting place between England and
West Africa, and it is not a bad plan to travel thither
by the Union-Castle steamer from Southampton, stay

a few days there and join the West African boat at
" The Islands," or, as they were called by the ancients,
" The Isles of the Blest." Usually the passage is
good, in spite of the proverbial Bay of Biscay, but
sometimes rough seas are encountered in the neighbourhood of Cape Finisterre, and upon this occasion
the waves reached nearly 50 ft. in height.

*   *   *   *

Las Palmas is the doorway of the Tropics, one of
the most cosmopolitan places on earth. Here call the
steamers of all nations, to and from the West Coast,
South Africa, and South America. Here you meet the
devotee of the desert, the adventurer of the Coast, the
millionaire from the mines, and the tourist who wants
to taste of the Tropics without risking its dangers.
It matters not that Canary geographically is not in the
Tropics, but only at its gateway. Its life and manners,
its plants and its people all savour of the Tropics. As
every steamer approaches the harbour it is met by
crowds of boats filled with picturesquely attired natives
and fruit and merchandise of all kinds for sale. A few
are allowed to come up on deck with their wares, others
bargain from below, hoisting their goods by ropes
thrown to the passengers. A charming sight it is,
never to be forgotten. The boats lapped by indigo
waters, the dark upturned faces topped by the broad
sombrero, the women with their immense earrings and
gaily coloured kerchiefs, and a background of rich
green foliage, golden sands, and azure hills rising into
the beautiful blue translucent sky.

The sun has appeared once more in Grand Canary,
and the people are glad. The Levanta wind blows,
and the Canarese are beginning to doze again. For
here, in Las Palmas, no one—no, not even the English
people who bask on the sunlit terraces, or dream under
the shady palms of the Catalina—takes life seriously.
To-day is everything, to-morrow nothing, among the

banana groves and the oranges—those oranges of
Tilde, the finest in the world. In the banana, the
orange, and the English tourist lie the hopes of a
harvest in Canary.

Almost everyone leaves the steamer for a jaunt
through the town on the electric tram or *tartana* (a light
mule trap), or for a repast at the Catalina. A few
pesetas (equivalent to about 9d. each) carry you a long
way in Las Palmas. If you arrive by the Union-Castle
Line and stay a few days awaiting the West African
steamer, a peseta will carry you by motor to Monte,
another peseta will convey you to Tilde and its beautiful orange groves, and quite a moderate sum will
transport you all round the island. The delightful
dances of the Nautical Club or the delusions of the
" Crystal Palace " will, of course, cost considerably
more. If you can spend but a few hours, a couple of
pesetas will take you by *tartana* right through and
around the town, giving you a far more comprehensive
insight into the place than by boarding the electric
tramway which runs from the port to the market-place
through the principal thoroughfare. The driver of the
tartana, by the way, will certainly take you to the
English cemetery and point out the graves of many
of those who have been laid to rest here on their
homeward journey from West Africa. I remember
my Canarese Jehu scanning me curiously, either to
see how I enjoyed his story or to hazard a guess as
to the probability of my candidature for the next
tombstone. He must have thought me a hardened
sinner; but, in truth, I had heard this kind of thing
so often, while Alpine climbing, from guides who
persist in pointing out and even halting at points and
precipices where someone has been killed, that I did not
even press into his palm an extra peseta for his prayers
on my behalf. He had his revenge, however, for he
nearly jolted the breath out of me when returning on
the wretched road between the Metropole Hotel (now
closed) and the port. This road the late Sir Alfred

Jones offered to make and maintain, an offer the Government declined lest the islanders might desire all their roads equally good !

* * * *

Once again we are on the ocean, with infinite space about and above us. The air seems full of idle dreamy thoughts and expectations. Sports beguile the morn, and music whiles away the evening. Within two days from Las Palmas we enter the Tropics. All the officers appear in white uniforms, awnings are up, and sunshine or sleep seems the order of the day. A sunset of saffron, scarlet, and sapphire ushers in the night.

The following day we enter the " death-trap " between Cape Verde and Sierra Leone. The name has been earned because many homeward-bound passengers are said to catch cold and fever here after leaving the Coast.

A more impressive sight could not be imagined. The ocean here appears immense in its loneliness. The South African liners have left for another track; and so silent and deserted seems the mighty deep that we could imagine ourselves traversing an unknown sea. Apart from flying-fish and porpoises, an occasional sea bird, and a few whales and sharks, nothing is visible but the dark blue waters and the bluer sky; but the old Coaster will tell you he can smell the Coast.

The Coast steamer preceding us was suddenly stopped in this part of the ocean by a whale 35 ft. long and 16 ft. broad, which jammed its head between two blades of the propeller and the upper part of the stern-post, so that the propeller could move neither way.

A couple of days more, at latest, we enter the pretty harbour of Freetown. A sea haze envelops the land in a mantle of white wool as the Coast first comes in sight, but this quickly lifting reveals a picture deeply green in spite of the relentless glare of an African sun.

Attractive though Freetown appears from the steamer, with its high hills clothed in verdure, its steep streets

teeming with life, and its many coloured roofs and
buildings interspersed with its precious palms, none
but those who have business or want a little relaxation
appear disposed to disembark. You hear the place called
" The Hole "; you listen to the uncomplimentary remarks regarding the impertinent natives, with fearful
tales of the deadliness of the climate; but if you are
wise you will nevertheless go ashore, and come back
alive and pleased, as I did.

CHAPTER II.

THE WHITE MAN'S GRAVE.

The Black Man's Country—Sharks and Vultures—West African
Esperanto—Means of Locomotion—Creole and Aborigine—
Black Belles—The Markets and Hill Station.

SIERRA LEONE is perhaps the most typical, most
representative Colony of West Africa, certainly of the
black man's country. For here the black man rules.
The municipality and many of the principal public
offices are in his hands. He is represented in the
Legislative Assembly. He preponderates everywhere.
Out of an entire population throughout Colony and
Protectorate, 1,505,000 are Africans, only about 850
Europeans. You become aware of this before you
leave the steamer. The Customs officer, who comes
on board in the regulation uniform, is black. His
gig is rowed by blacks, although they may be dressed
as British sailors. Everybody that you can see ashore
is black.

Around you are many European steamers, coaling,
watering, victualling, loading or discharging cargo.
The sight is superb. But only after you have visited
other ports along the coast do you realize why more
ships call at Sierra Leone than at any other West
African port. Accessibility to the shore, facilities for
coaling, and the possession of an excellent water supply
give it this pre-eminence.

But look up the broad waterway leading to the palm-
lands beyond, from whence the Rokelle and other
rivers flow to join in one fine estuary to meet the
sea! Gaze upon the magnificent range of hills which
gave to the Colony its name, and watch the palm trees

fan the fringe of hot and hazy green. Then you may
realize that Sierra Leone has other charms than that
of usefulness.

Mrs. Mary Gaunt, in recording her first impressions
of Sierra Leone in 1911, describes Freetown as "the
most beautiful spot on the West Coast." And, as
you are conveyed to the shore by electric pinnace or
native sculls, the picture she draws is certainly more
and more impressed upon you by its vividness and
beauty. In the real scene, however, are two features
which the artist forgot to depict, but which may dis-
concert the visitor—the occasional glimpse of a shark
in the waters, longingly awaiting an accident or mis-
chance, and the appearance of vultures and huge crows
on the roofs, likewise awaiting prey. But these are
only heralds of what is to be met in West Africa,
whetting the appetite of the adventurous Englishman
for more.

The harbour is formed by the Bullom shore—a long,
low strip of land to the north—and by the peninsula
terminating in the sandy promontory, Cape Sierra
Leone, to the south, the latter conspicuously displaying a lighthouse. The three bays or creeks, Pirate
Bay, English Bay, and Kru Bay, with smooth yellow
sand, are fringed by forests of palms, cotton trees, and
occasional baobabs. Above, the well-wooded hills rise
to form spurs of the Sierra Leone itself, the summit
of which is 2,500 ft. Milton describes Notus and
Afer, in "Paradise Lost," as "black with thunderous
clouds from Sierra Lona."

Next in conspicuousness is the Sugar Loaf mountain, which, with the Aruma hill, is a favourite resort
for picnics and gala days.

Getting ashore here is easy. There is no surf or
extortionate charge. The black boys are all licensed,
and the Government has fixed the charge at one
shilling. Compare this with other ports on the Coast,
at Accra, for example, where it costs nearly ten shillings
to land. The boat-boys also at Freetown are im-

measurably superior—except, perhaps, in physique—
to the Krus, who do all the beach-boating along the
Liberian, Ivory, and Gold Coasts. The Krus are pre-
eminently the sailors of West Africa, and are always
to be found on the liners. They are well built and
sturdy, and appear to be the most popular blacks
among the British, probably because of their marine
instincts; but they are despised by many of the Coast
tribes, who apply to them an epithet meaning "home-
less," "without a country," or "no patriot," because,
although originally coming from Liberia, they have
now no definite territory, but are wanderers and servants to any man. Afloat, the Kru has a reputation
for pilfering; but as a personal attendant he is regarded
as honest.

All the races along the Coast, in their dealings with
the white man, appear to speak a common dialect
known as "Kru English." You hear it first on the
steamer as she arrives in the harbour, when a few black
boys come aboard to offer themselves as personal
attendants. You hear it again while being conveyed
to the shore.

Once on land you are assailed by this quaint but
not unpleasant tongue, which is spoken among the
people of Freetown themselves.

"How do ma?" you hear one "mammy" (married
woman) say to another.

"Yes, ma, thank God," the other replies.

"Wass matter you? You go talk so," says another "mammy" to her boy attendant (meaning
What's the matter? Stop talking); to which the
impudent boy replies, "Ma, I no find you pyjama-
house" (I won't look for your nightdress bag).

If you buy something of one of the women selling
fruit, nuts, or other merchandise from a calabash, it
is ten chances to one that before you pay, her "boy"
comes forward from behind and, holding out his hand,
says, "Gie me heen ooman coppa all" (I take all
the woman's money). After a little initiation you

pick up much of this West African Esperanto and realize that " fit " means able or ready; " chop," something substantial to eat; " find " = look for; " look " = see; " kiddens " = kidneys; " lib " = free, or at home; " libba " = liver, or bad temper; " savvy " (a corruption of *savez*) = to know, or understand.

A prolonged experience is necessary, however, to fathom some of its eccentricities, *e.g.*, when your boy tells you your " sock catch leak," meaning your foot-wear has a hole in it.

And thus, amid this jargon and clatter of tongues, under a sweltering sun, I made my way from the harbour—after passing my luggage through the Customs and paying duty on my camera—up the toilsome steps which lead from the quay to the principal thoroughfare, Water Street, where the railway station is situated. Here some of the glamour of the picture from the sea is somewhat, but by no means entirely, dispelled.

The main town consists of three- and four-storeyed red and white stone buildings. The streets are wide and some are crowded, but grass still grows in patches on the sidewalks of a few thoroughfares, and all are lighted by kerosene lamps, although a concession to light the town by electricity was granted long ago.

The principal buildings are the new Law Courts in Westmoreland Street, the Bank of British West Africa, the Colonial Hospital, the Cathedral, and, of course, the Government and Municipal Buildings, and the large trading companies' depots. Some excellent new buildings are in course of construction.

Whatever disappointment may be felt in viewing some of the older architectural adornments of the town is amply compensated for in the people. There are about 850 Europeans in the whole of the Colony, and most of these live in Freetown and Hill Station; the whole population of the Colony proper being about 78,000, and that of the Protectorate about 1,500,000. Of this number there are nearly 3,000 Syrians resident around Freetown, and engaged in trading, and a black population of 50,000 is resident there.

The substantial tradesmen stand in their shops, but innumerable stalls line the thoroughfares, with women and children selling fruit, tobacco, cotton goods, and all sorts of merchandise. Stately Mandingoes in resplendent dress, white-robed Susus and Temnes, Mendis clad only in old breeches, and Creole clerks, professional men and traders, dressed in the latest European fashion, jostle each other in the crowded streets.

Here a European is carried along in a hammock, or saunters along under a pith helmet, and sometimes a white or green umbrella; there a rich Creole is conveyed through the streets by a rickshaw propelled by a couple of boys—for no horses are, as a rule, seen in Freetown, and even the importation of donkeys from Gambia has proved a failure.

These rickshaws, by the way, are very comfortable. On my return to Freetown, on the way home, Dr. Easmon, the cultured, clever, and well-known Sierra-Leonean doctor, placed one at my disposal while I remained in the capital, and very welcome it was, for in the wet season the state of the streets here is little short of abominable.

The motor-'bus is now suggested as a means of transport, and, perhaps, will be adopted.

The Creoles are, generally speaking, the descendants of the emancipated slaves from various parts of America, who were dumped down here first by British philanthropists and subsequently by the Government at various intervals during the latter part of the eighteenth and beginning of the nineteenth centuries, as mentioned elsewhere. Strictly speaking, the application of the word to the present inhabitants of the Sierra Leone peninsula is misleading. A " Creole " (from the Spanish *criollo* = native-born) is really " one of any colour born within or near the tropics of America," or, used in its more exclusive sense, " a

native of the West Indies or of Spanish America, but
not of native blood." Most of the original settlers
brought to Sierra Leone by the British would certainly
be correctly described as Creoles—although many of
these were African slaves liberated by British ships
before they reached America, and have practically died
out; but the present population would be more accu-
rately named Sierra Leoneans, as being born in Sierra
Leone. As, however, many of the people prefer the
term, and as the original inhabitants of the country
always call them by that name, it will probably remain.
Yet it is surely paradoxical that the three newspapers
run by these people, each more or less advocating unity
and larger powers of self-government for the black
races, should continue to designate the people they
represent by a name which is not only non-British,
but is absolutely alien to Africa and Africans.

Suppose that the Jews had adopted the name by
which they are said to have been known in the land
of their captivity, or any other Egyptian nomenclature!

For many years after the Creoles came to the Colony
they anticipated or "universally harboured a desire for
returning to America," and according to a Report of
the Sierra Leone Company, dated 1804, few of the
original settlers or their descendants remained after the
middle of the nineteenth century. Perhaps this was
the reason for their clinging to a name which their
descendants, with less reason, retain.

So much for the Creole. Of the other races I will
speak later. But the women of all types met in Freetown and elsewhere in Sierra Leone deserve a special
word. The African woman is perhaps the most
striking of all the inhabitants, possibly because she
seems more natural—possibly, also, because she forms
such a contrast among women whose lot is cast
in no easy path, and upon whom much of the labour
and responsibility of the world are thrown. Few girls
of the labouring classes of Europe can be described

as beautiful or shapely. The West African " tee-tee "
—as the young girl is called—is both. A jovial coun-
tenance, a perennial smile displaying conspicuously
dazzling white teeth, a well-poised head covered with
a coloured kerchief, a graceful, shapely figure scarcely
concealed by a gauzy gown wound round the waist
and flung over the plump, rounded shoulders, to hang
down on one side, leaving the fine arms and bosom
bare—such is the West African girl at the age of
puberty and, for a time, afterwards. Even when they
are "mammies," or married women, of some experience, they retain the teeth and smile. To please her
is to gain much. Cross her, and she will not rest till
her menfolk have avenged her. Of the position and
influence of women in the Protectorate more anon.

Freetown has developed remarkably within recent
years. The once vacant land at Upper Garrison Street,
known and called in native parlance " The Fort," is
now converted into the Victoria Park; the vacant land
at East Battery, formerly known as the Battery, is
now partly a fort and partly a railway market. The
land at King Tom's is now converted to a fort and
quarters of the Royal Artillery. The side now occupied by the railway compounds and quarters for
European employés of the railway was, until comparatively recent years, a wilderness known as the
Racecourse; in that locality land was not much thought
of, either on account of the barrenness of the soil or
its distance from the heart of the town.

Victoria Park was the outcome of spontaneous
loyalty of the people of Sierra Leone to the British
Crown at a representative meeting of the inhabitants
of the Colony, summoned at Government House by
His Excellency Sir Frederick Cardew, in 1897, when
it was decided by a large majority that the com-
memoration of the Diamond Jubilee reign of our late
Sovereign, Queen Victoria, should take the form of a
park in the city. Voluntary subscriptions were raised
for the purpose, and on June 20, 1900, Victoria

Park was opened to the public. The site is vested in the Municipal Corporation of Freetown, which is pledged to provide for its upkeep.

Freetown has five public markets : the Vegetable Market in Water Street, called in native parlance " big market," and dating back to 1861 ; the Meat Market in Garrison Street, colloquially named " Grain Market," opened in 1862; the City Market in Kroo Town Road, erected in 1899, at a cost of £2,000, by the late Sir Samuel Lewis; the King Jimmy Market in King Jimmy Wharf, Water Street, opened in 1909; and the Fish Market in Rock Street. There is also a slaughter-house in King Jimmy Wharf, Water Street.

The Freetown Municipality Ordinance of 1893 shifted the burden of providing markets in the city from the shoulders of the Colonial Government to the head of the Municipal Corporation of Freetown, and vested the then existing markets and slaughter-house in this native body.

* * * *

While contemplating the busy market scenes, a native dropped dead, apparently from exhaustion, and almost simultaneously a European trader was affected by sunstroke. These events reminded me suddenly that I was in "the White Man's Grave." But the next moment I assured myself that the two events occurring together and in my sight were but a coincidence which might easily have happened elsewhere. The heat and drought also were exceptional this year, as everyone was remarking, the thermometer registering 98° F. in the shade. At any time Freetown, in the dry season, is particularly warm, and, surrounded as it is by lofty hills, very little air finds its way into the town. Even the sea breeze seems to become heated and dampened by its passage over the burning ground, and its free entry is further checked by the many intricacies of the streets and buildings. The sea wind is said to be more dangerous to Europeans than the heat itself. Every evening it blows smartly landward, chilling the atmosphere and the bodies of unwary folk who avail themselves of these pleasant if dangerous draughts.

The Charlotte Falls, the Flat Stone, and the Mirimbo reservoir I was obliged to leave until my return.

The Freetown people are very anxious to have their town lighted by electricity. In the year 1894, about 107 years after Sierra Leone became a British Colony, there were only about sixty lamps, engaging the attention of four lamp-lighters, to light the whole of Freetown. Until December 31, 1895, the streets of the city were lighted by the Colonial Government.

The Freetown Municipality having come into existence in the month of August, 1895, became the authority responsible for the lighting of the streets by virtue of the provisions of the Freetown Municipal Ordnance, but it was not until January, 1896, that the City Council relieved the Colonial Government of the duty of lighting the streets of the city. At present there are about 332 lamp-pillars with street lamps, necessitating the employment of thirty lamp-lighters, and the actual sum of money spent each year in street lights is over £1,100. Despite these rapid improvements in the programme of the City Council, it is manifest to every citizen and ratepayer that the lighting of the streets by kerosene oil is most unsatisfactory and a waste of public money. It had always been the intention of the City Council, since its inception, to light the city by electricity, but not being in a position financially to install electric energy in the city for the purpose of lighting the streets, the City Council had, on three distinct occasions, granted to individuals the exclusive right of installing electricity in the city for a definite and specified period of time. The first two of such concessions lapsed through default on the part of the respective concessionaires to carry out their contracts. The last concession, though granted some years ago, was still, when I was there, *in nubibus* as regards its operation.

However defective in lighting Freetown may be, the same cannot be said regarding its educational establishments. There are about 100 primary schools in the Colony, teaching about 4,000 children, besides five Muhammadan schools (of which four are in Freetown), in which about 1,000 children are educated.[1] In addition there are secondary and technical schools, Fourah Bay College, and the excellent Government School for Chiefs, formerly at Bo, and now at Moyamba.

There is a course of lectures to school teachers on manual training at the Government Model School. About sixty-eight school-masters and teachers attended the 1913 course; about twenty-six of this number came from the suburban villages in the neighbourhood, and forty-two, including the Model School teachers, were city pedagogues. Punctuality and regularity were noticeable on all occasions. The lectures comprised the following subjects : Clay or plasticine modelling, paper cutting and folding, cardboard modelling, colouring, model drawing, practical geometry, and woodwork.

Most of the white people, however, live at Hill Station. Hill Station is a township designed exclusively for Europeans, and built at an altitude of 800 ft. near the western end of the half-circle of high hills overlooking Freetown and the harbour.

The mountain railway gives access to the station, while a pure water supply, beautiful scenery, and provision for tennis and other games enable the residents to live under pleasant and healthy conditions. Not in these things, however, does the distinctive interest of this place lie. The notable fact is that the Hill Station in Sierra Leone was planned and designed as a fortress against the mosquito, and was the first important tangible sign that war was to be waged against

---

[1] For further information on education in Sierra Leone see the author's "Local Government Handbook on Education."

malaria. The township is intended for European residents only, and this principle of segregation is carried out as far as practicable; thus, there are no houses with native children, and each resident has to comply with the Government rule that not more than one native servant is to sleep on the premises.

The journey there by the mountain railway takes half an hour, the return fare being 1s. 3d. first class, 10d. second class, 5d. third class. The freshness and healthful effect on body and mind are said to be as twilight is to the noonday sun, and it is one of the few places in West Africa where white ladies can dwell with comparative safety from fever. I only paid a flying visit there, however, finding the Bank at Freetown and the residence of one of the councillors quite comfortable enough for my short sojourn in the capital.

CHAPTER III.

From Freetown to Christineville.

Railway Travelling in Sierra Leone—An Educated Creole—
Kline Town and Kissy—Kissis and Mendis as Carriers—
Forests, Savannahs, and Ginger Farms—Hastings and
Rokelle—Laterite Hills—Devil Hole.

Clang! Clang!

Sipping tea in the cool and comfortable drawing-room
of the bank with one of the most genial and capable
Europeans on the Coast, the Honourable Isaac Slater,
of the Legislative Assembly and Resident Manager of
the Bank of British West Africa, I had almost forgotten
that I was in the Tropics.

Clang! Clang!

Again that universal sound, announcing the approaching arrival or departure of a train. In spite of its
familiar and European sound, it brought me back to
Africa. Involuntarily I looked at my watch. Four-
fifteen!

At four-thirty the last train leaves Freetown for
Waterloo, and I must catch it at all costs. A hasty
au revoir to the bank, with a promise of a longer rest
there upon my return, and I was speeding down the
hill to the station at a pace common enough in England,
but not understood in Sierra Leone.

* * * *

Freetown Station is an interesting but noisy place.
Always a crowd and plenty of chatter and colour. You
have to push your way among Europeans in white or
khaki, natives from the interior with striped hats of
various hues and almost destitute of other clothing, and
Sierra Leoneans or inhabitants of the Freetown district

in varieties of European dress. Only a small portion
of this crowd is actually travelling by the train; but the
departure or arrival of a boat or train always attracts
a large gathering of people. Very little notice is given
of the intention of the train to start; but possibly the
noise and excitement make the departure seem more
sudden than it actually is.

The ex-Governor of the Colony recently offended the
population by remarking that they were " born in noise,
live in noise, and die in noise." He was quite right.
Not the words, but the deprecating manner in which
they were believed to have been uttered caused the ill-
feeling. He was himself of a quiet nature, and had
come from the East, where the natives are less noisy,
Oriental languor and passivity lending different characteristics to mind, body, and language. The African is
absolutely different to the Asiatic, and requires different
treatment. I may have bad taste, but, on the whole,
I prefer him and his noise to many an Oriental, just
as I would a tiresome child to one sullen and suspicious.

*   *   *   *

Suddenly, while I was surveying this noisy interesting scene, and wondering when my luggage would be
put in, there was a shrill whistle and the train began
to move. Hastily I told the station-master to throw on
quickly what luggage he could, and send the rest on
to-morrow morning. Then, snatching the smallest
packet containing toilet necessaries, bush garments, and
some underwear, I jumped on the moving train to the
amazement of the whole assembly, who apparently had
never before seen a European in a hurry. Certainly
none of them had tried the experiment themselves.
Shouts and entreaties to remain I heard, but heeded
them not. Determined to reach Devil Hole that night,
off I went with the train. Then it occurred to me that
my medicine chest with the indispensable quinine was
among the packages left behind. Now I had been
ordered to take 5 gr. daily. The first dose I had

taken religiously the night before we arrived in Freetown. This evening I should have to break the in-
junction unless I could borrow some. But before night
had arrived I had forgotten all about it, and next day,
although my luggage did not arrive, I felt so well that
I decided that, rather than borrow, 1 would forego the
potion until my medicine-chest arrived. This event
occurred five days later, so I decided henceforth to
take only 5 gr. once a week, which I did. I am
inclined to agree with those medical authorities who
argue that too much quinine prepares the way for
blackwater fever, but of this a few words later.

*   *   *   *

The accommodation afforded to travellers by the
Sierra Leone Government Railway is by no means equal
to that given by the Nigerian railway authorities.
Travelling on the Lagos line is as comfortable as in
Europe. Corridor saloons, dining cars with plenty of
provender, electric light, baths, electric fans, and everything that can be desired, including reasonable speed.
On the Sierra Leone railway no such travelling arrangements are made. A whole day is expended in reaching
Bo, a distance of 120 miles, and if your destination be
farther you are obliged to stay the night at Bo and
continue the journey next day. First-class accommodation consists of two or three arm-chairs with
caned seats, akin to the "Derby" chairs of our great-
grandmothers, very comfortable and sanitary, but cold
and unattractive-looking. The floors are frequently
covered with a fine dust or sand in the "dries" and
flooded with rain in the "wets," for when it rains in
West Africa there is never a shower, but a deluge. At
such times—and, I am sorry to say, at almost all times
—the opposite chairs if vacant are used as foot-rests.
Nor is this all. The head also has to be protected
from the drippings through the roof of the carriage,
and your general atmosphere has to be guarded, or the
neighbouring second-class passengers will invade your

compartment to escape the equally bad or worse conditions of their horse-boxes. My advice to intending travellers up country in the wet season is to be well equipped with good temper, patience, endurance, rainproof coats, rubber Wellingtons, umbrellas, and uniform steel trunks on wheels or waterproof bags. I had neither umbrella nor steel trunk—no, and not even Wellingtons—but I was happy.

In West Africa, like India, the white man, even though he be but a trading assistant, must travel first class, if only to maintain his dignity and status, and enjoy a chair to himself. Unlike India, however, the West African first-class carriage is not the monopoly of the white man. The wealthy educated African can and does travel first class. There are many rich Sierra Leoneans, and very agreeable companions are many of them. I travelled some distance with a very cultured African, who had studied law, philosophy, and medicine in London after a preliminary education at Fourah Bay College, Sierra Leone. He had chosen the Bar as a profession, but we found a mutual basis of conversation and sympathy first in philosophy and ethics—particularly in the theories of Spinoza, Berkeley, and Herbert Spencer—and afterwards in the products and possibilities of the country through which we were travelling. I gained a fund of information regarding the land, which I could scarcely have obtained from the ordinary white traveller, and I hope I gave him a *quid pro quo* in my personal reminiscences of the late Herbert Spencer.

My black companion knew the history of the principal farms and villages which we passed *en route,* the trees, the soil, and even the minerals under the different soils, or where they are supposed or ought to be. Naturally, I discounted considerably his views as to the possible mineral wealth of the country—every educated native of any country always has an exaggerated idea of what may be found under the soil of the Homeland—especially when he talked of bitumen and even of gold; but, generally, his tone was rational and his information useful. Perhaps he was inclined to be dogmatic; but that is a common fault of scholars of all belief and colour, unless they have roughed it among all classes of the community and enjoyed plenty of physical as well as mental education.

*   *   *   *

In the meantime we were passing through the picturesque suburbs of Freetown to Kline Town, which is becoming quite a serious rival as a trading centre. To this place Lever Brothers have already transferred their port factory.

How different this business activity and the prosperous-looking houses from the picture of these parts presented to us by Surgeon Atkins, R.N., of H.M.S. *Swallow*, in 1721 :—

" The country about Sierra Leone is so thick-spread with wood that you cannot penetrate a pole's length from the waterside, unless between the town and fountain whence they fetch their water, without a great deal of difficulty. They have paths, however, through these woods to their lollas and lugars which, though but a mile or two from the town, are frequently the walks of wild beasts. Their houses are low little huts, built with wooden stockades (or forkillas) set in the ground in a round or square form and thatched with straw."

To-day the railroad pierces the groves of palm trees which have not been cut down by squatters, and crawls up the mountain-side, which is still covered by a part of the primeval forest. Upon the plains are dotted many villages. Trudging the roads are innumerable native traders.

Kissy is a particularly interesting place. Most of the people inhabiting the villages within ten miles of Freetown are descendants of the Creoles before mentioned. The people who founded the village of Kissy differ, however, from the inhabitants of the other villages. Their forefathers were natives of the district of Kissy, lying between Falaba and the sources of the Niger, originally a savage and barbarous race, who lived entirely on the sale of slaves, even their wives and children being sold into slavery. Several hundreds of this tribe having been captured from slave ships by British men-of-war, it was considered desirable to locate them in one place. They were therefore settled in this beautiful village, named after their own country.

These people—the Kissis—have a peculiar way of carrying their loads. A kind of basket made of twisted palm leaves, and in shape semi-cylindrical, is packed with kernels or other commodities and slung over the back by two braces, one passing under each armpit and over the corresponding shoulder, a third brace leading from the top of the basket and passing around the forehead. Men who carry loads in this way are not half so sturdy as the Mendis, who always carry their loads on the top of their heads.

*　　*　　*　　*

The train now takes its course over wonderful ravines fringed by beautiful palms, and occasionally refreshed by a small waterfall or stream. The Government has done much to retain this beautiful scenery, backed by the lofty hills, which give the Colony such an excellent water supply.

The forests here act as protective covering to the moisture in the soil, and are responsible for a high percentage of the total amount of water held in suspension by the atmosphere, thus increasing the relative humidity of the atmosphere in their neighbourhood. The effects of irrigation are negligible in comparison with the effects brought about by forests, so far as the humidity of the atmosphere is concerned.

The native of Sierra Leone, blessed with a water supply which is exceptional in West Africa, and which is admittedly one of the finest features of the country, is apt to forget this unless gently reminded by a wise paternal Government. Having found the destruction of forest beneficial for agriculture in the plain, the un-tutored native would eliminate even more ruthlessly the trees upon the hillsides. He realizes not that the dangers attending the destruction of forest in the mountains are more serious than in the plain. The mountains are formed of large masses of syenite rock covered with a thin layer of soil. This soil is held together by the vegetation that covers it. Once the vegetation is removed and the ground cultivated, there is nothing to retain the soil, which is washed down the sides of the mountains into the rivers and carried out to sea. The natives take two successive crops from virgin forest soil. This makes the total destruction of the vegetation possible in two years. Farther up the line, especially after the border-line between the Colony and Protectorate is passed, this evil has been amply demonstrated.

There the torrential tropical rains, instead of sinking into a bed of forest soil and down through the fissures of the syenite to break out in springs lower down, rush off the mountains into the valley, often causing short-lived but violent floods. During the dry season, on the other hand, where the forest has been removed, the springs dry up. Thus, instead of perennially running water, the rivers are converted into torrents in the rains and detached pools in the dry season.

Mountain ranges, offering a cold surface to the moisture-laden winds, increase the precipitation. This effect is more marked when the range is covered with forest, the reason being that the mean temperature in the forest is several degrees lower than the surrounding country. Even in some portions of the Colony through which I am now passing, and which came under British administration later, this is noticeable.

The forest here was no doubt formerly much larger, but the making of ginger farms on the slopes of the mountains has very much reduced the original forest, which probably extended right down to the water's edge where now the mangrove holds sway.

The underlying rock of the whole area is syenite, which crops out especially on the summits of the higher mountains, making very steep cliffs. In some parts laterite is found, especially by the plain just outside Waterloo.

The syenite weathers into a very good soil, reddish loam, forming an excellent natural seed-bed. The laterite, on the other hand, tends to harden at first on exposure, though it afterwards breaks up into small pieces varying from an eighth of an inch to an inch in diameter, and forms a very poor soil.

*   *   *   *

Time passed so quickly while noting the varied character of the country through which we were passing that Hastings and Rokelle were reached before I realized that in another half an hour I should arrive at my destination for the night.

Hastings is one of the four villages where the eighty-five settlers from Barbados established themselves in 1817, and were reinforced by the discharged soldiers of the 4th West Indian Regiment. It is therefore essentially Creole in character and not African.

The next, and far prettier village, Rokelle, is peopled by a mixed race, some Creole, some Temnes, some a hybrid production of the two races. The name of the village is essentially a reminder of the old Temne domination when Kwaia (Quiah) country embraced all this territory. There is another and larger Rokelle on the river of the same name.

From Rokelle the scenery again became wilder, and as we passed on a slender bridge over an impressive natural chasm, I assured myself that this was really a " devil " hole, and that my journey for that day was over.

CHAPTER IV.

First Night in the Interior.

Absence of Twilight—Charm of the Sunset Hour—A Scramble in
the Dark—Snakes and Insects—Telegraphic Eccentricities—
" Chop "—A Discourse on Drinks—A Romantic Rubber
Plantation.

NEVER shall I forget my first night in the interior
of Sierra Leone.

Arriving at the flag station called Devil Hole about
half-past six in the evening, and expecting to find the
assistant manager of the plantation waiting to receive
me, I beheld only two Africans. One was attired in
respectable European fashion, the other was in native
garb.

Apparently I was unexpected; but, having announced
myself, the first dusky stranger, with every deference,
introduced himself as the native clerk. Then, quickly
sending up his companion to the nearest *zimbek* to
announce my arrival and obtain boys, hammock, and
lamps to escort me to the European bungalow, he
hastily jumped upon the moving train and was
whirled away into the shadows,

"Leaving the world to darkness and to me."

This hasty retreat, I afterwards learned, was due to
his home being beyond Waterloo, the next station,
and this train being the last.

For a few moments I was dumbfounded, bewildered.

Day had now become night. For here twilight is
practically unknown. Once the day begins to decline
darkness descends rapidly. But though the dreaminess
of dusk is denied to the African, the silence of the
sunset hour has a weirdness all its own. The evening

meal is being eaten. The flare of camp fires and sounds of savage revelries have not yet broken upon the night. Tick, tick !

So still was the silence that I heard my watch ticking. The sound brought me back from a momentary dreamland. Here was I, alone in the gloom, in a strange land on the verge of forest and bush teeming with insect and animal life. Far up the hillside, above rows of trees, I could distinguish a twinkle of lights from the bungalow. On my right the hillside broke away into a chasm which had been christened by the unholy name of "Devil Hole." Before me loomed the pathway to the bungalow more than a mile distant; behind was the one thing which linked me to civilization—the iron railroad, unlighted and deserted.

Quickly I made for the *zimbek* to which I had seen the second native hasten. The apparition of a white man set feet scrambling, tongues talking, lights to appear in the gloom, and general commotion.

A *zimbek*, I should explain, is a native hut, often built only of mud, but sometimes of wood, bamboo and mud, with thatched roof.

In a few minutes two or three boys were ready to accompany me, but they had left the hurricane lamps, they explained, at the bungalow, and the hammocks were in the store half a mile away. I decided to dispense with both, and gave the order to proceed to the bungalow. The boys conducted me up with great speed. They do not love the darkness and they had hoped that I would not ascend without lights or hammock. Afterwards I learned that at this hour of the evening, and just before dawn, snakes prefer to peer about for their victims. At the time I was unaware that these reptiles frequented this spot. More than once after this did I experience in West Africa that "ignorance is bliss."

The journey up the hillside seemed interminable. The moon had not yet risen, and the silence which succeeds the sunset remained unbroken save for the buzzing of insects and the melancholy drip, drip, drip of the dew on leaf and branch. The wavy spear-grass lining the path and the tearful trees at each succeeding bend cast their quaint shadows across the path as here and there the flickering light from the bungalows shot through some side clearing or new plantation path. The general darkness prevented me from perceiving the cultivated parts on either side of the cleared areas as I proceeded, but I saw enough to assure me that it was not the swamp or bare hillside which a few ill-informed critics in the city had proclaimed.

At last out of the gloom of the trees lights loomed, and there came in sight a bungalow raised high upon wooden supports and platform in the midst of an open square, which was arranged, I could dimly see, like an English garden.

Arrived at the bungalow, I was accorded a hearty reception, with profuse apologies for my unceremonious arrival and escort. The telegram announcing my advent in the Colony had not been received. At noon the following day it was brought in by one of the boys who was sent to Waterloo for letters.

Waterloo, I should explain at this point, is the nearest town, about three or four miles distant. The telegraphs are under the railway and not the post office authorities, and the native station-master had apparently detained the telegram till he could see one of our messengers. Incidentally, he had pocketed the ninepence porterage which I had paid. Needless to say, the case was taken up and the money refunded.

A good rub down and a change into pyjamas soon refreshed me, and the first natural stiffness between the plantation managers and myself having quickly worn off, we sat down to " chop."

* * * *

" Chop " is the word used indiscriminately for breakfast, lunch, dinner, or supper. Presumably the term is derived from the old English chop-house, or it may be reminiscent of cannibal days. At any rate, it is a welcome word out here in West Africa, and without it the planter would be poor indeed.

The evening meal usually consists of soup, fish, meat (when it can be obtained) or chicken, cheese, or nuts, and perhaps fruit. Many people will not touch fruit here in the evening, but I did.

As to what constitutes " chop " at other times in the day, that depends upon the European's tastes and requirements. Some planters and traders eschew breakfasts altogether. The " no breakfast " brigade has quite a following in the Tropics, but I have never in that region come across an apostle of the " no hat " brigade. If that ilk ever had a representative in Sierra Leone sunstroke must have claimed him, for here even the natives wear caps or some sort of covering, or else they take care to keep in the shade.

However, to return to " chop." As I have said, some white people apparently prefer to be breakfastless. I never was one of that fellowship. I always enjoy a good early morning meal at home, and I made no change out here. Bananas, pineapple, or paw-paw, scrambled eggs and toast usually formed the nucleus of such a meal.

Midday " chop," which is partaken of between 11 a.m. and 1 or 2 p.m.—which time is a sort of siesta in West Africa—is much the same as an evening meal, possibly a dish less. The soup is usually composed of ground-nuts—of which a few words later —oddments of fish, meat, rice and herbs, wonderfully and excellently made by native cooks.

Midday and evening " chop " are frequently washed down by libations of whisky and soda, vermuth, bottled beer, mineral waters, or natural lime juice. Alcohol is usually prohibited on plantations before sunset, but it is difficult to enforce such a rule. If Europeans possess good sense, however, they adhere to this practice, which is best for everyone on the Coast. Half the trouble in the Tropics may be traced to its evasion or neglect. I am inclined to go further and say the less alcohol you consume at any time the better; indeed, where, as in Sierra Leone, the water is good, one can dispense with it *except as a medicine.* The notion that alcohol is a necessary drink in the Tropics is a superstition. So is the belief that you should *absolutely* dispense with it. Alcohol, like quinine, is an excellent friend when used sparingly. Unaccustomed to either, a little works wonders, and makes you feel another man. Habituated to them, both alcohol and quinine depress rather than revive. Whisky and soda and gin and bitters appear to be the most popular drinks upon the Coast. Bottled beer and bottled lemonade each cost a shilling a bottle, but whisky is actually cheaper than in England. Personally, I seldom took anything stronger than lime juice, though I quaffed palm wine with the chiefs and champagne with the Mayor of Freetown, and once or twice, after exhaustive days, indulged in a little whisky or vermuth and soda; vermuth, I consider, is preferable.

At a later date, when speaking to a wealthy Creole who seemed rather fond of the whisky bottle, I asked him why vermuth was not consumed more than whisky, as the former contained cinchona. To my surprise, he replied, " Oh! it's the general belief here that vermuth renders you impotent." I can candidly aver that this is another superstition.

"Chop" over, we adjourned to the verandah, and there, under a dark velvet sky and in the shadow of the palms, we gave ourselves up to the languor and loveliness of a tropical evening and talked of many matters.

Perhaps the dominant theme was the place and its history. For Christineville is almost the only European plantation in the Colony, the land of which has hitherto been considered sacred to the black man. Its history is therefore worth a passing notice.

*   *   *   *

Originally the estate was a Crown grant in perpetuity to Sir Samuel Lewis, a wealthy native lawyer, knighted by Queen Victoria on the occasion of her Jubilee—the only West African native, I believe, who has received such an honour. Sir Samuel devoted his leisure to experimental planting on a large scale. Throwing himself heartily into tropical agriculture and the development of the Colony, he planted not only indigenous trees and plants, but rubber of the Cearà and Castilloa varieties, the cashew, pineapple, annatto, and other useful trees and plants imported from various tropical countries.

Unfortunately, Sir Samuel Lewis died before his enterprise could be made successful. His wife and successors had neither the intellect nor character of the old man. Leased out to native tenants, placed under the supervision of inexperienced natives, the plantation speedily became half forest, half wilderness. A promising chapter in Sierra Leone history seemed to have ended, the book closed.

Then came the rubber boom. All sorts of wild schemes, useless tropical land, and unscrupulous promotions were foisted upon the public.

The opportunity was not neglected by some of the shrewder of the educated natives of West Africa. This plantation, among others, was sold in London to a small syndicate, resold to a larger syndicate, and again sold to a company at an inflated price. Considerable gambling ensued upon the last transaction. Then came the collapse of the boom. For a time it seemed as though this plantation would suffer the fate of many others bought by speculators at this time. Prudence, however, has preserved the place, and under its present control it promises to be a plantation with a future. One day, perhaps, I may write its secret history.

Since my return I might mention that a tragedy has overshadowed this place. A temporary manager, refusing to give up possession to the newly appointed

THE MANSION OF THE LATE SIR SAMUEL LEWIS
(with group of Temne, Mendi, Susu and Vai labourers and servants).

Face p. 34.

planting manager, shot at him, killing a native and wounding others. He was tried for murder.

*　　*　　*　　*

From conversation we turned to music. The assistant manager had brought out an excellent gramophone and some very fine and well-chosen records. The natives would be enticed to the bungalow by the welcome sound of music and listen enthralled for hours if it were continued so long; and the house-boys, though they could read no English, quickly learnt to distinguish the particular records which they liked best, and would always give them first place when they were asked to " put them on." " Mr. Black Man " was a special favourite.

And thus with the voices of Caruso and Melba in our ears, mingled with the distant drumming of the natives in the village below and the droning of innumerable insects around the verandah, we retired to rest.

CHAPTER V.

LIFE ON A RUBBER PLANTATION.

The Planter's Life—Managers and Assistants—Irrigation—Iron Hills and their Possibilities—Hevea, Ceará, Funtumia, and Castilloa Rubber Trees—Coffee and Cacao as Catch-crops— Ginger and its Complaints—Rubber Pests.

LIFE on a rubber plantation is never monotonous to the man who loves Nature and his work. From six in the morning to six at night there is always something to do, something new about which to think. At each roll-call of the labourers there is usually a new arrival or a falling-out. Barely a week passes but one of your " boys " falls a victim to some misadventure through mischievousness. Sometimes there is a boundary dispute, sometimes a forest fire, sometimes an attack by wild beasts, sometimes disputes and fights among your employés, principally over women. Such a quarrel occurred while I was there and knives were out and blood spilt before we could interfere. Even labour troubles are not altogether absent, and temporary strikes will occur, especially if there be much " clipping of the copper," an expressive phrase for a " fine."

During the wet season, from May to October, every nerve is strained to keep down weed and grass and plant up new stock. During the " dries," from November to April, clearing new ground and watering are the main occupations. Visits from officials, passing traders, and occasional journeys to Freetown fill up one's time. With good pay, generous leave, healthy quarters, this should be an attractive employment.

At daybreak the planter rises and by six o'clock he has inspected or taken the roll-call of his staff, and they have been allotted to their respective sections for clearing, watering, or planting. If clearing has been completed, and it is the dry season, watering will be the principal work of the staff; if the wet season, planting. Weeding can be performed in both wet and dry seasons, and in land of the evergreen forest type it is a never-ending industry, but in land of the savannah type it may be sandwiched in according to convenience.

Clearing can be effected with knife or by fire; if the latter, great care must be exercised, and it should never be attempted close to the planted area. Watering is always done before nine o'clock in the morning and after four in the afternoon. One boy can water ninety plants.

Holing and preparing the ground of a cleared area for planting in the subsequent " wets " is an industry which can usually be performed towards the end of the preceding wet season, or, if planting work be very heavy, at the beginning of the " dries." Not a little success in plantations is attributable to wise holing, as an inch deeper in drier soil, or in an area exposed to such dry winds as the *harmattan,* makes all the difference between success and failure. Directors of plantations in West Africa cannot be too careful in securing for their managers or assistants, men who are planters of experience and discretion, men also, if possible, with chemical knowledge of soils.

For the best results from manuring a knowledge of the chemical nature of different soils is very necessary, and if the managers do not themselves possess the knowledge, samples should be sent home for analysis and direction.

As the company owning the plantation was anxious to learn more of its property and the neighbouring country, and had given me *carte blanche* to go where I pleased or do whatever I desired upon the place, I took the opportunity during the next few weeks to make a thorough investigation of the estate, watching and taking a personal part in the planting, holing, clearing, experimental tapping of trees yielding rubber or gum, and extraction of oil from the various nutty trees, visiting the native huts, participating in the pleasures of the people, and touring in the vicinity on foot or by hammock.

At present, off the railroad, the only means of conveyance in this district is by hammock or your own feet. This part of the country, however, being apparently free from the tsetse-fly, cattle could be used for transport purposes. They are now being bred here with very satisfactory results. Hammocks carried on poles by four boys, two in front, two at the rear, are very comfortable means of travelling for short distances and on the level; very disconcerting on hills or after many hours.

*　　*　　*　　*

The estate, covering about 3,500 acres, lies about 8° North of the Equator, between the sixteenth and nineteenth milestone on the railroad which runs from Freetown into the interior. The main road from Freetown to Waterloo also runs through the plantation, which makes it rather difficult to police and divides it into two separate parts. Two up trains and two down trains each day stop at the flag station upon the property. There are several good private roads on the estate, and as the land is mainly of the savannah and monsoon forest type it should be easily maintained and kept clear. The European bungalows, one for the manager and another for the assistants, are picturesquely built at an elevation of about 500 ft., and both the position and conditions are conducive to good health. From the bungalows an extensive view is obtained over the plantation, the mangrove forests, the River Bunce, and the Bullom shore. Probably the place would prove of strategic value should a rebellion or invasion threaten the Colony. From the main road and the railway, which are quite close to each other, the plantation ascends gradually by four spurs of hills to the upper road, high up on the left of the bungalow, where it rises suddenly to a height of 1,400 ft. among dense uncleared forest, which preserves the moisture and cradles two excellent streams. There echo sounds of things unknown, while the mysterious murmuring of a million insects betrays a ferment of life more curious than beautiful. Here and there on the Rokelle hillside patches of open land appear where the forest has been felled by native tenants for planting cassava and ginger.

Through the less dense bush, the following week, we cut our way to the highest point of the hill hitherto uncleared or explored. The water from the two streams is dispersed through both the upper and lower plantations by irrigation pipes and an extension of boulders from three dams, built by the present proprietors. The soil varies in depth and character, but red gravel is predominant. The country rock which outcrops here and there is hornblende pyerite. Upon at least two of the hill spurs magnetic iron ore has been discovered in large quantities; but the percentage of titanium with it would render it unprofitable to work until electrical power is brought here to convert the iron into steel.

Hevea or Pará rubber has been planted upon two of the upper spurs. On one it is interplanted with coffee, on the other with cacao. Before the present company came into possession, only a few hundred Manihot or Ceará rubber trees were growing, and these on the lower estate. Many of these were destroyed when the dense bush around them was being cut down and fired by a gang known as " King George and his boys," employed by the first European manager to " clear " the forest by contract. The same manager declared later that Hevea could not grow here; but upon his dismissal after six months' tenure, Hevea was experimented with and has succeeded in vigorous growth, though its latex yield has yet to be proved.

Hevea rubber thrives only in an annual mean temperature of about 80° F., and best where the daily temperature is between 75° and 90° F., with an annual rainfall of from 80 to 120 in. It requires moist but not marshy soil, a red clayey or loam soil, well drained, being perhaps most suitable.

Latex in the Hevea tree is in tubes, which run practically parallel to each other and allow it to flow when they are cut, therefore it is desirable to cut as great a number as possible of these vessels as can be made to flow. With parallel horizontal cuts the greatest number of tubes is opened, but the latex does not flow, therefore the cut is made obliquely.

Several other kinds of rubber are being grown upon this estate on the lower plantation.

The Manihot or Ceará will thrive in places unsuited to any other kind of rubber, and seedlings from the original trees spring up like weeds and are being planted along the roadside and up the hills. The leaves of this species are five-lobed and of a curious bluish-grey, while the bark is like a silver birch and peels off in strips, but becomes very rough and jagged with years.

It is therefore more difficult to tap, the best method, perhaps, being to stab or prick it. On the other hand, it will yield when from two and a half to three years old, and the latex runs freely and coagulates on exposure to the air, while that of Pará, Castilloa, and Funtumia has to be collected in cups. Ceará rubber will fetch almost the same price as Pará, and is preferred by some manufacturers. I tapped the older trees of this species and found the yield very satisfactory. I noticed also that the latex in the Ceará appears to be in cells rather than tubes.

The Castilloa tree has a smooth, light grey bark and has peculiar branches bearing rows of large green leaves from 12 to 18 in. long. It is the handsomest but least satisfactory of all plantation rubber trees. Those upon this plantation are the seedlings from the two trees planted by Sir Samuel Lewis, and though no particular attention has been given to them they appear flourishing.

Funtumia elastica, indigenous to West Africa, has
white or yellow flowers, with seed like a silky plume
about 2 in. long. There are a few trees of the species
on the estate, and upon tapping some I found the latex
flowed freely.

The yield of rubber from *Hevea brasiliensis* trees,
over five years old, tapped on the " herring-bone " or
" V " system, may be taken as 1 lb. of dry rubber per
annum for each foot diameter of the tree, measured
at 3 ft. from the ground. In Castilloa trees, tapped by
hatchets, chisels or axes by the methods used for Hevea,
the yield is much poorer and does not exceed 6 oz.
per foot diameter, measured at 3 ft. from the ground.
Castilloa trees continue to yield latex for from ten to
twenty minutes after pricking, but the period of flow
can be lengthened to about fifty minutes by continuously spraying the pricked portion of the bark with
water, and in this way the yield of rubber can be
increased by from 20 to 40 per cent. The latex is
collected by means of an unbleached calico "apron"
of special form, attached to the tree about 8 in. from
the ground.

A tree is considered to be suitable for tapping when
the girth amounts to 18 in., and as soon as the tree
at a distance of 1½ ft. above the soil has this girth, a
V-cut can be put on it.

If one or two years later, at 3 ft. above the soil, the
tree is 18 in. in girth, then the tapping can take place
at this height, and a half herring-bone cut can be made.
The age is also taken into consideration, and Hevea
trees which are younger than four or five years are not
touched, even when the girth is sufficient. Castilloa
and Funtumia trees are of no use until after seven or
five years respectively.

The period for tapping is shorter in West Africa
than elsewhere because, during heavy rainfall, the
water washes out the latex, and the prolonged drought
dries up the latex, thus preventing an easy flow. Every
available fine day between the rains from June to
October has therefore to be utilized for tapping.

While it is the best in the long run to bring rubber into bearing without catch-crops, which all compete with the principal crop and remove a certain amount of available plant food, few companies can wait five years for a return. They therefore plant catch-crops.

A desirable catch-crop should be one yielding a good profit, and bearing early, while not being too severe on the soil; it should also admit of weeding so as to leave the land in a clean condition when it is taken out.

Tapioca yields a very small profit, if any, and it is so difficult to weed that the land is in a decidedly dirty condition when the crop is removed. Camphor keeps land clean, but the time to wait for a crop is too long, and then the profit is not much. *Coffea robusta* offers by far the best catch-crop. A small return will come in the second year and a good one in the third and following years. Therefore, for those who must put down a catch-crop, coffee is undoubtedly the best. The production of the *robusta* kind costs less per pikul than the *liberica*.

The cost of planting the coffee has, of course, to be added to the cost of bringing the rubber into bearing, but, on the other hand, the weeding will cost less than in Pará alone.

The coffee must not be allowed to die out. It should be ruthlessly *cut* out as soon as the branches of the rubber trees meet, and certainly in the beginning of the sixth year.

Cacao or cocoa, described in a later chapter, is another catch-crop, but takes longer to give a return and takes more out of the soil.

Although the girth of the rubber trees interplanted with coffee or cacao may be somewhat less than trees of the same age planted on jungle ground, the production of latex is quite as good. Coffee and cacao crops are obtainable for some years during the growth of the rubber, although they are, of course, a decreasing quantity as the Hevea grows. Furthermore, there is

YOUNG CACAO AND RUBBER BEING REARED BETWEEN BANANAS.

Face p. 42.

the advantage that the ground remains covered and maintenance accordingly is less; there is also an absence of fungus.

Besides the Hevea, coffee and cacao upon the upper part of this estate, kola, cassava, bananas, paw-paw, and the avocado pear are being cultivated, while fine specimens of the kamoot, lime, annatto, bamboo, *Xylophia æthiopica, Parkia africana,* and other oil and forest trees abound. All the upper portion is terraced to retain the moisture of the heavy rains, and the plantation is exceptionally fortunate in its numerous streams and irrigation pipes and its four fire belts, each 25 yards wide, preserving it from all kinds of attacks during the otherwise disastrous dry season.

The place is also singularly free from many pests, the cricket and woolly aphis being the most troublesome. These, however, seldom attack rubber.

Ginger is grown by tenant farmers all over this district, upon the hillsides, and in the poorer and shallower ground, where ordinary plantation products will not grow. It is generally thought more profitable to let the native grow ginger, the planter buying it at a halfpenny or so per pound less than can be procured at Freetown. In case, however, it should be taken up by white planters upon a large scale, a few hints may not be out of place.

Owing to the pungent nature of the shoots, the ginger plant is attacked by very few insect pests, and it has even been recommended that the crop should be planted in orchards to prevent the development of pests of fruit trees. The first indication of disease is a yellowing of the leaves, which droop and wither; the bases of the stems become discoloured and rot, and finally decay spreads to the rhizomes, which disintegrate to form a putrefying mass of tissue. To prevent infection of healthy plants every portion of an affected plant must be removed and burnt, whilst the soil itself should be treated with lime, or a light dressing of sulphate of iron may be applied.

In the case of a bad attack, ginger should not be grown on the land for at least three years. The disease is most serious on wet, heavy soils, or in exceptionally rainy seasons, and it may be prevented to a large extent by draining the land so that no water lies round the collar of the plant. Great care should be exercised in selecting only healthy rhizomes for planting purposes, any plants with even the slightest trace of disease being rejected.

After a bad attack it is advisable to steep the rhizomes for about half an hour in Bordeaux mixture before planting, to destroy any fungoid spores or lymphæ on their surface or in the soil clinging to them.

Speaking of pests and plant diseases, two serious diseases which have specially to be guarded against in most rubber plantations are fungus and white ants. The fungus lives on tree roots in the jungle and extends itself along the dead roots of rotten wood through the soil. Without the help of such conductive materials it cannot grow. The infection starts with the side roots of the plant, then to the top root. Only when the latter is affected will the tree bear exterior marks of the disease; then the leaves wither and the tree soon falls. Rubber trees of fifteen months to four or five years old are specially exposed to this, not because they are less susceptible beyond these limits of age, but because the fungus requires the first few months to obtain a hold, whereas when the plantation has remained free the first four or five years, it is evident that fungus is not present. The only method of combating fungus is to clear up as cleanly as possible; dead wood must be dug up, stumps must be taken away and burnt so that there are no sources of infection. A second and important pest is one special variety of "white ant" (*Termes gestroi*), of which mention is made elsewhere in this volume.

KOLA, YOUNG RUBBER, AND PINEAPPLES AT CHRISTINEVILLE.

(By permission of the Company.)

Face p. 44.

CHAPTER VI.

NATIVE LIFE, LABOUR, AND INDUSTRY IN THE COLONY.

The Canteen and the Compound—Different Races and their
Characteristics—Labour and Wages—Women and their
Work—Marriage—Children an Asset—Palm Oil and Kernel
Industry.

> " Wherever God erects a house of prayer,
> The devil always builds a tavern there."

So sang the English poet. The African has few
houses of prayer; but wherever there is a native village,
there is a canteen and store. If the store has not a
canteen to sell liquor, it will sell little else.

Once I met a director of a West Africa plantation
who was a total abstainer. He objected to selling rum
and gin to natives at their store. But the native tramped
another two miles to the next store whenever he wanted
anything, because he could buy intoxicating liquor
there also, so the director gave way and sold rum
and gin.

Sometimes the store is run by a Creole, sometimes by
a European company.

Someone who has written about West Africa—I
believe it is Mrs. Mary Gaunt—has spoken of " the
weary, dreary life of the trader " and its " ghastly loneliness." As though the trader were a forced exile, with
nothing to do except to sell cotton stuffs, gin, rum, and
tobacco to the natives and count the days for his return !
Of course, there are such " traders "—at least, they call
themselves by this term—but such men are usually
exiles through their own faults. They could never
obtain employment at home, and when they return they
are careful not to seek the port or town from which they
came. They sit down at a store from about seven-

thirty to ten-thirty in the morning, shut up shop for two or three hours while they eat their " chop "—just at the time their wares are most needed—return for an hour or two in the afternoon, sauntering up to their bungalow about four, and seeking repose from such terrible exhaustion in copious libations of whisky, or occasionally breaking the monotony by threats or actual attempts to fight the manager or other " boss." Even when they are selling goods they will seldom handle the stuff itself ; a native does this, the so-called " trader " merely taking the cash and giving change. The sooner this type leaves or is eliminated from the Coast the better for West Africa and its investors at home. The really good trader can usually secure a Creole clerk or trader to perform this counter business—of course, if he has a European assistant it is preferable—while he himself will boat up the rivers and creeks, securing the palm-kernels and any other produce he can lay hands upon, or he will be busy at the wharf receiving consignments, or entertaining at the store those natives who have come from various parts to trade with him.

To see life in a native village, go to the store on " pay night." There you will see one side of the picture. To see the other, visit the *zimbeks* and the women.

*　　*　　*　　*

The natives here are divided into tenants and labourers. The tenants, mostly Temnes or Creoles, are scattered about on the hillsides bordering on Rokelle or on the low-lying land by the Waterloo creek. The village, or compound of the labourers, is grouped around the store between the high road and the wharf.

The labourers include Mendis, Vais, Temnes, and Susus, but chiefly Mendis, the last-named being pure pagans. The Vais, Temnes, and Susus, who are mostly Muhammadans, are domiciled towards the Waterloo end of the plantation. The Mendis are the hardier labourers, the other tribes making better houseboys. Of the Mendis, Temnes, and Susus I shall have more to say later. The Vais are not natives of Sierra Leone. They come from Liberia, and are superior in many ways. They are the only black people in this part of the Coast possessing a literature.

They have, however, rightly or wrongly, an un-enviable reputation for homo-sexuality, and the epithet, *ollapojiba,* frequently bestowed upon them, although horrible, is significant. Like the Temnes and the Susus, they are generally clean and loosely robed—preferably in white.

The labourers receive from sixpence to ninepence a day, but they are at liberty to gather wild fruits like the mango, plantain, monkey apple, cashew, &c. The Government railway pays the labourer one shilling daily and gives him less supervision. The natural result is that in the dry season many of the plantation labourers leave for the Government service. Labour was so short when I was there that the plants were suffering from lack of watering. The watering, I should mention, is largely performed by hand from supplies brought down from the dams by irrigation pipes. Later, when I went up into the interior, I made an arrangement with the chief to supply the labour deficiency, and devised a scheme whereby they might bring their " mammies " and " pickins " (children) and settle on the waste parts of the plantation, growing cassava and ginger, as long as they worked for the owners. By this means a con-tinuity of labour is now assured, and a larger and model village is in course of development.

The labourers work from 6 to 11 or 11.30 in the morning, with a short interval for a " snack," and again from about 2 to 5 in the afternoon. The native " drivers " or overseers receive from £3, the native superintendent £7 a month, hammock-boys and house-boys about 25s. to 30s. a month. Gam-bling with dice and anything else to hand is a con-summate vice, and quarrels and fights are a frequent result. Rum and gin considerably diluted by the store-keepers are their favourite drinks, and when this and

the dice are in company together, or if the dispute be
over women, knives are out, and sometimes life is lost.
To pay gambling debts, the natives borrow at enormous
interest either from their drivers or from some rich
Creole in the neighbourhood, who often thus obtains
control over their belongings after a scrimmage.

Life in a native village is not, therefore, so monotonous as in many a rural hamlet in more civilized
countries. Further, both men and women frequently
tramp miles and miles from their homes in search of
more remunerative labour or for the gains of trade, so
strangers are frequently seen on the high road. Women
traders are many in Sierra Leone, especially in fish,
fancy work, and articles of dress or ornament. At
home, the women look after the piccanninies or children,
pound the maize or the coarse millet flour which is made
into *kusskuss* or porridge, cook the rice and fish, peel
and prepare the cassava root, boil in cauldrons the
palm oil, and sometimes help to crack the kernels. In
addition, also, they frequently attend to all the crops
around their *zimbeks* when their lords and masters are
labourers upon an adjoining plantation. The "mammies" of those who are independent tenant farmers in
the Colony attend only to the smaller plants in the
immediate vicinity of their homes—the tenant farmer
having his plots scattered perhaps over a wide area—
but they have to carry their husband's produce on their
heads—frequently very heavy bundles—to the nearest
store or town where it can be realized for cash.

I remember seeing a Temne tenant's mammy come
into a store carrying 80 lb. of ginger in a huge
sack upon her head, supported, of course, by her hands.
Her wretched husband—who was by no means a trustworthy tenant, and who received notice to quit while I
was there—followed her. He carried a stick in his
hand and a cigarette in his mouth. He sat down, while
she stood. Receiving the money, he promptly spent a
considerable sum in rum, part of which he consumed
forthwith without offering her a drop; the remainder,

after haggling about the price, he carefully corked up for future private use.

Probably here in Africa, as elsewhere, the lot of women whose husbands are attached to one particular spot, and therefore have not had their sympathies broadened by travel and contact, is harder than that of others. Certainly the wife of many a British working man is, allowing for our higher civilization, in no more enviable a position. Here in West Africa, at any rate, no woman is left destitute. There are no old maids, and few young ones. When a man seeks labour elsewhere on the Coast, or in some distant part of the Colony, he may leave his "mammy" or "mammies" in charge of anyone else. She or they become somebody else's "mammy" for the time being, but they have to be looked after properly. As for children, they are never encumbrances, but assets. The boys have to work for the father and the girls are sold in marriage, often fetching £5 or £6. Hence the possession of children is everything both to man and woman; and she who has had a child without being married is more respected than a childless woman. The only unhappy women appear to be those who are married but childless. These are not very numerous; but they are more frequent than would at first be imagined in a land where natural intercourse is less restricted. In few cases does the fault lie with the woman; entirely perverted sexuality is answerable for much. This is noteworthy from a sociological standpoint, indicating that perversion is not merely due to the economic pressure of civilization restricting or retarding marriage.

To return to the women's work. I have mentioned the food they prepare from cassava and plantain. Cassava is a shrub growing to about 6 ft. in height, the roots of which grow in clusters, and yield starch and tapioca. The "bitter" cassava root contains prussic acid, which is eliminated by heating, the boiled juice, no longer poisonous, being used for sauces, and called "cassareep." The "sweet" variety can be eaten raw,

and is very nice and nourishing when properly peeled
and washed. Prepared into meal or cakes, it is even
more appetizing.

The plantain is a kind of bitter banana, the shrub
bearing it resembling our dock weed. When peeled,
the plantain is cooked by being wrapped in leaves and
steamed like our potato. It is also eaten mashed like
our "mealie," usually with a meat or fish sauce.
Bananas, mangoes, and other fruit add to their menu.

Most interesting of all perhaps are the natives
engaged in breaking palm-kernels and extracting the
oil by huge boiling cauldrons, some for food and some
for sale and export.

A fine belt of palms lies between the railway line
and the store; and in the vicinity of the mangrove
swamps. While the women make the oil, the males
secure the kernels. The general practice among natives
in securing the nuts of the oil palm is to climb the
trunk of the tree by the aid of a stout creeper, steps up
the tree having been previously made by the bases of
the leaves cut off in the course of pruning or cleaning.
Arrived at the top, say about 60 ft., the boy severs the
bunches by an axe, then, descending, collects them in
a heap or heaps, covering them with plantain or banana
leaves, and leaving them exposed to the sun for four
or five days. The heat causes the fruit to drop away
from the stem and the porcupine thorns, which before
tenaciously held them. To force the oil from the fibrous
pericarp various methods are adopted. Some ferment,
some boil, others do both. Palm oil, as prepared by
natives from freshly cut fruit for their own use in cooking, is a pleasant-smelling and yellow-coloured fat,
which is sometimes eaten and relished by Europeans
residing in West Africa; but, as less care is taken in
the preparation of the large quantities of oil required
for export, together with the length of time elapsing
during transport, it is generally very rancid when it
reaches the European market.

Palm oil extracted from the outer fleshy portion of
the fruits of the oil palm is also exported in large quan-

SETTING OUT ON A PALM KERNEL EXPEDITION (note the apparatus).

Face p. 50

tities. The kernels or seeds contained in the nuts or
" stones " of the oil palm are obtained by cracking the
nuts by hand or by the aid of a nut-cracking machine,
after the orange-coloured palm oil has been extracted
from the outer pulpy portion of the fruit.

The kernels are exported, and the extraction of the
kernel oil carried out in Europe. Palm kernel oil is
white in colour and of rather softer consistence than
palm oil. It is largely used in the manufacture of
soaps. The best grades can be employed for the preparation of margarine and other modern foodstuffs.

Another product of the oil palm which is not so
generally known is fibre; this fibre is of very good
quality, and realizes as much as £60 a ton on the
Liverpool market.

It is the only fibre that is sufficiently fine and strong
to make fishing lines, and this is the only use to which
it is put by the natives. It is obtained from the young
pinnæ, the older leaves being too strong and coarse to
permit the hand-extraction of the fibre.

The process of extraction is laborious, and therefore
unremunerative, the cost of the production being as
high as £75 a ton. There remains, however, a possi-
bility that a mechanical or a chemical process may be
introduced to separate the fibre from the pinnæ cheaply.

There is an enormous supply of material in the
country which at present rots on the ground, and which
might be turned to profitable account by very shrewd
enterprise, working on more economical lines than the
majority of present plantation companies in West Africa.
The oil palm, which is indigenous to West Africa, is
found generally throughout the country from the sea-
board towards the interior, diminishing in those districts
where the climate becomes drier, or where rocky and
mountainous tracts intervene. It is rarely found beyond 200 miles from the coast. The most suitable
situation is where the soil is generally moist. Swampy,
ill-drained land is not favourable. In those parts of the
country where there is gravelly laterite over a deep
substratum of syenite, trees may abound in considerable

numbers, but the trunks of such trees do not acquire the same thickness as those growing in damper or lighter ground. The trees in this district, for example, are not such fine specimens as in the damper Sherbro country. No distinct varieties are recognized by the natives, although distinctive names are applied to the same fruit in different stages of development. Yet there is great disparity between oil palms, both in yield and quality, to the extent of 30 per cent. The oil palm does not thrive in heavy forest, but in open valleys with low undergrowth. The seeds or nuts, which are large and heavy, are distributed by the agency of birds and mammals.

The full-grown oil palm attains a height of about 60 ft., and consists of a stem covered throughout its length with the bases of dead leaves, and bearing at the apex a crown of large, pinnate leaves, each of which may be 15 ft. long with leaflets 2 ft. or 3 ft. long.

The tree is very slow growing, reaching a height of 6 in. to 9 in. in three years, 12 in. to 18 in. in four or five years, 8 ft. in ten years, and 13 ft. to 14 ft. in fifteen years, and attaining its full height of 60 ft. in about 120 years.

The fruits are borne in large bunches termed " heads " or " hands," which are small and numerous when the tree first begins to bear, from the fourth to the eighth year. The oil palm requires little cultivation, but there is no reason why the white planter should not take his place beside the trader, provided he knows the country, the palm, and the people. But he must be wary. Not only must his labour not be handled on the " plantation " system, but his cultivation of the palm must not be indiscriminate.

There is great disparity between oil palms in yield and quality, some having thin pericarps and thin-shelled kernels. The first is almost universal in Sierra Leone, but only personal investigation on the spot can say to which variety particular palms belong. Hence the planter and shareholder should be satisfied with no report which does not state this.

MATURE KOLA TREES (IN BEARING).

Face p. 52.

CHAPTER VII.

Among Kolas and Coconuts.

The Value of Kola—How to grow it—The Kamoot and its Oil
Product—The Coconut : How to Plant and Utilize.

BETWEEN the store and wharf lies the Christineville
kola plantation, interplanted with Ceará rubber and
cacao, while between this and Waterloo creek a coconut plantation lends real beauty to the scene.

The kola nut, sometimes called the bissy or guru
nut, has a bitter taste, but a high commercial value,
being used by Muhammadan and pagan natives alike
as a stimulant and as a symbol at almost every religious
or social function. To present two red kolas signifies
war; a white nut, broken in two, proclaims peace. To
decide one's luck in hunting or any other business for
the day, a kola nut is taken in each hand and tossed in
the air. If they fall with both pointed ends towards the
thrower, all is well; if the reverse, it is ill; if each should
point a different way, three throws decide the matter.
So indispensable is kola to the daily existence of the
Muhammadan natives that some will travel from
Northern Nigeria to the Gold Coast, Sierra Leone, and
even to Gambia and the Senegal Valley to barter or
buy their favourite fruit.

As coffee is to the Arab, beer to the English, and
opium to the Chinese, so is the kola nut to the Hausa,
the Songhay, the Fulani, and other native tribes from
Gambia to Nigeria. The Hausas—the native traders
par excellence of Africa—are to be found in all the
Africa ports, and they convey the kola or guru nuts,
delicately wrapped in leaves and packed in large
baskets, to sell at a large profit in Kano, Zaria, and

Gando, from which places they are often retransported to Wadai, Borum, and even to Khartum. These nuts are white or crimson, and number five to fifteen per pod. When deprived of their seed coats, they are masticated while fresh, being very stimulating and sustaining, and consequently are used in medicine to prevent fatigue and to stimulate the nerves. The prices at Freetown vary from about £6 10s. to £13 a measure (176 lb.). There is, however, a huge and constant local demand. The annual value of the kola nuts exported exceeds £100,000, but only the throw-outs and under-sized nuts reach Liverpool or London, where, selling at 2½d. to 4d. per lb., they are used as an adulterant for cocoa.

The kola of Sierra Leone is more prized than that of any other West African Colony. The trees are extensively grown throughout the Protectorate, almost every village having its kola grove, and each tree bearing a value of about 30s. With proper cultivation, therefore, a kola tree should yield nearly double that revenue.

The native propagates the tree from seeds which he germinates in the mud of the marshes. As soon as it starts sprouting he sows it at stake. He always chooses a well-shaded spot in the forest that surrounds his town. Unfortunately, he plants his seeds too close together; instead of 18 ft. to 24 ft., he puts them 5 ft. apart. Having established a few trees, he continues the propagation by layering down the lower branches, and so obtains two or more young trees growing round the larger ones. Thus his kola grove is finally planted with trees 2 ft. apart. The native never attempts to prune off the forked stems, but seems to prefer a number of weak stems and sucker shoots to a healthy tree. In short, he so works his plantation that he gets the minimum possible yield from the maximum number of trees. He also surrounds his trees with " medicine " and makes deep cuts in their stems, and these he believes will cause the trees to bear more fruit.

Some of the natives believe red ants help to fructify

the tree, but the Temnes surround the tree with the blood of chickens or cattle to attract the red ants from the tree, and then kill them *en masse.*

Kola is being extensively grown here, and will one day afford a handsome revenue. Pilfering, however, is very prevalent, and watch-dogs from England have been imported to prevent it. They may catch a few thieves, but will never make dishonest men honest. Even the ruses adopted by native chiefs, mentioned later, are not always successful, and upon a white man's estate dishonesty is apparently not blameworthy to the native, even when followed by quick retribution.

Walking from the kola to the coconut plantation, I noticed a boy trespassing on the fish preserves by the river bank. Turning round to keep his eye on me while he devised some means of escape, he forgot his legs were dangling over the bank. Suddenly I saw him disappear. I heard a howl, a splash. Hastening to the spot I saw nothing; but one of the labourers near told me that the river-god had taken him. I guessed it was a crocodile, yet the following week I saw another trespasser there.

Closely allied to the kola is the kamoot, or butter and tallow tree. The fruit of this tree closely resembles the *Kola acuminata,* and is often placed among genuine kola nuts as an adulterant; but it does not contain theine like the kola, and it yields fat and tannin, neither of which are to be obtained from the genuine kola. The fat is edible, and can be profitably used in candle-making, margarine, and soap manufacture. As much as 41 per cent. of oil has been obtained from the seeds, and £10 a ton has been obtained for the commodity.

The Sierra Leoneans and the Mendis do not use the tree; but the Temnes, from whom the name kamoot is borrowed, extract the oil for food purposes in the same way as palm oil. They dry the seeds, parching them over a fire, then pound them in a mortar, add water, and boil, skimming off the fat or oil as it rises to the surface. The tree is propagated by means of seeds, and is usually found near streams, being plentiful in the savannah districts of Sierra Leone, and particularly on the Christineville rubber estates between Rokelle and Waterloo, where it is called by the Mendis "jorrah" or "black mango." It is also plentiful on the Niger River and Congo district, where the natives call it "Ngoumi," and a trade is done in it with Europe from French West Africa, where it is called by the name of "Lamy."

But it is to the coconut that many people look for wealth in the near future.

The coconut is essentially a tropical palm. Though it will grow up to the 25th degree North or South latitude, it rarely ripens fruit beyond 15° North or South. It should never be grown among Hevea rubber, though it makes an excellent addition to rubber plantation revenue if grown on a separate portion of the estate, as at Christineville. The germination of the seed is not injuriously affected by the immersion of the fruit in sea-water for a considerable period; it is assumed, therefore, that ocean currents played an important part in dispersing the seed from this region over wide areas prior to the intervention of man. The tree rarely bears profitably until nearly seven years old, and the fruit itself takes nearly a year to mature. Although introduced by man to all the warmer coastal regions of the world, the coconut has never become truly wild, but is always dependent upon human care to enable it to compete with Nature's vegetation. The trunk has been known to attain a height of 100 ft. and a diameter of 18 in., while the leaves are usually 15 ft. to 20 ft. long The coconut palm is not only one of the handsomest, it is also one of the most valuable of tropical economic plants, its products being of great importance not only to the natives of the countries in which they are produced, but also to the commercial and manufacturing communities of the world, the price of its fruit having increased more than a hundredfold during the last few years. There are many varieties of the tree, causing difference in habits of growth, periods of maturity and yield, and, more markedly, in the size, shape and colour of the mature fruits; but, generally speaking, the coconut palm is a light-loving species intolerant of shade, delighting in a maritime climate where the light is strong and there is a constant breeze. Essentially a tropical plant, it requires a considerable amount of heat and moisture to attain full development. An average mean temperature of about 80° F., with little variation throughout the year, is perhaps the most suitable. An average annual rainfall of from 60 in. to 80 in. is advantageous; but as low a rainfall as 45 in., evenly distributed throughout the year, is found sufficient when the palm is growing on fertile, moisture-containing soils. If less than 45 in. is received, artificial irrigation becomes necessary; while on poor, sandy soils a rainfall of not less than 70 in. is essential, unless there be a flow of water in the subsoil.

The soil best suited to the coconut palm is a deep and fertile sandy loam, such as is found in alluvial flats along the sea-coast at the mouths of rivers, or in wide river valleys. It is in such situations and on such soils that the coconut palm is most commonly found to flourish, but it can be grown inland, especially if situated by the banks of a tidal river, the ebb and flow causing ideal conditions. The principal products derived from the coconut palm are: coconuts, copra (the dried kernel of the nut from which coconut oil is expressed), desiccated coconut (prepared from the fresh kernel, and largely used for confectionery purposes), and coir fibre, which is prepared from the husk of the fruit.

In tropical countries where the coconut palm is grown, nearly every part of the tree is utilized by the natives. The roots are used as an astringent in native medicine, and are sometimes chewed as a substitute for betel or areca nuts, sometimes interwoven with fibres to form baskets. The trunk, which, when mature, develops a very hard outer shell, is used to form rafters and pillars of native buildings. The inner portion of the trunk is too soft to be of value as timber, but the outer portion is capable of taking a fine polish, and is sometimes used in this country in marquetry work and cabinet making. From its peculiar markings, consisting of ebony-like streaks or short lines irregularly disposed over a reddish-brown grain, it is known as " porcupine wood." The leaf-bud or " cabbage " is much appreciated as a vegetable or salad by both natives and Europeans, but to obtain it or to tap the palm for wine the tree has to be sacrificed. Planters need, therefore, to keep a sharp look-out. The fully grown leaves are put to numerous uses. They are formed into mats, baskets, roof-coverings for native huts (*ataps* or *codjans*), fences, articles of clothing, and ornaments. The petioles or leaf-stalks are used to make fences and handles for tools, and when cut into short lengths and frayed at the ends they serve as brushes. The midribs of the leaflets furnish a strong elastic fibre that is used for making basket strainers and native fishing tackle. The sheaths produced at the leaf-bases consist of triangular pieces of fibrous material having a woven appearance; these are cut into various shapes to form mats.

The flower spathes, when dried, are used as torches, and are also twisted into coarse ropes after being soaked in water.

The water contained in the unripe nut is a cool, refreshing drink that is much appreciated in tropical countries, and constitutes the only available drinking water on some of the smaller oceanic islands; while the soft creamy kernel of the unripe nut, when flavoured by spices and lime-juice, is eaten as a delicacy.

The ripe nuts enter into the composition of numerous native sweetmeats and curries. Coconut milk is prepared by grating the fresh kernel and mixing it with a little water and then pressing through a cotton cloth. The liquid which passes through the cloth is an emulsion, consisting of oil suspended in water with a little mucilage and sugar. It resembles milk in appear-

A COCONUT PLANTATION BEING CLEARED NEAR WATERLOO.
(These trees are over 20 years old.)

Face p. 58.

ance and consistency, and is extensively used in India
in the preparation of curries and as a substitute for
cow's milk.

The oil obtained from the' kernel of the nut by boiling with water or expression is used as an article of
food, and also employed for culinary purposes. The
husk is utilized as fuel, and sections are used as brushes;
the fibre of which it is largely composed is made into
brushes, yarn, cordage, and matting. The coconut
shells are used as fuel, and are also formed into drinking vessels and numerous other articles of domestic
use, as well as being carved and polished for ornament.
I have seen Kru boys on the steamer using the natural
husk, cut into pieces, as a scrubber.

Rubber plantations sufficiently near the coast would
do well to nurse any coconuts they may possess, and
there is room, in spite of the difficulties mentioned, for
individual European enterprise in coconut growing,
especially in Sierra Leone, in the lowlands surrounding
the tidal waters in the Protectorate. Here the Government have tried to encourage the coconut industry,
failing only because of native antipathy. They raise
the trees planted by the Government, but neglect to
water them, arguing that, because the nuts contain
liquid, there is no need to water the young plants. Only
the insufficient supply of trees in that part of West
Africa and lack of European capital prevent the copra
and coir industries from being taken up there by
Europeans. Once there is a move in this direction, the
possibilities of the coconut, also, of the piassava palm—
at present recognized only in the Sherbro district—as
well as the utilization of the mangrove bark, will become
more than problems.

CHAPTER VIII.

Adventures in and about Waterloo.

Mountain Climbing and Forest Clearing in the Tropics—A
Mirage—The *Harmattan* and its Effects—A Snake Adventure
—A Boundary Dispute—Land Law of the Colony—A Night
of Alarm—Gambling in " Haunted " Spots—Waterloo—The
Ascot of Sierra Leone—Church Parade—Native J.P.'s—A
Devil Dance—Meeting a Kwaia King—His Followers think
I take him Prisoner—Invitation to the Temne Territory.

A THIN *harmattan* haze hung over the hills as, one
morning, we ascended to the highest portion of the
surrounding country about 1,400 ft. high. Apparently
we were the first white men to tread this territory. In
anticipation of our climb, much of the forest had been
cleared during the preceding days, and temporary
boundary posts fixed. The highest portion was still
clothed in primitive forest, and through this we had
to cut our way. Through the grey mist the sun peered
out like a fiery ball, presently bursting out in burnished
gold. Half-way up a wonderful vision in the haze like
a mirage in the desert met our eyes. The range of hills
opposite, on which was situated the bungalow, was
reflected in the sky—a curious sight which I never saw
again.

The *harmattan* is a hot, dry wind blowing from the
desert, and brings with it infinitesimal grains of sand
which cause the peculiar haze. Sometimes you can
feel the sting of these particles, but often you are unconscious of them till you rub yourself down. Your
towel then appears sand-coloured. This wind is very
trying to those with any weakness of chest or lung.

The summit was reached in the afternoon and a

splendid view obtained. On the way down a little adventure awaited us.

The snakes in this district are not to be despised. A week before I came hither a boa constrictor of considerable size had been captured. Now I saw a struggle between man and snake (a large kind of viper called by the Mendis *tuper*) which was dramatic and startling. Only by mere chance did I become a spectator, or rather a secondary, instead of the actual object of attack. Half-way down the hillside is a private road, but as it is a short cut over the hills to a native village, it is frequently used without permission by neighbouring people visiting their hillside friends. Two such trespassers we suddenly met, and one of my boys went up to warn them when a snake, lying unnoticed by a timber log, and until then apathetic, was suddenly aroused and, stretching itself out, made as though it would coil round the group were it possible. One of the intruders' boys and I successfully evaded it, but the other dusky stranger was not so fortunate. The reptile buried its fangs in one of his arms, and was only prevented from doing further damage by our united attack upon the enemy. The boys, applying a chisel and piece of stick to its mouth, tried to obtain the release of the victim, but this proving useless, only one resource remained. The two boys seized the snake, the victim's companion and I caught hold of the man. Both parties pulled this living rope until the biter and the bitten came asunder at the weakest place, the victim being thankful to escape with the loss of a larger pound of flesh than Shylock would have exacted. He was so overcome, however, with shock, horror, and exhaustion that he became unconscious, and remained thus for a time. We applied a tight ligature, and forced banana juice, taken from the trunk of the plant, down his throat. I heard afterwards that a native medicine man supplemented our efforts by treating him with the leaves of *poni gbeho* and preparations from the head and gall-bladder of the dead snake.

The next day a neighbouring people sent a messenger with a letter in Kru English, asserting that we had trespassed upon and damaged their property, placing boundary posts on their territory. The people insisted on their removal and threatened reprisals.

The land in the Colony, I ought to mention, is held by the Crown. All grants made, contain reservations with regard to roads and other public requirements. The tenure of Crown lands is fee simple, but occupation is also sanctioned under squatters' licence at a nominal rent, and the tenure is then in the nature of a tenancy at will. Under Ordinance No. 14 of 1886, real and personal property may be taken, acquired, held, or disposed of by any alien in a manner similar to that allowed to a British-born subject. Fields or waste lands outside town or village limits in the Sierra Leone Peninsula and Sherbro Island must be taken up in lots of not less than 20 nor more than 200 acres. Such lots are disposed of at auction at an upset price of about 5s. per acre in the former and about 10s. in the latter locality. In the Protectorate arrangements may now be made with the chiefs for the lease of tracts of land for long periods on an annual rental agreed to between the applicant and the tribal council, the title requiring the confirmation of the Government. According to native law, the lands of a chiefdom are not the property of the chief, but are held in trust by the chief for the tribe. A chief cannot alienate any portion of the land of a chiefdom, or grant to anyone perpetual rights to any portion, but the lease of land by arrangement with a tribal council, and having Government sanction, should satisfy all requirements with regard to legal title.

The land on the other side of the boundary posts we had erected was Crown land held by members of the commune of Rokelle, but they had been encroaching upon this neighbouring territory and did not like the new boundary marks. Their messenger was detained, and a note sent to the headman of Rokelle by means of a passing native, stating that we should hold the whole village responsible for any removal of the boundary posts or any antagonism.

That night was an anxious one. The assistant manager considered we had acted high-handedly. Barricades were prepared, guns made ready. Presently, after chop, lights were seen moving about near the high road leading from the next village to ours, close to a spot which was supposed to be haunted. The assistant manager declared that the antagonistic villagers were coming to attack us. I maintained that if they proposed reprisals on our bungalow they would not come near the high road, but through the bush over the hills. It occurred to us, however, that the store on the lower plantation might be their objective. We therefore divided our strength. Two of us, with a house-boy and hammock-boy—the two latter very reluctantly—stole down the path towards the lights. Before we had gone any appreciable distance, the house-boy suddenly turned round and tremblingly blurted out, "Dem our boys, massa, go gamble." Amid much laughter and great ease of mind, it half dawned upon us and was half explained that the plantation labourers, having been forbidden to play outside the store, had for some time taken dice and hurricane lamps to the spot supposed to be haunted, guessing that there they would be undisturbed.

After this little episode the night passed quietly. The next morning the headman of Rokelle and his supporters waited upon us, and, after apologies and lengthy arguments, agreed to leave our boundary marks untouched until the District Commissioner's decision was taken. Their kinsman released, they repaired with us to the store. A little gin and rum wisely distributed clinched the compact. Later on, in the Protectorate, I was asked to act as referee in another boundary difficulty, and since my return home there has been an inquiry as to whether I were coming back, as another dispute required settling.

* * * *

The following day I hammocked into Waterloo to
obtain the District Commissioner's sanction to the new
boundaries.

Waterloo is the second town of importance and size
in Sierra Leone, the seat of the District Commissioner
for the Headquarters District, the residence of several
wealthy Creoles, and the favourite week-end or holiday
resort of many of the Freetown population. Picturesquely situated and well watered, it will probably
rise in prestige and popularity as the Colony advances.
At present the District Commissioner is practically the
only white resident, and he is not always there. When,
therefore, I hammocked into Waterloo my entry aroused
no little excitement. White officials and traders are
comparatively so few in this land that in places like
Waterloo and Freetown a white stranger is at once
detected, and speculation is at once rife as to his
identity, mission, and manner. An African is quick
to recognize friend or foe, and is fairly accurate in his
shrewd guesses at character—guesses which he frequently does not forget to verify by some subtly devised
test. Astonishing also is the rapidity with which your
fame or ill-fame, and sometimes even your movements,
precede you and circulate even into places which you
have no intention of visiting. I discovered later on,
when I had left this district for the Rokelle River, that
my travels were known, and the precise hour at which
I left and returned to Devil Hole duly recorded in many
a native mind.

The boundary dispute, which I had assured myself
I had definitely settled, was sure to be reopened when
the next new white man or manager came upon the
estate, if only, as it were, to test his mettle—so, at least,
the District Commissioner seemed to think, as he
formally approved and accepted the boundary lines I
had laid down, and promised his support in case of
difficulty. Since my return his words have proved true.
The relentless law of competition is nowhere so strong
as in Africa, and the average black is always striving

to get the better of the white man, even as the average white man seeks to enclose his neighbour's or the common land, or beat his brother in bargaining. Hence another reason for securing good men for management in West Africa.

I spent one Easter in Waterloo. Easter is the principal festival of the year among the converted Christians in Sierra Leone, and right royally is it kept. There is a service in the church with all kinds of musical accompaniment, and plenty of psalm-singing, in which the converted black man delights. There is a pompous procession of black priests and black choir-boys in white surplices and black cassocks.

After this follows the church parade. This is the finest or quaintest sight of all. Bond Street, Hyde Park, and Ascot have serious rivals in Waterloo at Easter time. The immaculate white collars, cuffs, and spats, glossy silk hats, lavender gloves, morning coats, fancy waistcoats, and carefully creased trousers of the masculine portion of the congregation are, to use a colloquial expression, " great." Even the monocle and the gold-knobbed cane are not wanting. As for the " mammies " and " tee-tees," how shall I describe the many-coloured shades of their dresses, ribbons, parasols, and hat millinery, or the languishing effect upon the dusky Reginalds of black Amelia's dainty ankles under cream open-work stockings?

The scene was kaleidoscopic and chameleon-like in colour. Nor did I think the European dress looked so incongruous upon these people as many travellers aver. Upon some of the blacks, I admit, it seems misplaced; but this remark equally applies to certain white people in Europe. Many of these blacks at Waterloo are of families which have been wealthy for more than one generation, and have probably made more than one journey to Europe. Several do not possess the flat nose or the extra thick lips usually associated with their race, for there are many exceptions to general race physiognomy here as in Europe. The only incongruity

I was conscious of was the uncomfortableness of such dress in a temperature of 90° F. or more in the shade. I suppose I looked a fearful heathen in white flannels and helmet among this fashionable crowd, but I enjoyed the festival, nevertheless.

On the Easter Monday the town was given up to festivity. There is but one proper hotel, and half a guinea a day is charged for accommodation. On Sundays and holidays it is crowded, likewise its gardens. The owner is a rich Creole who possesses much property in Waterloo, and of whom the poorer people stand in great awe. He is a Justice of the Peace and Headman of Waterloo.

After watching the various sports—many organized by British soldiers who come up to Waterloo for the holiday—I turned in to tea with Mr. Nicol, another Creole Justice of the Peace, who has a store opposite the hotel. He was an interesting old gentleman, who spoke English well, and had a charming wife and daughter, whom I photographed. His humour was dry but delightful. Asked his opinion concerning another Creole at Freetown, he replied, " Well, I think he must have been born on the Sabbath." Then, seeing my puzzled look, he added, significantly, " On the seventh day God rested from all his work."

He also told me a story of a neighbouring Creole who prosecuted a native trader for stealing a monkey from a batch which the former was conveying for sale. Addressing the magistrate, the prosecutor asked for an example to be made of the accused because " there has been a lot of monkey-stealing lately, and none of us is safe."

*　　*　　*　　*

Easter is a festival of the pagans as well as of the Christians. Only a mile or so on the other side of Waterloo I met a festival party of the Bondu Secret Society, the functions and dances of which I have described in a separate chapter. The devil dance was

TEMNE AND SUSU CHIEFS WITH DISTRICT COMMISSIONERS.

(*Photo by W. H. Seymour.*)

Face p. 66.

in full progress, and all went well until, in a moment of indiscretion, I opened my camera and tried to snap the "devil."

Instantly I was surrounded by yelling women using every artifice to screen their idol. It was unnecessary. Quickly I realized that I had made a mistake, and at once rectified it. I explained that I had wanted to photograph the most beautiful woman and had chosen the "devil."

The result was electric. The women thronged round their "devil" and communicated the compliment. But the sense of the mysterious, fear of the white man's spell, and fidelity to the cult triumphed over vanity. The inner group encircled their "devil" so as to screen her completely from the camera, while the *mensu,* or "mistress of ceremonies," explained that her devilship would not permit herself to be snapped. Naturally, I did not press the matter; but I regretted losing so unique a picture. A friend tried to console me later by saying that if all I wanted was a devil any woman would do. I could not share his misogyny.

*   *   *   *

A second visit to Waterloo a week or so later is even more indelibly impressed upon my mind. I hammocked into Waterloo to "chop" with Mr. Lane-Poole, the able Director of Forestry, who spent a few days there during his periodical tour up country. He is one of the most enthusiastic of officials, and I was sorry I could not stay longer with him. The next day, after visiting the creeks and riverside, I proceeded to the hotel for refreshment. As I was being ushered into the best room I noticed a picturesque personage attired in flowing robes being escorted out, apparently to leave the room for me. He saluted me with an English "Good afternoon." Seeing he was a native chief of some dignity, and anxious to interview such a person, I motioned him to stay, and invited him to return to the room and partake of some refreshment. He seemed much pleased, and accepted with marked breeding.

Scarcely had we started our conversation, however, when there was a tumultuous noise outside. The chief, quickly divining the cause, hurried to the verandah, and, leaning over, addressed a few words to the noisy ones below. A short harangue followed, and the chief, returning to me, asked if I would permit his two head-men to come up and sit in the room, as his retinue outside had seen their chief return into the room with me, and, jumping to the conclusion that I had taken their king prisoner, were clamouring to come in, and were having an angry palaver with my boys. Much amused, I at once acquiesced. The two headmen came up and the commotion ceased. The headmen had to be pressed considerably before they would accept each a drink. They were still suspicious of me, and they could speak no English, not even the Kru English.

Their qualms were soon dispersed, however, when they saw how composed and friendly their chief appeared to be towards me. He spoke English quite well, having been educated at the Chiefs' College, and was gifted with very good intuition. His name signified "smart," and was appropriate to the man. He had plenty of labour available in his domains—the upper reaches of Kwaia country—he said, and invited me to visit him there, offering to send down carriers to Songo Town to convey me through the bush, or a war-canoe to transport me by water. Knowing that I should have considerable hammocking to do in visiting places off the railway line, I chose the water, and after a few exchanges of compliments he departed for Songo with his retinue.

CHAPTER IX.

CANOEING ON THE BUNCE AND SIERRA LEONE RIVERS.

Arrival of a King's Courier—Mangroves—The Bullom Shore—
Electric Launch Service—Possibilities of the Waterway, and
a New Port—A Temne's Devotion—Tasso and its History—
Bunce Island, Tombo, and Gambia.

SOON after daybreak one morning there was a stir
of excitement in the compound or village around the
store. The blast of a bugle was heard among the trees
leading from the wharf and creek. A few moments
later a courier from the native king arrived at the store
and was soon speeding up the plantation towards the
bungalow, preceded by two of my boys and followed
by the native overseer. He was attired in clean white
linen loosely wrapped around him. Upon his head
was a long knitted woollen cap of many colours. In
one hand he carried his most precious possession,
a military bugle, which had seen better days but had
never probably been better blown. It had been purchased second-hand in Freetown. In the other hand
was the missive from the king, his master. I opened
the letter, written upon English notepaper, and in
English style. It contained a warm welcome to his
territory and informed me that his captain, who was
the bearer of the missive, would escort me thither with
any attendants I might bring.

The spelling was absolutely faultless, and the whole
epistle should put to the blush many a youth who
emerges from some of our schools with a so-called
" finished " education and a snobbery and ignorance
which classify all people of a darker hue as " niggers "
and " uncivilized." The courier was courtesy itself.
His natural ease, his low obeisance, the graceful

manner in which he doffed his cap and handed his master's message were worthy of a European Court.

Ordering " chop " to be given to the captain and crew of the boat, I hastily partook of some fruit, scrambled eggs, toast, and tea tempered with lime juice, which I used in place of milk. My house-boy meanwhile gathered together a hurried outfit for river and bush, with provisions, presents, guns, and, not least, fresh water. There was no time to lose. Unless we embarked by 8 o'clock or 8.30 we should miss the tide at the junction of the Sierra Leone and Bunce Rivers, and have to spend an extra night on the water.

The assistant manager of the plantation decided, not without some reluctance, to accompany me. He considered my proposed expedition a mad freak, and in this he was supported by a Government official who arrived on the scene that morning on a tour up the railway line. " As long as a European is on the iron road," said this representative of a race which is second to none in enterprise and exploration, " he is safe; but to visit a native chief, sleep on a native boat, explore unknown bush—why, my dear sir, it is absolute madness, especially at this time of the year, the hottest of all months. Besides, sir, these very people you are visiting are the people who gave us the most trouble when they rose against us in 1906. It's not safe; it's uncanny."

Since my return I have remembered his words and admit that there was some reason for them.

But my mind was then made up. Nothing could deter me. With us went three boys, one Mendi and two Temnes. The first of these showed some fear at first, as he did not like the idea of being the only Mendi boy in the land of a rival tribe. He was, however, quite of a superior order among his race, and a very faithful and trustworthy servant also, and his fears died away with the excitement of a long journey and appreciation at being selected by me to accompany us.

The boat was something between a canoe and a surf-boat, and was not at all uncomfortable. There were six oarsmen and a coxswain, besides the captain. The inevitable drums were on board for the accompaniment to the bugle.

A large crowd of boys working upon that part of the plantation nearest to the wharf assembled to see us off, and, as usual among natives, each wanted to carry an article—but not more than one—to the boat in the expectation of a " dash."

Before 8.30 we were well away. As the landing stage of the wharf and the fine old coconut plantation adjoining faded away, there came a momentary reflection that possibly we were taking a hazardous journey and might not see this spot again. Such a feeling, however, rapidly subsided as we gave ourselves up to the pleasures of an African river, the diversities of the aboriginal Temnes, and the opportunities afforded for observation of the adjacent country and its possibilities for future enterprise.

The Bunce itself gives but a few glimpses of the sport and delight of a tropical river, and our boys reserved their liveliness till it was left behind. We shot a few wildfowl and tried to distinguish other birds which flittered over from the mangroves which hid us from the mainland of the Colony on our left to the low-lying land of the Protectorate on our right. Once only did we see a crocodile. Sport and the dangers of an African river awaited us farther on.

For the first few hours, therefore, the surrounding country absorbed our greatest attention, except when the sandbanks in the river caused us occasionally to divert our course and take soundings.

There is a good wharf here in a sheltered spot hidden from the main river by the island of mangroves already mentioned. Emerging from this bend of the river and leaving the coconut plantation upon the right, the Bunce flows onward towards Waterloo, losing its name as a river and becoming known as Waterloo creek. When I returned to this district later I explored the creek, following the mangrove banks along to Waterloo, demonstrating that a large boat carrying about 3 tons can get up there even in the driest of dry seasons, though not so easily or so quickly as at the wharf, where the water is 6 ft. deep at low tide, affording a good channel for a larger boat or even a small steamer.

At this end of the river, on the Waterloo side, are many traces of the evergreen forest. This, by constant clearing in the past, has given place to the intermediate type, fast merging into the secondary or savannah forest where left in the hands of the native, but preserved to a large extent where, as on the adjacent estate, the land is under European ownership and supervision. On the other side, on the flat land opposite, is a large kola farm owned by a Creole.

Farther down the Bunce the mainland on the left is almost hidden by the mangroves, but the hills behind, many of them clothed in primeval forest, render the scene very picturesque.

The mangroves are an interesting group of trees which inhabit the swampy foreshores of tropical countries, where they form forests frequently of vast extent. The barks of all the mangroves appear to contain more or less tannin, but the principal species yield barks containing from 40 to 50 per cent. of tannin. The bark is merely stripped from the stems and branches, broken up into small pieces and dried in the sun, preferably under cover. When dry it is packed into bales weighing about 1 cwt.

On the right the low-lying land is dissected by another river, the Robunce, the source of which apparently lies in the hills behind Polamatot. A little engineering would doubtless join this stream with those running into the Rokelle River and cut a by-way into the latter, thereby saving the long and often treacherous journey round the sandbanks at the junction of the Rokelle and Bunce.

From the Robunce our course lay almost right across

stream, until the junction was reached, when the wind caused us great trouble, and the oarsmen made little headway. There are sharks in the channel here, so we were naturally anxious lest mishaps should occur. Before us, however, lay a fine sea- and land-scape. The deep blue of the sea and sky, the orange-red of the soil, and the brilliant green slopes of the hills, developing into darker green and brown as they rose higher and higher, made a scene never to be forgotten. On the left, Kline Town glistened in the sunshine, while the mountains behind receded into distance, and the Rokelle River flowed rapidly out to sea. On the right was the broad expanse of water that forms a highway of two or three separate channels to the palm lands of Makene, and the lesser-known territory of the Temnes, in the further reaches of the Kwaia country. This estuary is frequently called the Sierra Leone River. In front of us lay the Bullom shore, a low-lying territory with distant hillsides upon which firewood is cut and from which the leopard frequently saunters to make havoc in the villages of the plain.

Of this Bullom shore an early adventurer records :—

" Under the shade of a tree sat the king in an armchair, dressed in a suit of blue silk, trimmed with silver lace, with a laced hat and ruffled shirt, and shoes and stockings. On each side sat his principal people, and behind him two or three of his wives. This river was formerly a place of great trade for slaves and ivory, but the slave merchants now take a different route.

" The natives are originally Suzees, but the principal people call themselves Portuguese, claiming their descent from the colonists of that nation who were formerly settled here, though they do not retain the smallest trace of European extraction. Immoderately fond of liquid, they part with everything they are possessed of to acquire it, and when those means fail they pursue the same course which idle drunkards do in every part of the world : rob and plunder their neighbours, for few apply themselves to trade."

Much export produce comes down these rivers by native canoe and surf-boat, the loaded down trips being made on the current, the tides extending for about forty miles. In the wet season ocean-going cargo boats might ascend the river here for about fifteen miles, but in the " dries " this would be impossible.

An electric launch service is, however, run in all seasons between Freetown and Port Lokkoh, the most northerly town of any importance, and a similar service might be arranged between Waterloo and Mahera on the Rokelle River. If a port were established on the Bunce, or farther up on the Rokelle River, much of the riverway commerce would be diverted there, for although the fifteen miles or so to Freetown on the current is nothing to the native, the return journey is no easy matter, the current at this part being very strong.

*   *   *   *

Here occurred an incident trivial enough as it seemed, but of more importance, perhaps, than I then realized. The vice-captain of the boat, whom I had previously noticed regarding me curiously when not issuing his orders in lordly style, came to sit behind me in the stern to take his turn at the rudder. The boat gave a lurch as he passed over. Involuntarily I put out my hands to steady him, and his lithe body slipped through them to the seat in the stern. Quickly touching my hands, he expressed his thanks. Then looking full at me, he added, with the little English he had picked up at Freetown, " I love you, massa ; you like me !"

How could I do otherwise than like this impulsive, outspoken child of Nature?

From that moment, Fodi, who, I discovered later, was the chief's nephew, and whose name, though common among the Temnes, is usually only found among those of royal or warrior descent, took me under his special protection. Although we had brought our own house-boys, Fodi was always at hand to get anything I wanted. When we landed anywhere for any purpose, as we were obliged occasionally to do, Fodi alone carried me to dry land, although two natives are usually required to perform this service for a European. Imperious to his subordinates, surly even to his captain, to me he was always cheerfully obedient and obliging; for me his mouth relaxed and his white teeth were ever showing. From him I learnt all the Temne dialect or language which I could retain, as well as the story of Bai Bureh and the particulars of the Porro Secret Society narrated in subsequent chapters.

Nowhere, perhaps, more than among primitive races and where Nature reigns supreme, does luck, chance, coincidence, fate, or whatever else you may term it, play so great a part in one's success, and even in one's continued existence. Personal predilections or unconscious affinities are important enough in all European walks of life, and everyone knows how much both faith and distrust are inspired by the subtle forces of attraction and repulsion; but we Europeans are too much inclined to place ourselves on a pinnacle and conceive it impossible for black and white to feel anything but repulsion or, at least, indifference towards each other. Yet here was an aborigine taking a sudden fancy to me and asking reciprocity. And here was I, usually over-cautious if anything in placing my confidence, trusting this Temne as I should never trust some Europeans, and afterwards sleeping soundly and securely on a boat among ten Africans, knowing that one at least was devoted to me and would watch though he could not pray. I should not have dreamed of sleeping similarly among strange Europeans in a strange land without one eye open and one hand on a revolver.

The first break of our journey was at Tasso.

Tasso is a very pretty island, and, judging from the number of boats which touch there and its geographical situation between Freetown and the convergence of the Sierra Leone and Rokelle Rivers, the petty trade must be enormous. Yet only black or rather Creole traders are there, and the bottled beer and lemonade bore, without exception, German labels.

Here was established in 1663 the English factory or store of the " Royal Adventurers," a Company which had for its founders the Queen of England, the Duke of York (afterwards James II), and the mother of Charles II. One of the conditions of its many concessions was that it should supply 3,000 negro slaves annually to the British West Indies.

Tasso, with factory and port, was captured in 1664 by the Dutch under De Ruyter, but by the Treaty of 1667 was restored to the English Adventurers. The subsequent African Company maintained a large slave plantation on this island. Then it fell into the possession of the Bullom natives, whose domains lay on the north side of the river. Finally, with Bunce, Tombo, and other islands adjacent, together with a strip of territory a mile in breadth on the north Bullom shore, it was ceded to the British Government in 1824.

Along the southern banks of the mainland between Tasso and the next few islands are mangroves in plenty, the branches touching and trailing the water, encumbered by oysters and barnacles, while fish is abundant in the river.

Three other islands are very conspicuous and notable in this highway of rivers. They are known as Bunce, Tombo, and Gambia.

The first formed the refuge of the Royal Adventurers' Company after the capture of Tasso. The fort of lime and stone was on a steep rock, the only access to which was by stairs cut in the rock. The walls were mounted with forty-four guns, and over the gate was a platform with five or six pieces of artillery. The trade was in elephants' teeth, beeswax, gold, and negroes, but nothing of this exists to-day. The French pillaged it in 1704; pirates sacked it once more in 1720, seizing the Governor.

Tombo, a little farther up the river—now nominally under female domination, the chief being Mammy Karu —is historically celebrated as the island to which

CATTLE BREEDING WITHIN 20 MILES OF FREETOWN.

(A contradiction to the Official Handbook.)

Face p. 76.

Governor Plunkett escaped from the pirates in 1720, and from which he was ignominiously brought back. The story goes that the Governor cursed and swore so furiously at the pirate chief, who was using similar language, that the other pirates declared their chief to be out-matched. Plunkett, by this means, saved his life and was left with the ruined fort.

Gambia Island was formerly in possession of the French, who had a garrison and battery of six guns there. It was ceded to Britain in 1802. The soil is rich, but mangrove swamps surround it.

———————

CHAPTER X.

CANOEING ON THE ROKELLE RIVER.

Effects of the Dry Season—130° F. on the Water—The Devil
Rocks and Port Lokkoh—The War of the Temnes and the
Susus—A Weird Boat Dance—Barbaric Boleros—A Crocodile
Adventure—Hippopotami—Stoicism of the Native.

" *Numant, Numant,*" replies the captain, when I
inquired why we seemed to be travelling miles out of
our course after leaving Tasso and the islands.

Numant means " with water," and water is a word
full of meanings, just as it is to us. Involuntarily I
called to mind that we speak of a person in a predica-
ment as being in " hot water " or unable to " keep his
head above water," or " all at sea." Could this be
the captain's meaning? That we were in " hot " water
was certain, for the thermometer I carried registered
130° F., and some of the natives were beginning to
feel ill-effects from it, as was also my white companion.
But I dismissed this interpretation. Equally unfitting
to the occasion were the mouths which " water " at
dainty things, or arguments that " won't hold water."
Finally, I came to the solution. In the dry season
here, boats require clever navigation, good piloting,
and inexhaustible patience, for the Rokelle River is
full of sandbanks, rocks, and narrow channels. The
captain meant that he followed the water.

The dry season was at its height. The exceptional
drought was causing anxiety at Freetown lest yellow
fever should again break out as in a previous year of
extreme drought. I had been in Sierra Leone a month
and not a drop of rain had yet fallen. Personally, I
had felt no inconvenience, but I began to understand

that one must get tired of living in a place where for long lapses of time no rain falls.

Sunlit day after sunlit day apparently palls upon one. The regular coming of the glare and brilliance of the sun in time appears to jar and disquiet the nerves of Europeans. Without rain, light is death, even as darkness is death. There is no stillness and desolation such as the stillness and desolation of the parched plain; no silence like the silence that here abounds on a wide expanse of water with no shady bank. Dead seem the places where no rain falls; dead as the bright shining moon which accompanies our world on its voyage through the heavens. In contemplating such a country one involuntarily conjures up a remote future, when the rain will no longer fall in this world of ours, when seas and oceans, brooks and rivers will be dried up, and the world will journey through the heavens, arid and dead.

* * * *

Our course had led us almost within sight of Port Lokkoh, some miles farther ahead up another channel of this wide confluence of rivers. Now we turned our course to the right. As we did so, the boat-boys seemed to want to air their knowledge of the river and country we were leaving, and thus we heard the story of the war between the Temnes and the Susus which many years ago was waged for the supremacy in this district.

* * * *

Bacca Lokkoh, or Porto Lokkoh, the port from which many Lokkoh people were shipped to be sold at Bunce Island as slaves, is situated about forty miles from Freetown up the Sierra Leone River. At the entrance to this branch of the river are two large rocks called the "Devil Rocks," which are never covered by the highest tide. The natives have a legend that these rocks travel. In past times sacrifices were offered to them.

The Temnes, the owners of the country, resided on

the north bank of the river, and called their town Old
Porto Lokkoh.   About the year 1700, permission was
granted to the Susu people, who were engaged in the
slave trade, to settle on the south bank of the river,
which they named Sain Dugu.   In process of time the
Temnes built another town called Ro Marung, and the
Susus built Ro Batt.   The Susus, Muhammadans from
Mellacouri, in the Morea country, usurped the chief
authority in the district, while the Temnes, who were
at that time unable to resist, gave them wives and
placed many of the children of the principal men at
schools under them to learn the Koran.   Thus many
Temne children were carefully brought up according to
the Muhammadan creed, and acquired wealth and power
in the country.   The Susus at Sain Dugu were of the
Sankong family, with a chief called the Almami.

This state of affairs continued until about the year
1815, on the assumption of the government by Brimah
Konkori Sankong.   He was an arbitrary ruler, and the
Temnes, thinking themselves oppressed, took up arms
in 1816 under Momba Kindo, son of one of the principal kings of the country.   Before taking active
measures, Momba Kindo visited the Susus' country to
gather information concerning them.   Whilst at
Malaghea he heard the title of " Alikarlie " used; learning that it meant a magistrate or judge, he said he
would like to have the title introduced into his country.
His wish was granted, and upon paying merchandise
to the value of seven slaves (about £20), a turban worn
by persons of that title was placed on his head.   This
was his coronation.   As soon as it was over he returned
to his country and summoning all the principal men of
the Temne country to a private meeting, he bound
them individually by oath not to reveal what they
should hear.   After they had been sworn he proposed
that they should take up arms and expel the Susus from
the country.   This was agreed upon, and he was
acknowledged as Alikarlie.

An influential Temne chief of Mandingo descent,

called Fatma Brimah Camarra, was nominated to be his second in authority for carrying out their plans. Bai Foki, the king of the country, having been offended by the behaviour of the Susus, placed the country under the Alikarlie's management in these words : " My son, you are my son, the country is yours as it is mine. I and your people can no longer bear the insult of these strangers. I place the country in your hands that, with my assistance, and that of the whole country, you drive the Susus out of this land."

The Alikarlie said, " Thank you, father, that is all I want. I shall call to my assistance a dear and true-hearted friend, one that will be able to take my place if I fall in the struggle and carry out your wish."

The Alikarlie then had a drum, called tablay, made, which was to be in possession of none but the king or chief in authority. The plan for attacking the Susus having been made known to all the Temnes, the Alikarlie one morning ordered this drum to be beaten. Hearing this drum for the first time, the Susu Almami at Sain Dugu sent to see if his own tablay was in its place. Being told that it was, he ordered 150 armed men to proceed to Ro Marung and bring the offending tablay, the person who was beating it, and the person who ordered it to be beaten.

The Susus proceeded, unaware that more than 500 Temnes were in ambush in a thicket which divided Ro Marung from Sain Dugu and Ro Batt. They were all captured, their arms seized without a gun being fired, and they themselves taken as prisoners to the Alikarlie. Some of the principal men were killed, and five sent back to inform their chief of the intention of the Temnes. From all quarters the Temnes poured into the town. Engagements succeeded one another day after day. The Susus fought desperately, but were defeated, and the Temnes having besieged their stockade until the Susus had exhausted their supplies of water and provisions, the latter surrendered. Sain Dugu was then entered, and the Almami, Brimah

Konkori, and his chiefs beheaded. Others were sold into slavery. None of the Temne women who were wives to the Susus, nor their children, were killed, but were allowed to return to their own families and their adult children given the privilege of citizens. Amongst those who were thus spared were Lamina Lakai, Misfarray, Booboo Sankong, Adamah Lahai Momoh Sankong, and several others, who afterwards became leading men and Muhammadans. Several of their descendants I met while in the Temne and Susu country.

The Susus once played an important part in the history of the Niger Valley, living side by side with the Fulahs or Fulanis, with whom they have intermixed. Both races were given to pastoral pursuits, and some authorities have endeavoured to trace their descent to the Hyksos or Shepherd Kings of Egypt. Many of them are prominent by their somewhat aquiline features, straight hair, and oval faces. They retain also their love of cattle-dealing and nomadism. A favourite occupation also is the making of linen and silk costumes, at which they are very adept. I was so struck with their cleverness in this respect, and also with their picturesque garb and apparently clean habits, that I placed the hospitality of a little unused trading shanty on the Waterloo road, near Christineville village, at the disposal of a few of these Susus wandering round that country, in the hope that this would form an attraction in that spot and bring in more trade there. While I was there the experiment was answering satisfactorily, but I hear it was discontinued soon after I left, innovations of this sort not being appreciated by the average European.

Another race worth mentioning at this juncture, because he is often met in the Port Lokkoh country and higher up, is the Mandingo.

The pure Mandingo is tall, with long arms, lean, active, intelligent, brave, clever in trading and as an artizan. These qualities make his race dominant among

the tribes of North-West Africa. His marked features
are the low brow, long head, and prognathous jaws.
The eyes also of this race are longer and narrower than
those of the pure negro.

*   *   *   *

With the estuary behind us, and their native Rokelle
in front of and around them, the boat-boys became
extremely lively. The bugle rang out, the kettle-drums
were beaten vigorously, and various noises were added
to form an accompaniment to the weird boat-dance in
which they now indulged.

Instead of sitting in the boat to row, they would
stand on the bottom and place one leg upon the seat.
Then they would lift themselves upon the seat with
both legs and, while still rowing, each would throw
one foot backwards and upwards into the air, balancing
upon one foot and not relinquishing the oars.

At the same time they chanted a dirge-like ditty
or sang some song, which, although evidently to them
inspiring, had yet to me a mournful cadence. Some-
how I always detected a strain of sadness or mnemonic
of melancholy in the music of West Africa, whether
it were a barbaric bolero or fierce fantasia on horn or
drum.

*   *   *   *

We were now out of salt water and into the brackish,
between salt and fresh. The wind was with us,
although rather squally, and the boys put up a sail
to speed our journey.

Rayel Island and Mabombo were passed. Forogudu
was in sight. With fresh water now around us we
raced through it joyously, when suddenly we were
again reminded how near to life is death.

Close to a wooded bank was a " hippo " pool. Our
captain directed our attention to it as we sailed rather
close to shore. For a few moments we watched these

huge, harmless monsters lazily lolling in and out of the water, now exposing their heads with a snort, now disappearing in an almost unrippled pool. So cumbersome are these beasts that they take nearly twenty-four hours to float after being sunk by a shot.

Suddenly our boat gave a lurch. Our sail dipped heavily in the water, and a young hippopotamus, till now unperceived by us, disappeared towards the bank. It had evidently wandered into the river too far from home and, frightened at our boat standing between it and the bank, had made a dive to reach the shore and slightly touched our boat.

To add to our comfort, or discomfort, we saw at that moment, close at hand, two or three crocodiles basking on a sandbank, anticipating, possibly, a feast.

To be capsized in waters infested by these ugly and rapacious reptiles was too horrible to contemplate. I remembered the boy I had seen disappear with a crocodile. I recalled the many stories I had heard concerning these tropical pests, and reflected that a mere blow from one of their tails might mean a broken limb, even if one escaped their jaws. Strange, is it not, how many memories in a moment of peril revive instantaneously and crowd together in the mind?

There was no time, however, for reflection. Instinctively all of us threw our weight upon the side of the boat most above water. At the same time one of the boys dexterously unfastened the sail and let it go—we recovered it afterwards. Then with the boat half full of water we made for the shore and baled out.

Finding a little ammunition dry we tried some ostensibly on the hippopotami, but really upon the crocodiles. Many of these repulsive reptiles are 12 ft. or more in length, and prey upon all fauna, including monkey and man.

The crocodile's head is nearly one-fifth of its total length, and from the eyes it tapers down to a blunt snout with a bulbous nose, on the top of which are the nostrils. In basking on the top of the water, all that is seen is the piece of the head between the eyes and the bulb of the snout above the water-line. When alarmed, he sinks silently below the surface.

Like other reptiles, the crocodile takes a long time to expire, even after a fatal wound. When a good shot tells in the spine, heart, or brain, the tail only quivers gently. A bad shot simply hurries him into the river, in which case, even if mortally wounded, he can only be secured after a day or two, when he floats upwards on his back. When alive he always swims against the stream.

In the event of a good shot, the boat is grounded noiselessly, the loom of an oar placed across the snout, and two boys stand on the flat portion of the oar to keep the jaws closed, while a rope is placed under them, by which to haul him up.

There can be little doubt that the crocodiles in some of the rivers are intelligent and possessed of great skill in upsetting light canoes and obtaining a meal. They have been known to seize the arm of a single occupant of a canoe as he stoops to his stroke, and pull the paralysed victim to the depths. Natives are consequently very superstitious in crossing infested rivers.

A few yards from the bank just here is a large oval-shaped stone, before which a heap of leaves is piled. To ensure safety in crossing, some of the leaves are plucked and rubbed over the forehead, while an incantation is muttered, which, being interpreted, means : " I am coming across the river ; may the crocodile lay down his head." The same fear of the crocodile is manifested by Gold Coast and Nigerian natives.

The meat of the crocodile is much appreciated by some African peoples. In this district, however, the crocodile and alligator are, apparently, regarded with superstitious veneration. If a man's evil genius should be supposed to be a crocodile, and he happened to eat some of its flesh, he would contract some skin disease.

In some parts of French Guinea, a crocodile is kept in a tank in the centre of a village, fed carefully and worshipped. Generally, however, the crocodile is loathed, both by the black and the white men.

* * * *

The danger from which we had just escaped had not damped the ardent spirits of our boat-boys, and we had not proceeded far before our craft grounded on the sands, and the boys had to get out and shove her off. They took the opportunity to have a good swim and to wash all their clothes. The Temnes, I ought to mention, are very cleanly; all the time I was with them I never saw an indecent or unclean action. Those with me in the boat were typical Temne war-boys. When the hippo-crocodile incident occurred, my throat, curiously dry, did not lend itself to conversation, yet they never ceased chattering.

The West African is certainly stoical. Seldom does a sigh of regret escape from him. Sorrow is forgotten the day after to-morrow. Faithfully does he live Long-fellow's " Psalm of Life." He lets the " dead past bury its dead "; he " trusts no future howe'er pleasant," and he " lives in the living present." With a laugh, a jeer, or profound nonchalance, he steps ashore into swamp or jungle, or sports in a crocodile-infested river. A man must live and a man must die—how or where it matters little. And his spirit is infectious. You forget the many Europeans at home and in the Coast towns feeling their pulses and examining their tongues, with palpitating hearts and grim visions of malaria and coffins—people who would live painlessly like the worm, or prolong indefinitely their rapid existence like the carp, yet unconsciously hugging the shadow of death because they dare not enjoy to-day through trembling piteously for the morrow. And there, there on the Rokelle, enjoying the languor and loveliness of a tropical afternoon, listening to the lapping of waters and watching the nodding palms and the boys disporting themselves, there is revealed to you the secret of the happy boyishness of these natives, the defiance of death, the joy of life.

CHAPTER XI.

IN A NATIVE CHIEF'S PALACE.

Patriotism of the Temnes—Reception by the Chief—My European Companion becomes Incapacitated—Superstitions and their Usefulness—Alone in a Strange Land—Equipments of a Native Palace—Amusements—The Principal Wife and her Children—The Position of Women—Polygyny—Tracing Descent through the Mother—Marriage of Cousins.

TOWARDS sunset, after a long day's journey, there was a cry from the boat-boys—" Mahera ! Mahera !"

Before us upon a small hill, nestling among palms and profuse tropical vegetation, there appeared a very superior native village, in which the abode of the chief or king stood conspicuous. The sight gave me no less a thrill of pleasure than it did the boat-boys. The heat upon the water had been very trying, and the nearness to death to which we had approached during the day made more welcome the haven of rest to which we were approaching. The enthusiasm of the boys upon seeing their home also added to my sympathy for these natives. Europeans are too apt to treat the African as though he had no fine feelings. Yet there was a ring in those voices, a gleam in those eyes, a reanimated vigour in those tired arms and legs which revealed a patriotism more natural, more inspiring than the utterances of many an educated European upon a political platform.

A few minutes more and our boat ran alongside the short towing-path, from which mangroves were entirely absent. Down the steep hilly path winding from the village to the waterside through an evergreen avenue of palms, there descended slowly and majestically a picturesque procession, the chief or king, in robes of state, with his headmen and suite, in gala attire. The chief was clothed in a long flowing robe of white linen, over which hung, like a priest's stole, over either shoulder, a blue silk breadth. Embroidered slippers, which many an English curate might envy, a gold-mounted stick carried as a sceptre, a tinsel crown, and a white umbrella held over him by an attendant, completed an outfit at once dignified, becoming, and artistic.

We were received with a warm welcome by the monarch and conducted up the steep and evergreen path. We were offered hammocks and carriers, but I preferred to walk. My European companion, however, gladly availed himself of the conveyance. He felt the heat badly, and the same evening had an attack of malaria, which confined him for the next few days, thus leaving me alone in my wanderings through the Temne country. Two of the boat-boys and one of our attendants were also very much exhausted, and our hosts appeared very surprised that I did not feel the effects of the intense heat.

I discovered next day that I was given an un-pronounceable nickname which signified "sun-beloved," because they said "The sun must love massa much." This sobriquet proved very useful to me in subsequent travels among and in dealings and relations with the peoples of the Protectorate, for next to courage and equanimity, and sometimes, perhaps, even in preference to those qualities, there is nothing the West African reveres so much as power or ability to cope with the forces of Nature. Of course, his reasoning is all objective, *i.e.,* he attributes it not to any inherent or acquired capacity in the person possessing these qualities, but as a gift from the gods. Thus it was "the sun that loved massa," not massa who was able to stand the sun. Similarly, when my Mendi boy felt ill, it was not his stomach or digestion that was out of order. No! his illness was caused by the Temne tribe in whose country he found himself who were poisoning him, or using their medicine charms upon his food. Yet another example I noticed later when in the Mendi country. A native had an accident with a gun which exploded and deprived him for a time of the use of his eyes. Instead of telling us he could not see, he informed us " The sun gone dam."

Arrived at the top of the hill, we were surprised to find quite a compact village of good-class native dwellings, evidently those of the headmen and councillors, an excellent little store, run by the chief, and a comfortable well-equipped building of stone, wood, bamboo, thatch and mud, which was both roomy and picturesque, as well as sanitary. The walls were detached from the roof, which not only covered the building, but protruded on either side, triangular in shape, to wooden supports at front and back, forming porticos on either side, affording shade from the sun, protection from the rains, and a cool and well-distributed ventilation throughout the building. A large reception or court-room, tastefully furnished in semi-African, semi-European style, occupied the main part of the building. On the left side were bedrooms, furnished with European bedsteads and bedding covered by mosquito nets, enamel toilet sets, and a native rug. On the right were the chief's domestic quarters.

After a refreshing meal of soup, chicken, rice, omelette, native fruits and palm wine, a musical box (made in Germany) was set in motion, the chief's principal officials assembling to meet the white man and enjoy the music. After the music there was a display from a cinema lantern (also made in Germany). The pictures were not good, and sometimes could scarcely be distinguished, but the audience did not mind; in fact, they seemed to enjoy any failures of the lantern as much as its success, and were particularly hilarious when the picture appeared upside down.

This performance over, the assembly broke up, but not the merriment. Drums and bugles, chatter and laughter continued outside and in the vicinity for hours afterwards.

While the merriment was in progress, and afterwards, I had time to observe and converse with the chief's principal wife and advisers. With the former this was easy. She spoke English almost as well as her husband, though she had not the advantage of his college education. She had picked up all she knew from her parents, the Bondu Society, and Freetown; but never had woman so profited by all she learnt. Her household was a model one. Though no longer young, she was still a dusky beauty, and her intelligence and skill were amazing. She had heard of and longed to talk about Europe and England, the ways and thoughts of the white people and their children, the streets of London and its amusements, the electric light, the shipping, the parliament, and the churches. Then she showed me her basketwork of many colours, exquisitely plaited and tastefully dyed. Involuntarily, one could not but contrast her with a white official's lady farther down on the Coast, whose conversation always hovered between lumbago and the depravities of the black race. Meantime, two of her young boys had calmly seated themselves on my knees. One of these future Nimrods was very loth to let me go when, days afterwards, I took my leave. He wanted to come to England with me, and the chief had to promise that when he was older, and I came again, he should go. Altogether the scene was more like an ideal English home than a remote African palace. All the women of the household seemed happy.

The incident related in a previous chapter concerning the tenant's mammy is, therefore, indicative of one side only of the African woman's existence, and that probably after years of married life, and when she has ceased to have children. For, generally speaking, the married woman of Sierra Leone does not begin cooking her husband's meals at once, or even after the first baby is born. Social etiquette demands that the man shall procure somebody to wait upon his wife and fetch water at this time.

Further, as an indication that all the natives are not wanting in little courtesies to their women, let me narrate another little incident. In the course of my travels into the interior, I halted one day in a shady nook by the roadside by a little village, where an Arab named Moses supplied lime juice—slightly diluted with an intoxicant—to travellers. A group of Susus—a tribe nearly related to the Temnes, and mostly Muhamma-dans—were on the march with womenfolk; they stopped to take refreshment, and I noticed that in each case the draught was handed to the females before the men partook. I remarked also that among this group the burdens appeared equally shared between the two sexes.

Among the more important members of the Temne tribe, the lot of the women is still lighter. Frequently a young wife is secluded from the sunlight for about nine months after marriage, doing no work, but re-ceiving guests and becoming much lighter in colour. Many of them are clever with their fingers, especially at basketwork and dyeing. I brought back one or two handome specimens given to me by the chief, which were worked by his " mammies." Some of the wives of the chiefs, as I have already indicated, are decidedly superior women.

Polygyny is the custom, even among those chiefs who have nominally adopted Christianity. Frequently, however, polygyny is more a name than a deed. The chief with whom I was staying, I soon discovered, had a wife in each village we visited, but in many cases she seemed but an emblem of his authority.

Among some West African tribes the wealthy man may have four or more permanent or temporary wives, although actually cohabiting, perhaps, with but one or two, in which case the remainder are leased to other male members of the community. Both permanent and temporary wives take care to secure proper treatment for themselves, and the husband who attempts to avoid

this finds himself in an unenviable position. The
woman in most West African communities asserts herself and exercises choice even in temporary marriage
arrangements.

Among the Mendis, and some other tribes, there are,
many women "chiefs." Each is styled "Madame."
Madame Yoko was one of their most famous recent
chiefs. She was exceedingly progressive, and the
Government found her ever ready to co-operate in their
experimental planting schemes. Madame Humonyaha,
of Nongowa, is perhaps the most noted of female chiefs
to-day. At Blama also there is another enterprising
Amazon whose name I have lost; while at Lubu there
is Madame Margow, at Bagbeh Madame Mabaja, and
at Nomor Madame Jungar, all excellent women.

In the deportation of King Prempey of Ashanti, the
queen-mother was exiled also, she and not Prempey's
father being of the direct royal stock and therefore the
source of that king's authority and heirship to the
"stool" or throne of Ashanti.

Ask an African chief of those tribes among whom
matrilineal descent is still prevalent, why the people
prefer the devolution to pass through the females instead
of the males. He will look at you with a curious smile
and say, "Everyone knows the particular woman who
gives birth to a child, but it is more difficult to know
the father; therefore, by tracing descent through the
mother, there can be no mistake." Not that the
children of West Africa, any more than in Europe, do
not know their own fathers! As a rule they do; for
even where women maintain relations with several men
consecutively, such relations are not simultaneous.

Marriage seldom takes place among blood relations.
Some tribes object to marriage even between second
cousins, and are surprised to learn that such marriages
are not prohibited among Europeans. On the other
hand, those who can read the English newspapers, or
extracts from them in the native press, smile when they
hear that Christian ministers will not celebrate a

marriage between a man and his deceased wife's sister, although such a marriage is recognized by law.

Women are not permitted to have relations with a man except with the full knowledge and consent of her parents, husband, or other guardian. A breach of this rule means social ostracism for the woman, while the man is tried in the local court and damages awarded to the injured party. If he or his relatives cannot pay he is handed over in pawn to the injured party, to work for and pay the necessary amount.

The only excuse for irregular relations or laxity on the part of the woman is in a case of childlessness. If she has been married for any considerable time without signs of becoming a mother, the other women will excuse her among themselves. There is no excuse for the man; he must pay damages.

Incest is extremely rare, and is entirely against native custom, being punished by death in the olden days.

*   *   *   *

In this particular chiefdom the advisers to the " stool " or throne were not so easy to comprehend as the chief's wife and nephews. In the first place, the advisers were old men and less inclined to be communicative. Secondly, they only knew a few words of English, and therefore could only speak through the chief or one of his boys or wives. In this chiefdom also the chief was indeed a king. Elsewhere, particularly in French Guinea, where certain chiefs are allowed by the Government to wear swords as a mark of rank, this symbol is often the only vestige of authority they possess. Perhaps that is why they are allowed to wear a sword, so that they may really look distinguished. Certainly, in palaver, they seem quite extinguished by their advisers, who really rule, and chime in with answers to questions asked of their chief, before he has time to grasp them (the questions).

CHAPTER XII.

In the Temne Country.

Contrasts between Chiefs—Products of the Country—Quaint Devices against Theft—Story of Muhammad and the Palm—Agricultural Implements—Cacao, Bananas, and Mangoes—Rice and Benniseed—Improvidence of the Natives.

The next few days were devoted to touring the Temne country. My host tramped or canoed me to all his villages and afterwards conducted me to another native chief some miles away, whose hospitality was as generous, although wilder and more barbaric. My first host was primarily and essentially a lover of agricultural and pastoral pursuits, the second was evidently a warrior and lover of the chase, so I had ample opportunities of enjoying both these aspects of native life and custom.

First, then, as to the products and methods of these interesting people.

My host was naturally anxious to show me his rubber, his palm and his kola trees. His rubber was immature, his palms and kolas in good bearing condition. Most interesting was the ingenuity displayed against theft.

In order to keep their subjects from plucking the fruit of their more valuable trees, especially before complete ripening has taken place, the chiefs resort to several devices, each of which indicates a "taboo" and is called a "porro." Upon the kola trees I noticed sheets of parchment hung. Upon them were Arabic characters, but when I tried to decipher them, the chief smilingly assured me that they formed no sentences, but were sufficient, by the "porro" or curse which was attached to the characters, to warn both followers and travellers from interfering with the trees. This chief was not a Muhammadan, but many people in this district have embraced that faith, and this, coupled with the fact that the kola nut is very much prized by the Muhammadans, may account for the interdict being in Arabic, and, unless I am much mistaken, in characters deemed sacred by the more superstitious followers of that religion.

A more subtle sociological reason attaches to a taboo or " porro " of another kind which is used to preserve the oil palm and the coconut palm from depredations. A branch of another palm is hung head downwards with strips of white calico fastened to it. The strips indicate the virginity or immaturity of the tree, and the hanging position of the branch is said to indicate the punishment which will fall on the head of one who steals therefrom. But the tying of the branch of another palm to the tree during the time of fruition is evidently a survival of the customary method by which the date palm is fructified by the Arabs.

The date palm, as everyone probably knows, is of two kinds, the pollen-bearing and the fruit-bearing. In its wild state the wind carries the dust of the one to the flower of the other. Where the date is cultivated, the branches of the former are tied to the latter during the flowering season so that the pollen falls upon the flowers and fertilizes them, each of the pollen grains emitting a little tube which penetrates the pistil and fructifies the flower. Of course, the majority of people who tie the branches of the wilder palm to the more cultivated tree are ignorant of the botanical reasons; they do it because it is the custom, justified by experience and results. The story goes—I will not vouch for its authenticity—that the great Muhammad, noticing that his people practised this little device—probably with a ceremony in earlier days—and regarding it as a superstition, forbade it. Consequently his disciples had the mortification to see the dates of the unbeliever ripening and yielding a harvest, while their own flowers withered on the trees. At that time, being practically dependent upon the date, it was a choice for them between starvation and faith-surrender. Realizing his mistake, Muhammad issued the famous edict that Allah allowed the true believers to pillage the property of their enemies, and his immediate followers forgot the date palm in their successful career of conquest.

To return to the " porro " on the palm kernels and kolas, which prohibits the multitude from plucking a single nut. This practice was at one time indulged in by the chiefs, not merely to safeguard the fruit from premature picking, but to prevent it being picked at all by any except themselves or their favourites, the " porro " being placed upon the trees for years together. This interfered so much with trade that the Government passed an Ordinance in 1897 forbidding this imposition upon indigenous products.

Besides rubber, palms, and kolas, the chief was growing cacao, and on the way to his maturer cacao plantation I was able to observe some of the tools used by the labourers. The native agricultural implements consist chiefly of a straight-handled, narrow-bladed hoe, called " kari " (Mendi) or " katala (Temne), and one formed from an angled stick with a charred point, called " bawoe " (Mendi) or " kelal " (Temne). This last is used for drilling. In addition to these, a large broad-bladed hoe, called " karu wai " (Mendi) or " katala habana " (Temne), is employed for cleaning out weeds and scraping the soil surface, which is often the only cultivation the growing crop receives.

The chief was rightly proud of his cacao, but the results would be better for wider planting and weeding.

The native planter sows the seeds in small patches or in roughly prepared beds in the vicinity of water, often so closely as to choke a number of the young plants.

Native plantations are for the most part formed of irregular lines of trees, generally planted too closely. The evil effect of this becomes apparent when the trees

A CACAO PLANTATION IN SIERRA LEONE SHOWING PODS ON
SPECIALLY PRUNED TREE.

Face p. 96.

attain a large size. Then the excessive shade they afford to their fruit-bearing branches, which, in cacao, consists of the trunk and main structure, prevents the fruit from forming and induces rot through want of evaporation of moisture.

The native planter is slow to recognize this, and disinclined to remedy the matter by removing some of the trees. I noticed the cacao trees were frequently but 7 to 10 ft. apart, whereas from 12 to 15 ft. apart would be more suitable for the best results; the density of foliage, however, with such close planting soon makes weeding practically unnecessary.

The native cacao grower collects the pods from his trees at the time when he can gather the most, and, in consequence, many over-ripe and under-ripe fruits are taken with the ripe ones. This gives an irregular product which can never possess the attributes of a good cacao.

The pods are usually pulled off the tree, a knife being seldom used, and in the action of pulling off, the cushion upon which the pod is borne is often torn and injured. As it is from this point, or near it, that the successive crops of flowers and fruits proceed, the bearing power of the tree is thus frequently diminished.

The pods after collection are thrown into a heap upon the ground, and are often left without further attention for two or three days, after which they are broken open with the aid of a " cutlass " and the contents are scooped out into a basket. The result is a mixture of beans, in their surrounding pulp, in different stages of maturity.

After washing, the beans are spread thinly upon mats raised upon rough frames in order to dry them in the sun.

In plantations directed by Europeans, the first flowers are not allowed to produce pods as this exhausts the immature tree. Bananas are used for temporary shading purposes, affording also a paying catch-crop. Rubber is sometimes adopted as a permanent shade tree, but during the rubber boom, cacao has been cut out for the sake of the growing rubber.

Cacao is worth more attention from planters. It produces a crop in the fourth year and bears nearly all the year round from that time, with an average crop of from 1 lb. to 7 lb. per tree. From the seventh to the tenth year it arrives at full maturity. Cacao plantations shaded by the handsome broad-fringed leaves of the banana plant present a pleasing picture.

Banana trees yield but one cluster of fruit, but this alone weighs nearly half a hundredweight. The natives use the outer part of the stem as manure and the inner portion as sponge and soap and as an antidote to snake-bite. With the ripe fruit they make beer. Farther in the forest you may find the wild banana with its large bitter seeds and tasteless pulp. All that remains of these seeds in the plantation banana are the tiny specks which have lost their function, the cultivated plant reproducing itself by shoots from its base.

The mango is another fruit tree abundant in Sierra Leone, but the fruit of the West African mango has a more oily taste than its eastern brother. If you want to eat a mango get into a bath. As you bite it—the fruit, not the bath—you will find the inside fibre comes out and smears your face with the luscious pulp. From the kernel of the wild variety, which I have mentioned with more detail in my book on " West Africa," is made the celebrated " Dika " bread, and its oil would make a good substitute for butter.

Here in the Temne country and the vicinity of Port Lokkoh, the finest quality of rice is grown, and the husking of this is a prolonged process of drying, without previously soaking, this rice only requiring to be thoroughly dried before the husk will separate on pounding. Though a large quantity of rice is grown, much remains unharvested, owing to the improvidence of the native. The price just after harvesting may fall as low as 3s. 6d. per bushel, but a few months later it may reach three times that amount, for the Protectorate native realizes at once upon his crop, without taking the precaution to lay in a store for his future requirements. In consequence of this he is compelled to buy back supplies for his own consumption at a much enhanced rate. The Creole or other trader at the Coast takes advantage of this improvidence and profits considerably. A corner could easily be made in rice by an enterprising trader with adequate storage accommodation, the rice being stored as "paddy," as hereafter explained.

The crop is reaped by cutting the stalks in practically the same way as wheat. Then the crop is tied up into bundles and placed to dry on the field, or piled up on the earth banks, or arranged over bamboo poles. The grains are removed by some simple form of threshing, or by drawing the stalks through a narrow slit so that they are pulled off. Each grain is now separate and covered by the outer brown or otherwise coloured husk. Rice in this state is called " paddy," and may be, and often is, stored in this condition, as it is found to keep better in the Tropics than when the husk is removed. The disease " beriberi," believed to be due to the condition of rice, more frequently attacks the men of a village, away perhaps on a hunting or other expedition, than the women who remain at home. The women at home can pound daily the rice they require, whilst the men take a supply of cleaned rice to last the whole time of their expedition. This cleaned rice, being stored for some time, is more likely to become infested by the fungus which appears to play a part in producing beriberi than the small quantities prepared daily. Hence the reason for storing the grain as " paddy."

The West African frequently renders rice more appetizing by boiling with it a piece of salt fish or salt pork, large quantities of which figure in the list of imports of a negro population. Rice cannot by itself be made into bread, as it contains little gluten. But it is very easily digested and of great benefit to invalids who cannot readily take starchy vegetables, such as potatoes.

It is used almost universally by black and white people in place of "mealies." The straw of the plant is a fairly good fodder for cattle. The husks or chaff are useful for manure and in a variety of other ways. Rice, bran, and the mixture of broken grains, dust, &c., are valuable cattle foods. Rice polish is the most nutritious of the by-products which result from the milling and cleaning of rice.

Benniseed and cassava form side-crops which come to maturity at different periods of the year. Cassava I have already described. Benniseed is like the "til" or "gingelly" of India. The seeds are pale or dark brown in colour, according to the variety of the plant, and the oil extracted from them is yellow, clear, and non-smelling, besides possessing the power of preservation for a long time without becoming rancid. It could be used in Europe for making butter substitutes and for mixing with olive oil, although it appears only to be used locally for food purposes at present. The seedcake forms a valuable cattle food and good manure, but as cattle are scarce here it is only used for the latter purpose, and frequently wasted. In Northern Nigeria the plant is grown in separate fields, but here it is grown as one of three crops, each coming to maturity at different periods of the year.

GATHERING OF MENDI, TEMNE AND KONNOH CHIEFS AT MOYAMBA.

Face p. 100.

CHAPTER XIII.

Native Amusements by Daylight, Torchlight, and Moonlight.

Reception by another Chief—Hospitality of the African—The Balangi Music—The Courier and his Horse—The Tsetse-fly and Sleeping Sickness—The Hammock Dance—The Sword and Torch Dance by Moonlight—The Story of the Hut Tax and Temne Rising—Bai Bureh and his Exploits.

Towards midday, under a sweltering sun, we arrived at a clean and prosperous village, from whence the echo of much music and merriment proceeded. From the *zimbeks* on the outskirts we were reinforced by a number of native stragglers, who were apparently unused to seeing a European with a native chief and his retinue, and naturally anxious to know our business. Thus we made our way to the chief's abode. In a commodious verandah, reclining in a hammock, enjoying some music and dances, and surrounded by wives and attendants, I saw a broad and ponderous figure, every inch a chief. He left his hammock slowly to greet his brother chief and me, but as he could speak but a few words of English, the other chief acted as interpreter. Chickens were at once slaughtered, eggs sprang up like mushrooms, and palm wine appeared as at the rubbing of a magic ring.

The hospitality of the Africans has been noticed by almost every traveller who has been much among them, and I cordially endorse their verdict. In travelling through many parts of their country, when seeking refuge from the rains, or tired with heat, fatigue, and hunger, I have met with a welcome and hospitable reception on arriving at their villages : mats have been brought out for us to repose on, and if it happened to be meal-time, we have been at liberty to join them without ceremony, or to wait till something better could be provided. If we intended to spend the night there, a house has been set apart for us, and on taking leave in the morning a guide has generously offered to show us on our way.

Reciprocating their delicate attentions, and wishing I had brought more presents, I passed round tobacco and cigarettes—always appreciated in West Africa— and asked that the musical festivities might not be interfered with. Accordingly the players, who were seated in the roadway, struck once more their balangi instruments.

The " balangi " is usually made from the wood of a dead rosewood tree, cut to the proper size, and then laid in the ground to season; after about six months it is taken out, cleaned up, thoroughly oiled, and placed in the sun (during dry season) for a few weeks. It is then ready for use and the strings are fitted.

A similar instrument is made from a gourd, partly covered with goat skins, and narrow cross-pieces of bamboo nailed over it. The music is produced by striking the bamboo pieces with sticks.

Two men played and two girls danced. When the latter rested, those around joined in a kind of chorus chant, at once weird and fascinating.

Suddenly the music ceased. The players made a hasty retreat to the nearest hut behind them. The villagers drew up on either side of the road. There was a clatter of hoofs. A horse—the first I had seen in Sierra Leone—came galloping in at racing speed. Suddenly it was reined in by its rider, stopping before the chief's residence. The rider, evidently a courier of the chief, was arrayed in a long white robe. The horse was decorated with gay trappings, but was practically saddleless. The bit in its mouth was of rough iron with a ring through which its tongue was thrust. The rider, who carried a kind of spear or lance with white ribbons attached, alighted from his curious iron stirrups, saluted and delivered his message. Whatever it was, the chief received the communication without any relaxation of his muscles or other sign of interest. The courier retired with his steed; the villagers re-squatted; the musicians again plied their instruments and repeated their melancholy and weird airs.

But the music had no longer any charm for me. That picturesque rider, his sudden entrance, and the steed he rode had distracted my thoughts and fascinated my interest.

Here was another contradiction of the Government handbooks, which tell you there are no horses in Sierra Leone, and that they cannot live in this country. I discovered a few more mis-statements before I left Sierra Leone. The horses that I saw were young—indeed, I should say they were ridden at too young an age—and some of the bits used had a spike which pricked the roofs of their mouths, lacerating them in time. From the information I gathered, the horses are bred in and imported from the French Sudan. The horses are never castrated as the natives have a superstition that a gelded horse always dies.

The idea that the horse cannot live in Sierra Leone is probably due to the knowledge of the prevalence of the tsetse-fly, which is believed to convey the disease "trypanosomiasis," so fatal to horses and cattle. The truth is, however, that this insect and its accompanying disease are quite local, certain districts being exempt from their ravages. In such districts cattle are more frequently found than horses; but it must be remembered that horses being used for covering long distances might pass through an infected zone and catch the disease. Perhaps it would be as well to record that the other districts in which I noticed the absence of the tsetse-fly were—(a) in the Konnoh country, by the Meli River on the Guinea and Liberia frontiers, and (b) in the Colony area between Waterloo and Rokelle, where cattle are being bred and reared with success. Yet in both of these districts, and especially

in the latter, the antelope is plentiful. Now the antelope is considered by some theorists on "sleeping
sickness" to be the chief reservoir in which the virus
is stored, because, "in these animals, the trypanosomes
or parasites which cause the disease flourish plentifully,
while the animals themselves are immune."

A Royal Commission is now sitting to inquire into
the causes of this disease and suggest remedies, but
like the Commissions on the Civil Service, Post Office
servants, and other similar Commissions, it has apparently pre-determined its verdict, as, before inviting a
witness to give evidence, inquiry is made from him as
to the kind of evidence he wishes to produce.

*   *   *   *

In the cool of the afternoon I was privileged to
witness a native dance known as the "hammock
dance." Upon two upright poles, 20 to 30 ft. high,
strutted in rather primitive fashion, an ordinary
grass hammock is stretched. A number of men
and women, forming a kind of orchestra and chorus,
then commence playing a series of weird tunes, and
singing songs, extolling the virtues and wonderful
powers of the person about to dance. As the music
continues, the crowd grows larger and larger, the
newcomers join in the chorus and increase the din
and excitement. The principal performer dances round
and round, gesticulating and shouting to his admiring
audience and arousing himself and them to a high state
of excitement. Suddenly he rushes towards one of the
poles and clambers up into the hammock. First
balancing himself while standing erect, he appears to
fall, but saves himself by catching the hammock, or,
dropping from the erect position, will hang on by one
leg and one arm or by both legs. As a kind of encore
he revolves the hammock almost on its own axis, winding himself up, and then unwinding himself again.
Between each feat there is an interval, during which
orchestra and chorus beguile the admiring audience,

which competes with the music by its chatter and criticism. The performance lasted about an hour, but I am told that it sometimes continues for hours, until performers and audience alike are exhausted or overcome with drink.

Another dance, a kind of war dance, is even more vividly impressed upon my memory.

A spacious ring is formed by the spectators. At the beating of the tom-toms or *sang-bois,* each warrior steps into the centre, stripped naked but for a cloth about his loins. Magnificent muscular specimens they appear as they move in the light of the flickering torches. Caps or coloured handkerchiefs circle their heads. The arms, knees, and ankles of every dancer are hung with bunches of fetish charms. Each man is armed with a heavy-bladed sword, which, before the people could afford guns, was their favourite weapon in war. On first entering the ring each warrior advances to the centre. There he stands like a chocolate statue, gazing, sword in hand, at the assembling audience. Meantime the beating of drums and throbbing of tom-toms continue and grow louder. The performer holds out his blade at arm's length, and with the point describes great circles with a sweep and a swiftness that the eye can scarcely follow, cleaving the air in lightning flashes above his head, or flitting in fiery arches round his body, while the thud of tom-tom and drum is redoubled and the onlookers enthusiastically applaud.

The dancer has, by this time, worked himself into a fearful frenzy. One can see naught of his whirling blade save a few steely sparks in the moonbeams. Then twirling and dancing round the circle, when excitement is at its height, and the dance at its climax, the warrior suddenly bounds across to where you or his chief is sitting, and driving his weapon, point foremost, into the ground, crouches at your feet.

As this move was quite unexpected, the reader can guess the sort of shiver I experienced momentarily as

the warrior rushed thus in my direction. Before the
end of the dance, however, I was able to endure it
without feeling a throb or moving a muscle.

No sooner has one man finished his frolic than his
place is taken by another, the people crowding round
the ring and becoming more and more excited as the
dance proceeds, while the quick throbbing tom-toms
lend an adscititious accompaniment to the general din.
The scene that night under a tropical moon was indeed brilliant and bizarre. In front the cleared ring,
looking like an enchanted circle, in which, instead of
fairies, chocolate warriors danced and pirouetted;
around it a restless, chattering, shouting crowd of
fantastically garbed natives; behind, the dim outline of
the village huts, and, in the background, the dark forest.

*　*　*　*

Around the chief's table that night there was explained to me the story of the rising of the Temnes
in 1898.

In 1896 the Governor held a big meeting at Matina-
for, in the Kwaia country, to explain the Protectorate
Ordinance and also the proposed scheme of taxation to
several paramount chiefs. Every owner of a habitable
house in the Protectorate was, from January 1, 1898,
to be liable henceforth to an annual tax of five shillings,
and for houses of four rooms or more, ten shillings;
whilst for every village whose number of houses was
under twenty no tax would be imposed. The amount
could either be paid in cash or kind, that is, one bushel
of rice or one bushel of palm kernels, taken at its trade
value, as equivalent to cash.

The tax was not a hard one compared with similar
taxes in Liberia, British Central Africa, and Basuto-
land, and the majority of the people could probably
have met it, as they since have done. Yet it was
more strongly resented than the Indian tax in Natal.
Probably the manner in which it was imposed, the
overwhelming officialism with which a decree or new

rule is promulgated, whether at home, in a Government office, or in a Crown Colony, caused the first spark. The Temnes refused to pay. The Mendis followed the lead of the Temnes. Soon all along these banks there sped the messengers of death bearing the burnt palm leaf, emblem of destruction, and the two red kolas, signifying war. Some of the horrors of that futile war I have recounted in another chapter. To the credit of the Temnes, be it said, that atrocities are not accounted against them. They are truly soldiers, and they fought gamely and well. Their casualties were few, considering the ammunition spent upon them, and they sent down the white people from their midst when war began, without perpetrating the deeds which blackened the Mendis.

The rebellion was ultimately suppressed, and a portion of the Temnes' territory was added to the Colony. But one West African chief at least left a lasting name behind him as a result of the rebellion. Bai Bureh, who ruled over the Kassi country, was not only a man of keen intelligence, but a renowned and successful leader, whose warlike influence extended beyond the confines of his own kingdom. The Bai Kabalai, as he was sometimes called, was an ally of the British in the 1892 campaign. His military qualities had also been proved and established when he led the Temnes to victory against the Susus in 1873. His name was a household word for miles around, and, like that of Napoleon in Europe, was used by village mothers to still their crying babes.

Bai Bureh led the Temnes in revolt against the hut tax and successfully defied the power of Britain for many months, thereby making for himself a name that will never die among that tribe. Like many another renowned warrior, Bai Bureh was not born to leadership, and was not even of chiefly rank. Entirely through his own ability in warfare he rose to command.

CHAPTER XIV.

Hunting and the Chase in Sierra Leone.

Licences, Laws, and Customs relative to Big Game Hunting—
Elephant Hunting and its Dangers—The Pigmy Hippo.—
The Leopard, and how to trap him—Giraffes—A Monkey
Hunt—Story of the Origin of Monkeys—The Antelope and
Kob.

Among other sports in this interesting country is
one common to all sorts of men from time immemorial,
the hunting of wild beasts and game. In this the
native enjoys more privileges than the European, being
exempt from most of the restrictions imposed upon the
latter.

With the exception of guinea birds or other fowl, no
non-native may hunt, kill, or capture any wild animal
in the Colony or Protectorate without a licence from
the Governor, and once granted a licence, must keep
within the strict terms of such licence. The Governor,
before issuing a permit or licence, may require the
applicant to sign an agreement, promising first to
observe native rights, giving the forequarter of the
animal killed to the chief or headman of the town at
which the licensee is residing; and secondly, that
during the residence of any hunting expedition in the
district, every licensee shall apply to the chief or headman of a town for the necessary accommodation for
himself and his followers, each house being paid for
at the rate of 1s. per day. All such payments to be
made to the owner of the house.

The Governor may also require a deposit (£100 or
any less amount) as security for one's compliance with
the terms of the licence.

The Governor, before issuing a licence, may modify

it by prohibiting the killing or capturing of more than one of the wild animals, or the hunting of any particular wild animal mentioned in any licence; or by adding to the list of wild animals in any licence prohibited to be hunted, the names of any other wild animals.

Every licensee before he begins hunting has to register his licence in the office of the District Commissioner in whose district he intends to shoot.

If a licence be lost or destroyed, the licensee may, on payment of a fee not exceeding one-fifth of the original, obtain a fresh licence for the remainder of the term for which his former licence was available.

Licences are either " qualified " or " full " licences. The former gives permission to hunt any wild animal except elephants, rhinoceroses, and hippopotami. This costs 10s. a year to a Government officer, £3 to others. The full licence to include the killing or capturing of not more than two of each of the three classes of big game just mentioned costs £5 to a Government officer and £28 to others. Every licensee has to make a return of his sport each year, the penalty for breach of this or other clauses being £25 fine or six months' imprisonment.

Licences to hunt elephants are issued only upon the following conditions :—

(1) The applicant shall produce a certificate signed, in the case of a military officer by his commanding officer, and in the case of other persons by the Colonial Secretary or a District Commissioner, that he is in possession of a rifle which will fire a charge of not less than 70 gr. of cordite or other explosive of equivalent force, and a bullet of not less than 480 gr. in weight, and that he is in possession of a licence to carry the said rifle.

(2) The applicant shall sign an agreement containing the following conditions :—

(a) The licensee shall under no circumstances in the first instance fire at any elephant with any weapon which shall fire a lesser charge of explosive or a lighter bullet than those hereinbefore described.

(b) The licensee will not employ any person to hunt elephants on his behalf.

(c) The licensee shall report the killing of every elephant by him to the District Commissioner of the district in which such elephant is killed, within thirty days from the date of the killing of such elephant, and the licensee shall at the same time furnish to the District Commissioner the name of the chiefdom in which such elephant is killed.

(*d*) The licensee shall give a present of £2 for each elephant killed by him to the paramount chief of the chiefdom in which such elephant is killed.

To provide for the payments mentioned, the licensee may on his arrival in any district be required by the District Commissioner of such district to deposit the sum of £4 by way of security for the proper carrying out of the last-mentioned condition; and the District Commissioner is hereby authorized to pay to the paramount chief of the chiefdom in which the elephants are killed from the amount of £4 deposited with him as aforesaid a sum not exceeding £2 for each elephant killed. If the licensee does not kill any elephants the amount of £4 deposited by him will be returned to him, or if he kills only one elephant, £2 of the amount deposited by him will be returned to him.

No elephant's tusk weighing less than 25 lb. may be sold or bartered, or attempted to be sold or bartered, and any person selling or bartering or attempting to sell or barter any such tusk is guilty of an offence, and every such tusk sold or bartered or attempted to be sold or bartered is forfeited to His Majesty.

This last regulation applies to natives as well as non-natives.

The West African elephant differs from that of East and Central Africa in its smaller and more rounded ear, in the shape of the body and relative height of the back.

Elephant-hunting in any form is not a game for weaklings or cowards. Even with a 470 D.B. Express you want all your wits and your nerves in encountering the elephant, for he has much sagacity at the back of his enormous strength, and defends himself when attacked with a counter-attack which, for resolute ferocity, is more dangerous than that of a tiger or a lion. Elephant-hunting with the best of armament is dangerous, and only a very cool brain and steady hand can successfully encounter the charge of a wounded tusker, for even at close quarters the vulnerable spots are few and only to be reached by deliberate well-placed shots. A slight inaccuracy of aim in the case of other animals might not affect the stopping power of the bullet, but it may cost the elephant-hunter his life.

Sir Frederick Lugard, Abel Chapman, and the late Samuel Baker, all redoubtable African sportsmen, considered the elephant the most dangerous of big game to hunt, though Selous and Roosevelt give the palm to the lion. Lions, however, are not now to be met with in Sierra Leone, so the specimen in the London Zoological Gardens must be a curiosity of a bygone age.

Hippos. are plentiful in the Rokelle and Kittam Rivers; and here also is to be found the pigmy hippopotamus, walking on the two middle toes, and possessing only one pair of incisor teeth in both jaws instead of four, like the ordinary hippo.

The best and cheapest equipment for the " full " licensee is probably a ·303 magazine rifle with soft-nosed cartridges.

Sierra Leone, however, is not exactly the place for big game hunting. Elephants have been driven to the northern extremes of the Colony, though they abound in the Gola district, as mentioned later. The buffalo may also be found, especially among the hills of Hastings, in the Colony. Four hundred guineas has been offered for a live specimen, but no one has yet claimed the money.

Leopards, however, are plentiful. I found them here in the vicinity of the higher reaches of the Rokelle River in the Protectorate, around the forest-clad hills at the back of Christineville and Hastings in the Colony, and on the Bullom shore, where they were making considerable depredations when I was there, raiding native farms and carrying off young children, as well as chickens. They usually roam about in couples, and as the skin of the West African leopard is handsomer than that of the Asiatic, it is in great demand.

As a rule, however, the leopard is a difficult customer to meet. He rarely comes out of his lair until dark; his step is stealthy, and he seldom attacks you from the front, except when wounded, when his spring is so sure that he who can evade it at close quarters must indeed be favoured by the gods. As it is practically impossible in the ordinary way to secure personally a good leopard skin, except at close quarters with a good revolver, leopards and similar marauding beasts are sometimes destroyed by the following method. A Long Dane gun heavily charged is securely fastened to two posts, with its butt resting on, and its muzzle about 2 ft. therefrom; a large piece of meat is placed round the muzzle, while a string passed round a post connects the meat to the trigger. Provided he is standing in the proper position when he tries to pull the meat from the muzzle, the leopard is shot.

One other way to secure a leopard is to entice him to a bungalow by tying up a goat outside, say on a moonlight night, when a good shot may be obtainable from the verandah or a mud hut door.

An occasional giraffe may be seen near the French Guinea frontier, but the natives do not seem to hunt them. There is a story that once a man trapped and shot a giraffe, but his body became swollen and his skin cracked and split. Finally he died in great agony (probably from elephantiasis).

During my stay in this neighbourhood my hosts had prepared a special hunting amusement for me—one, moreover, which had the greater fascination for them because it was profitable. The natives, by the way, scarcely ever kill for sport, but for utility. Now monkeys fetch a price, besides being mischievous to planted areas; occasionally, therefore a special hunt is organized.

The monkeys usually take to special trees, in which they pass the night; in this way a troop is marked down and surrounded at night by the young men of two or three villages, accompanied by every available dog or dingo whenever such is possessed. Fires are lighted until daybreak, when the monkeys are driven out of the trees, and the hunt commences. No guns are allowed (for obvious reasons), but swords and sticks are used, and if the hunt is well organized less than 50 per cent. of the troop breaks through the cordon. The dogs are of the greatest help, and in their excitement tackle the monkeys quite fearlessly. After one of these drives I saw eighty " captives " brought in, tied hand and foot, and hung on poles. Most of these were quite young monkeys, but there were also a few grown ones, all of whom died in a day or two, probably from injuries.

The young suckling monkeys are generally carried clinging underneath the stomach of the mother. When pursued and hard pressed the mother will retain them in that position as long as possible, but when she considers herself about to be caught she snatches them out and flings them aside without abating her pace.

Two other kinds of monkey are found in the Sierra Leone forests, the tailless lemurs and the chimpanzee. I never saw a gorilla, and I am informed his chief home is in the Cameroons.

Here is a story prevalent concerning the origin of monkeys. Many years ago, white, black, red, and yellow men lived together, feeding upon fish, in a country through which a river flowed. The fish prayed to the gods that for one day in each week men might be prohibited from catching or eating them. The prayer was granted, and man was commanded accordingly. All went well for a time, but one day several men of different colours disobeyed the deity and caught some fish. For this they and their wives and children were changed into monkeys.

The antelopes to be found in Sierra Leone are chiefly

of the Cobus Kob variety, recognized at once by the distinct black line on the forelegs. Only the bucks carry horns, but several of the female beasts stand 30 in. at the shoulder and weigh over 100 lb. So fond are they of lying in the grass during certain seasons that the bucks will not attempt to rise until the guns are nearly on them. Herds of Kob usually consist of from six to twenty females and young animals, with one or two big bucks only, or else entirely of males—old bucks, and half-grown animals which, as their horns are small, are often mistaken for does. As soon as the males are old enough to interest the females of the herd, they are turned out by the regular herd bucks to triumph elsewhere. They are beautiful animals and cover the ground rapidly, but they have a fatal habit of curiosity, and will turn broadside to their pursuers to stare at them.

Native hunting of the antelope or duiker is crude, cruel, and confusing. The hunters congregate on a path, with the wind for preference, armed with flint-locks, old metal, sharp stones, and iron nails. Boys carrying tom-toms or old tins on which to make a noise rush into the bush and set the grass on fire, beating their tins or tom-toms at the same time. The scared animals rush against the wind into the hunters' path, and are there assailed by deafening and deathly volleys. The carnage is great, but it is a marvel that some of the natives do not maim each other.

Sometimes, also, pits are dug to a depth of several feet with a sharpened stake inserted to impale beasts. Strangers have been known to fall into these traps. Such pits were extensively used during the war in 1898.

All sorts of deer abound in different parts of Sierra Leone, so that with a " qualified " licence those enjoying or having time for hunting can obtain good sport.

Many primitive hunters venerate the beasts they slay, and their veneration appears to be próportioned partly to the power and partly to the utility of the creature.

A BONGO. KILLED NEAR YONNIBANA.

Face p. 114.

Many African tribes take the utmost pains to propitiate an elephant or a lion after he is killed, lest his
ghost should haunt them, or his tribe carry on a vendetta to avenge him. In this respect they resemble
the people of Kamchatka, who take elaborate pains to
persuade a dead bear that Russians and not natives
killed him.

Totemism and the imitation of animals for the purpose of semi-religious and magical purposes also pre-
vail. I have dealt with this phase of West African life
in the chapter on " Secret Societies."

CHAPTER XV.

Sleeping in the Bush and on the River.

Rokon, Mabundu, and the higher reaches of the Rokelle—
Bivouacking in the Bush—The Fascination and Dangers of
the Forest—Sleeping among Natives on a Canoe—A Forest
Fire—The Sacred Fire—Makana and its Oil Palms—The
Sele River—The Konnoh District—Novel Cow-driving—The
Lime and the Ground-nut—Back at Mahera—A Tornado—
Return to Christineville—My European Companion contracts
Sunstroke.

The Temne country stretches for about ninety miles
from west to east, bounded by the ocean and the
Koranko country respectively. From the north—where
it is bounded by the Mandingo and Limba countries—
to the south—where Yonnis and Mendis meet—it is
about fifty miles. At one time it was much larger in
extent. There are four districts, each ruled by a paramount chief.

From Rokon the Rokelle River takes a long winding
course to Yonnipet, and a far more winding ramble
from there north-east to Lungi and Rosint, then dropping south to Mabundu; but there is a forest path from
Rokon to Yonnipet, through which one can hammock,
and a more circuitous cut from there to Mabundu
through which you can only scramble. But it saves
miles of river journey, and in the hot, dry weather is
cooler. More comfortable also the bush would be, but
that at night, when you are obliged to bivouack as
best you may, you have to chance being attacked by
wild beasts and scorpions, not to speak of mosquitoes
and other insects.

During this journey, and on the return, I had the

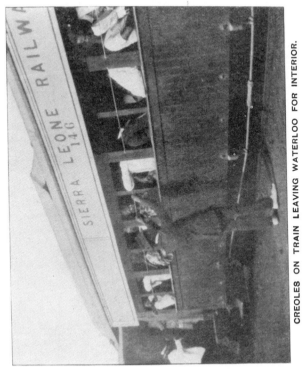

CREOLES ON TRAIN LEAVING WATERLOO FOR INTERIOR.

BOAT IN WHICH AUTHOR SLEPT.
PORRO BOY (ON RIGHT).

Face p. 116.

experience of spending a night both in the bush and on
the river, and I can honestly say that I enjoyed the
latter better and slept sounder during the night on the
canoe, although my resting-place was harder and more
uncomfortable.

There is something unearthly about the bush,
although there, after all, one is only with Nature in
one of her primeval moods. The African forest is not
the sylvan wood in which poets revel, or to which, as
Nietzsche remarks, "Men go not to find but to lose
and forget themselves, because the desire to get away
from oneself is proper to all weaklings and those who
are discontented with themselves." Verily one may
lose oneself here in an African forest, even in the
elephant grass of the half savannah land, where each
successive open space tells you nothing, when you are
lost, save that you are lost. But to forget yourself you
dare not! Far worse is it in the jungle still to be found
near the Nimmini mountains and along the Liberian
frontier. There the huge trees groan beneath the
weight of lianes intertwined, while the ground, greasy
with plantain fruits and kindred juices, suddenly dips
down into some unseen valley, where bats hang like
withered leaves, or flap past like spectral gray shadows,
and the hum of insects fills the air with gloomy gloat-
ing symphonies. The uncanny silence of the midday
is succeeded by the weirdest of noises in the evening,
when the animal and insect world seeks its prey among
mankind.

But evening on a tropical river is yet more fascinating. Never shall I forget one night spent upon the
Rokelle River with naught but the dark blue velvet dome
of a tropical sky for a canopy, none but a native chief,
his seven boat-boys, and my own black attendant for
companions.

The night was clear and starry, yet the waters which
lapped lightly beside us seemed almost black. Occasionally a sandbank would appear white and clear in
the moonbeams, and lights would gleam from the river-

bank, where natives indulged in music and merriment, the sounds of which came floating upon the breeze.

Here and there a forest fire lighted with lurid glare the heavens, and silhouetted the trees and huts upon the banks against the dark blue sky. One such fire was a splendid spectacle of leaping, hissing flame, enveloping everything and terrifying alike the beasts of the forest, the insects, and the birds, except perhaps the hawks, which seemed oblivious of the heat, and hovered above selecting the most tempting victim scared upward by the forest's funeral pyre.

These bush fires are both a bane and a boon to West Africa. Forests are destroyed, and the face of the country spoiled for many a year. Yet swarms of insects, which multiply during the rains, are thereby suffocated.

To sleep in the bush also is impossible without lighting a fire and maintaining it. Only those who have tended a fire for twelve hours can realize how much wood is needed where coal is not used. Such fires, by the way, are watched by a woman—usually an old woman—when natives are tramping for trade with their womenfolk; and it is a disgrace—once attended by very severe penalties—to allow the fire to expire. From this very ancient custom, perhaps, was derived the cult of the Vestal Virgins in Rome, the custom of keeping the sacred fire burning still being retained in some Roman Catholic chapels and convents.

I am afraid I should have made a sorry Vestal Virgin; for, while watching one of these forest fires from the boat, I fell asleep, and knew no more till the morn. I have often thought since that that sleep might easily have been my last.

* * * *

This portion of the Rokelle River, and the forest district spreading through Yonni, is less frequented and known than the succeeding portion. To the latter part the railway has been gradually creeping up, until now it has reached Makomp and Makene. The Makene country is rich in oil palms, scarcely tapped, and there should be a rich harvest from these later on if the native is properly approached.

A few miles farther north the Rokelle River, now called the Sele, flows through a narrow valley between high forest-clad hills. The forests are rapidly being destroyed and erosion has begun in several places. The timber is difficult to get out and therefore is not at present of any commercial value, but a reservation of these forests has now been made in order to check the erosion and the formation of torrents, which in a narrow gorge like this would have a disastrous effect. As it is, farther down stream the River Rokelle rises very rapidly in the rainy season, and falls with equal rapidity in the dry season, owing to the fact that there is very little forest vegetation on its banks, so that the falling rain immediately runs into the river.

Farther to the east, in the Konnoh district, there is a large patch of evergreen forest. To secure the Konnoh trade, a neighbouring woman chief, Madam Humon-yaha, has cleared some excellent roads in her district. The people in the north-eastern districts of Sierra Leone appear to deal in cattle, though the trade is small compared with that of French Guinea, from which country come most of the beasts.

The animals are usually of the feminine gender, the natives apparently believing it wrong to geld.

It is amusing to see natives getting these animals across rivers or streams. A rope is tied round the cow's horns. Then she is led to the water edge. Some of the native drovers then spring into a " dug-out " or " bullom " canoe. Others remain behind and be-labour the beast until she enters the water. Then, with shouts and yells, the drovers behind jump into the stern, while the men in the forward part of the canoe paddle rapidly. Those in the stern drag the cow, which begins to swim after them. So skilful are the boys, that the job is generally completed without mishap of any kind.

Among the useful fruits grown are the avocado pear, the paw-paw, and the lime.

The first is found on a tree which grows to a height of 25 ft. The flesh is yellow and green, soft, greasy, and—to some people—delicious. The fruit is usually eaten raw with pepper and salt or lime juice. The paw-paw is, to my taste, superior, being of the flavour of a melon. Further, it contains pepsin and is therefore excellent for digestive purposes. The tree is of rapid growth and will thrive in any soil.

The lime tree is one of the most valuable and one of the most neglected of the trees flourishing in Sierra Leone. The fruit was lying about in quantities all over the place, and no use was made of it. I found the juice invaluable for lime drinks, and almost invariably used it instead of milk for my tea, as it steadies the stomach and helps one to perspire freely. This is one of the habits to which I attribute my exceptional health while in the White Man's Grave. Apart from its value as a drink, the juice of the lime has many commercial uses.

The fresh and the pickled fruits are an efficient substitute for the lemon, and the trade in them between the West Indies, New York, and London is growing rapidly. Of this the European and native out here appeared quite ignorant. They were, however, beginning to utilize this waste product before I came away. The raw juice was being crushed from the ripe fruits for drinks, and I concocted a new beverage from the lime, cashew, and one or two other fruits upon the place which the natives appreciated very much when it was "dashed" with rum.

The ground-nut, pea-nut, or monkey nut, as it is variously called, is another plant, flourishing where superior cultivation has taken place; but it is not grown on a large scale, as in Gambia.

Ground-nuts are largely used as human food, either

in the raw state or roasted. The native races here use them in soups and mixed with millet and rice in the preparation of various foods. The demand for roasted nuts in America is so great that, after large local crops have been consumed, some thousands, if not millions, of dollars' worth of nuts are imported from Marseilles. Besides being roasted, various other methods of preparing the nut as food are adopted in the United States; they are blanched and salted; mixed with syrup, and sometimes with pop-corn and puffed rice, they are made into candies; and ground-nut meal is made into various confections. A recent development is the manufacture of " pea-nut butter " by roasting the nut and removing the thin seed coat, the kernels being ground up into a paste and salted. But the ground-nut is now being used principally for the expression of oil.

*   *   *   *

Returning to the Kwaia country, we reached Mahera just in time to witness, and avoid being caught in the open by a tornado.

The rainy season is usually heralded by one or two tornadoes. A soft and peculiar breeze is the harbinger that this tropical terror is at hand. Instantly there is a chattering and twittering in the trees, a shrieking, growling, rustling in the bush, a scamper of natives on the plain to the nearest hut or refuge, or a flat prostration on the ground. Dense black clouds sweep along the sky. Thunder is heard, not as a rumble, but in sharp cracking clangs. A screaming wind follows, uprooting trees, whirling away roofs, destroying homes, spending its fury over the land. Woe unto man or beast whom it encounters!

Then, when the storm has passed, wreckage lies everywhere.

But life uplifts itself again.

As every cloud has a silver lining, so every tornado has a gleam of gold in its train. The terror of the tumultuous torrent the native can understand. That which he can scarcely comprehend is the music and magic in the myriads of raindrops which appeal to the white scientist or lover of Nature. To the former, rain is indeed a gift from the gods; but it is one that is half snatched or forced by incantations, half given in anger. To the latter each raindrop is a world distilled by the mysterious alchemy of the ever-moving clouds.

But to both, and to all life on plain or in forest, the advent of the rain heralded by the tornado spells a new lease of life. For the dry season here is lengthy, and, perhaps, the one great drawback to greater vegetable wealth. The natives suffer from the intense heat preceding the tornadoes and the rainy season, almost, if not quite as much as the Europeans. Scarcely a week passed but there was a casualty among our escort. Native traders also, when travelling in the hot, dry season, prefer a moonlight night for their journey, and thus avoid the later morning sun.

A lively, noisy crowd, these traders. The loads they carry considerably exceed the regulation 60 lb. per carrier, but they take their own time and do the journey in their own way. A few passing through the Kwaia country to the Colony can speak English and even understand a joke in that language. To test one of them, I hazarded the question: Had he ever seen a pink palm in Sierra Leone. Instantly he replied in the negative. When I opened the palm of my hand and pointed to it he laughed heartily, and nodded his head sagaciously.

*   *   *   *

The chief at Mahera insisted upon accompanying me back to the Colony with his boat-boys, and the journey back was performed in good time. At Mahera I had found my European companion quite himself again, and able to appreciate the return journey to the Colony. Misfortune seemed, however, to dog his footsteps, for we had no sooner set foot on Christineville, the hospitable estate from which we had started, than he collapsed

from a touch of sunstroke and was obliged to return
to England.

After a brief entertainment the chief who had escorted
me so courteously took his leave.   Little did I dream
then that his reign was so soon to be terminated, and
that I should never see him again.

After a short rest I set out again to see something
of the eastern and southern portion of Sierra Leone.
Before describing this journey, let me devote a chapter
or two to the native laws, customs, and secret societies
fairly common to all the aboriginal tribes.

CHAPTER XVI.

Secret Societies in Sierra Leone.

The Bondu and its Devil's Dance—Penalties for leading Girls astray—The Yassi, or Society of Spots—The Kofungs and Resurrection—The Porro and its Powers—The Human Leopard, Alligator, and Baboon Societies—Cannibalism— Legislation and Arrests in connection with Secret Societies.

Secret societies are a feature of West African life and customs. Among the most important in Sierra Leone are the Porro, the Yassi, the Kofung, and the Bondu. The last named belongs exclusively to women, and is of great importance, particularly among the Mendis of Sierra Leone. Its headquarters are always in the bush, and known only to its members. Young native girls who join it at a certain age are trained, it is said, in certain feminine matters, taught the medical use of herbs, and all the mysteries of the dance and subtler arts of graceful carriage and attraction. Certainly the excellent figures of the higher class Mendi girls and " mammies " who have belonged to the Bondu are an excellent advertisement for the training received; and when one reads in European newspapers of the fearful " white slave " traffic in our civilized countries, and of the fearful ignorance of some European maidens, one begins to wonder whether the Africans cannot teach us something in the matter of preparation for womanhood and maternity.

The only ceremony of the *Bondu* at which men are permitted to be present is the dance. As I was privileged to be present at one of these affairs, I can assure my readers that it is almost as artistic and certainly more quaint than an Alhambra ballet, even though the costume, perhaps, is a little more abbreviated. The *tee-tees* or young girls are adorned with bracelets of palm leaf fibre encircling the arms and wrists, their body nets being made of cotton to which are attached small iron plates jingling as their owners dance. The faces of the performers are smeared with an animal fat called *wojah,* which acts as an equivalent for our rouge. The dance is sometimes weird and fantastic, especially the " devil " dance, and is accompanied by the inevitable *sangboi* or drum, and a *sehgura* or kind of guitar made from a hollowed gourd with seeds threaded on strings to make that sharp metallic sound so dear alike to the real nigger and the amateur minstrel. At the end of the dance many women spectators rushed into the circle and embraced the dancers, and really the dance works so upon one's feelings that you are half inclined to do the same.

The " devil " is dressed entirely in black, and no portion of her body is visible under the thick fibrous matting, giving her the appearance of a shaggy, hairy animal. The head and eyes are hidden by a hideous mask of stained wood. One of her attendants, called the *digba,* carries a large mat by which the devil is completely hidden when she sits down, thus enabling her to remove the heavy head-dress without disclosing her identity..

The " medicine " which the devil is supposed to have at her command is much feared, and no man who has transgressed a Bondu law, and is pointed out by the devil, dare refuse to follow her, and to pay the fine or other penalty which his headman metes out. A flogging is one of the penalties inflicted for leading a Bondu girl astray.

When a weird sound reverberates through the forest like one long-drawn low note, gradually loudening, then gradually dying away, the Bondu bush is not far distant.

The Kofung is a secret society which is very popular among the Limbas and Korankos, and also among

some western tribes. Its rites are mournful and morbid.
A candidate simulates death, and is supposed to be
made to return to life by the officiating members at
the initial ceremony. As he lies on the litter apparently
dead, the members dance around, raise him, and wash
his eyes with a lotion prepared from the bark of a cork
tree. When the dance is over, the novice stands over
a fire, the chief of the sect holding a burnt stick before
his eyes, and forcing him to swear the sacred oath of
the society.

The " Kofung " man may be recognized by a brass
ring on his toe, thumb, or wrist. A member is recognized by a brother in the order, if he cross his arms
or two twigs. Every member of this Society is supposed to have an attendant spirit who can be summoned
if required by uttering certain magical words and calling the spirit by name seven times.

The Kofungs believe they can transform themselves
into animals unless tied up to a piece of cork wood,
when this power of enchantment is broken.

The " Yassi " or " Society of Spots "—so called
because all its drums, swords, knives, or other instruments, and even its medicine are spotted with different
colours—appears to exist chiefly for the provision of a
select hospital for those who have been affected by
some " medicine " of their own or an enemy's fetish,
and can afford a decent fee. Only men from the
" Porro " and women from the " Bondu " are apparently admitted, so, like the other secret societies, it
is distinctly a caste or class organization. The West
African delights in every distinction, and loves rank
as much as the Spanish Don. The headman of the
Yassi is called *Behku*, the second *Yaman*. Then there
are the *Kambeh mama*, the *Kambeh mamsu* and the
Kambeh Kehwai. I did not get the opportunity to
inquire so fully into this society, as I did not actually
meet any of its members as I did those of the " Porro,"
" Bondu," and " Kofung."

The " Porro " is by far the most powerful secret

society in the Sierra Leone Protectorate, for by its laws the whole community may be said to be governed. Males only are eligible, and the revelation of its secrets means death or complete tribal excommunication and ostracism. At one time, the inner section of the " Porro " which, among other rites, indulged in forms of homo-sexuality, held up all the roads and passes, exacting toll from those who traded or travelled, and often offering death or membership of their society as alternatives to their victims.

Of this most important and most elusive secret society in Sierra Leone it is said that no European has been able to penetrate or understand its inner mysteries, or estimate its power. This is probably true; but I am quite sure from the special facilities I had for observing, noting, and conversing with members of the " Porro " and living with them on my canoe trip into the interior, that much that has been written about them has only to do with outer rites, laws, and customs which have practically been forced upon the community by the long domination of the original " Porro " Society; and that the secrets of the inner ring or real " Porro " are in no ways complex, but very simple, although at one time it meant death to divulge them, and even now they would not be betrayed even by a European, as they could never be known except by actual participation or affinity.

Suffice it to say, that the " Porro " is quite a body of freemasons, but that so dreaded and powerful has it been, that its name and its general laws have become common throughout the community, and many a boy who is carried into the bush and circumcised, or has even a few words said over him, is frequently called— but in a wide and honorary sense only—" porro." The " taboo " also, which is placed on particular trees to prevent them being tampered with before their fruit is ripe is also called " porro." Again, a conference to decide peace or war is called a " porro." Hence the real " porro " boy often escapes identity.

Roughly speaking, there are now three main divisions of the " Porro " Secret Society. The religious or mystical, the civil or exemplary, and the Semu, apparently confined to the Susus and some of the Temnes, which is better imagined than classified. Like the Freemasons, this secret society has its various orders and degrees; the Kaimahun or " big men," *i.e.*, chiefs; the Missi or Binina, medicine men corresponding to the Eastern fakir; and the Wujanga or Yugira, corresponding to the masses. According to his degree so is he mulcted of fees immediately upon admission to the *Kamehra* or Porro House, which, like its Latin equivalent, indicates the secrecy to be enforced. Even that entrance is not effected without a mock struggle with the guardians of the place, reminding one of the wrestling of Jacob with the angel. Drums and shouting are, of course, the inevitable concomitant. Inside the Kamehra he passes from one apartment to another, paying a fee at each. Finally, the last rite of the initiation is performed—always at night—and he is sworn to secrecy on powerful " medicine."

In the morning there is a procession headed by a " devil," which walks and dances round the town or village, much in the same way as our religious, charity, or strike processions promenade, with, of course, the inevitable collection. In the Porro processions, however, the subscriptions and donations are made, as a rule, by the headman of the town or village, or " commandeered " by the boys themselves; as everyone has to disappear inside their huts and close their doors, while the women kneel, shout, and clap their hands at the approach of the " devil " and his noisy retinue of initiated boys. The dancers are called *Lakas*. After the procession the boys have to return to the bush. The " bush " remains open for about four months each year, and the ceremonies are repeated each time a candidate joins, so the civilized idea of the happy savage immune from rates and taxes is very imaginary.

The society meets in the dry season, from the end

ENTRANCE (GUARDED) TO THE SACRED PORRO BUSH.

Face p. 128

of October to the beginning of May, and Porro boys have to live in the bush during the greater part of the rainy season. During this time the devil is supposed to be "pregnant," and to be giving birth to the "Porro" boys, a weird belief which is shared by certain Congo tribes. "Porro" boys wear a twisted rope of leaves resembling fern, wound round the waist during their novitiate; and when they finally emerge from the bush they are allowed a day's freedom to purloin poultry or any other property they fancy and can obtain. Naturally, the villagers on such occasions, as in early English days when our kings and their retainers wandered round the country for similar purposes, take care that little is left for annexation.

Two other important personages in the "Porro" deserve mention. Every important chief is accompanied to the ceremonies by a Tasso, arranged in a startling costume consisting only of skulls and thighbones, feathers, and fibre network. On their knees and ankles are plates of native iron, which clang and jingle as they walk. When one of these interesting creatures dies all the women in the town are driven out until he be buried.

The other personage is the *Marbori, Debhoi,* or "man-woman." She is not a native suffragette, as one might at first expect from this extraordinary combination of names, but a woman who has inadvertently, or, like Peeping Tom of Coventry, out of curiosity, gazed upon a Tasso and consequently been taken into the "Porro" bush and "medicinally" treated. The Mende chieftainesses who do not marry but have consorts are also admitted to the "Porro."

Whatever the past of the "Porro" may have been, the Government recognizes it as a real power in the land, the mysteries and rigorous methods of which really regulate public opinion and form a sort of moral tribunal to which the community is forced to bow. Both in the past and present also, it has undoubtedly extended protection to many who, individually, might have fallen victims to the Human Leopard, Human Alligator, and Human Baboon Societies, whose reprehensible practices and tendencies to apophagism have caused special legislation to be enacted since 1900.

The first-named of these associations is said to have originated thirty or forty years ago among crafty traders in the district of Sherbro, led by prominent people who wished to remove certain rivals from their path.

Probably it was a superstructure on a more primitive religious or fetish organization. Disguised in a leopard skin and armed with a knife shaped like leopard's claws, the man deputed to perform the murder would lurk in the bush and strike his victim in the back of the neck, usually causing instant death. This institution proved very attractive to the savage mind and the body was cut up and certain portions abstracted to make " medicine," which was supposed to render the individual and the society immune from detection. This cannibalism and the fact that new members were initiated at a feast at which, often unknown to them, human flesh was part of the *menu,* has induced the Government to legislate and take action against this society and similar organizations.

Until recently it was thought that these kinds of secret societies had been suppressed. Then, when I was in the interior of Sierra Leone, there was a sudden scare of cannibalism and murder. In some districts the people were in a state of terror, nobody knowing whose turn might come next, and no one daring to speak what they knew lest vengeance might fall upon them. Only when the dread of death overcame fear of the Society did several murders come to light. Then I suddenly awoke to the fact that deeds of darkness lay in the forest around. As I was the only white man in the neighbourhood for some miles the situation was cheerful.

However, the Government acted swiftly. Hundreds of arrests were made, including influential chiefs. Several suffered the capital penalty, several more were exiled, and many sentenced to various terms of imprisonment. The Human Leopard and Alligator Ordinance of 1900 has been amended to deal drastically with future outbreaks.

Although the arrests were, almost without exception, among the Leopard Society, the Alligator Society and the Baboon Society are very similar organizations, though with different rules. The former society, it will be noticed, is included in the Ordinance, and since I have returned to England several arrests have been made of members of both.

The procedure of the Alligator Society is conducted on somewhat similar lines to that of the Leopard Society, except that the murderer is disguised as an alligator and his special form of murder consists in tearing out the victim's stomach.

The Leopard Society operates south of the Government Railway, the Alligator Society on the north, particularly in the Rokelle River district.

In a creek far up the Rokelle river I saw in broad daylight a runaway black who was being tracked as a thief seized by what appeared to be an alligator. But instead of being sucked down into the water he was literally " carried " along the reeds into the bush. The boys who were following him up instantly gave up the chase and stopped me, saying the river god had taken him. I had seen enough alligators, however, to know all their movements, and I guessed the truth, though I allowed them to think I believed them, as I had no desire to become a " dangerous " person in a secluded part of the world where Nature rules.

The observation of this last incident, however, in which the victim was distinctly an outcast, led me to inquire into some of the Alligator Society's operations. From the sparse information obtainable, I am inclined to regard the Alligator Society, at least, as an institution primarily for putting out of the way by a kind of lynch law a dangerous or undesirable member of the community, whom it would be difficult to arraign before the District Commissioners, many miles away, and against whom it would be, perhaps, impossible to

establish sufficient direct evidence for conviction. The
distribution of the body or blood in such cases is merely
an act of propitiation to the gods, an offering to the
*borfima** of the community, to prove that the act is not
from personal but from social motives. In many cases
the actual body and blood is not partaken of, any more
than in our " Holy Communion." That this inner idea
lurks behind many of these secret societies is probably
the cause of their survival against all attempts to sup-
press them. The Governor, in his last despatch upon
the subject, remarks : " The eating of human flesh, is
only part of some ceremony which is believed to have
the effect of increasing the mental and physical powers
of the members of the society." And the *African Mail*
notes that " its religious symbolism is a medicine of
which an indispensable constituent is human fat."

There is another aspect. There are human " bears "
among the North American Indians, who group themselves in societies, with the bear as totem, and a young
man, at his initiation, will prowl through the woods,
growling realistically in a bearskin. It is only natural

---

* " Borfima," a contraction of *Boreh fima* (a medicine bag), is
a special fetish consisting of the blood of a cock, the blood, fat,
and other parts of a human being, and a few grains of rice,
tightly bound up, as a rule, in a leathern package smeared with
human blood and fat. The possession of such a fetish is supposed to give its owner power and wealth, and an oath adminis-
tered upon it is of the most binding character. Should its
efficacy appear to wane, it is because, according to the medicine
man, resuscitation is needed by reanointment by human blood
and fat.

Probably this special bag was originally entrusted to the chief
for the community and, like the Ark of the Covenant or a
modern mascot, was credited with mysterious powers. Later
each powerful man had his own Borfima (like the Biblical
Micah). The constant tribal wars then assured the frequent
human reanointment of such a fetish, but the *Pax Brittanica*
brought such replenishment to an end. The old and principal
men found their authority waning, their borfimas irresponsive,
and their own virility needing resuscitation. Human leopards,
and perhaps also alligators and baboons, brought them " young "
victims, whose blood and fat revived the borfimas, and whose
flesh and blood were believed to restore virility to the old.

that the leopard and alligator should be as important to West Africans as the bear is to American Indians. For a secret society to take either for its totem is not strange, nor is the dramatic instinct which causes the members of the society to dress themselves as leopards or alligators and to imitate the motions at all unusual. The Vikings from Jutland, who followed Hengist (the stallion) and Horsa, did the same thing. The great white horses on the chalk hills of our southern counties could repeat for us a tale no less curious of the human horses among our own ancestors. As one eminent writer has pointed out, " The savage hunter who identifies himself with a bear and regards the bear as his ancestor, kills his god and eats him. One of the reasons for this is that, by eating the bear, he acquires his many admirable qualities. The logic of Sierra Leone is more cogent, more straightforward, more honest in its downright bloodthirstiness. If you be a leopard you should do as leopards do. Bears do not eat bears, nor do leopards eat leopards. But leopards do eat boys and girls when they get the chance. They spring upon them from the jungle, and sever their spines. So regarded, there is no sort of mystery in the performance."

Sometimes it would seem that a secret society springs up as protection from, or for a vendetta against, another secret society.

Several .years ago the " Tongo " Society, existing for the detection of persons connected with the Human Leopard Society, had promoted the death of many persons to such an extent that the Government had to interfere.

Mr. Reginald Brett, Master of the Supreme Court, was sent up to the Protectorate to make some inquiry, and reported on his return that the Tongo Society had colluded with other persons and prostituted its usefulness to political ends, using it for the removal of influential or prominent persons in the Protectorate not connected with any unlawful society. Thus this identification of members of alleged unlawful societies by means of marks on their bodies has frequently been made a contrivance to subserve the removal from the Protectorate of influential persons not really connected with any unlawful society.

The " Tongo " Society has been forbidden, but so long as secret societies exist, others will spring up in self-protection, and abuses are bound to creep in.

The District Commissioners and judges have great difficulty in deciding justice in such cases, especially in discriminating voluntary members and those forced into such secret societies.

If any person has been compelled to join these societies, or if he has stumbled upon them in the bush and has been compelled to become a member of one of them, that is a matter which could and probably would be proved to the Court, and due consideration would be given to it by the judge in awarding punishment. The punishment for belonging to an unlawful society is fourteen years' imprisonment. It is not to be supposed for a moment that the Court would give a man fourteen years' imprisonment if it had reasons to believe that that man was coerced into becoming a member of such a society.

Government officials, as a rule, do not encourage the dissemination of any information about secret societies, regarding them as *taboo;* others give them too important a place, and ascribe all sorts of esoteric doctrines, astronomical knowledge, and abstruse philosophy and calculation to them and the mystery which is sometimes supposed to be behind the black man's mind. A medium attitude is better adopted. The average black man's mind is not at all complex, but very simple. A little knowledge, however, and the desire to impress the average man with that knowledge leads to elaborate and mystic formula signifying little, and as most men, black or white, love mystery and, often, secrecy, the existence of these societies is soon explained. They might, perhaps, be utilized more for social development.

CHAPTER XVII.

Native Law and Custom.

Native Courts—Paramount and Sub-Chiefs' Punishments—
" Kassi "—Contempt of Court—Women-palaver—District
Commissioners and their Influence—Regulations for Tribes-
men out of their own District—Ordeals and Charms—
Funeral Rites—Birth Customs—Superstitions regarding
Twins—How Death came into the World—Circumcision.

In most of the native states within the Protectorate
where native law prevails, the court is formed of the
king or paramount chief and his sub-chiefs and san-
tiggies, or in small towns by the sub-chief and his
principal men, who assist in threshing out the matter,
and may make remarks on, and offer suggestions concerning the cause, but have no voice in the final
decision, the king or paramount chief's word being
absolute and final. He may, however, delegate his
supreme power to some other member of the assembly,
who upon this being done, exercises the functions belonging to the king during the inquiry. An appeal
may be made from the decision of a sub-chief, but
from that of a paramount chief there was none, excepting, perhaps, an appeal to arms.

In these courts, crimes of murder, arson, adultery
(commonly called women-palavers), theft, assault, debt,
and other criminal and civil causes are inquired into,
and the decision is generally arrived at after consulta-
tion between the king and those of his principal men
who sit with him.

The punishment meted out for offences differs considerably, in purely pagan districts, fines being more
generally adopted than any other form of punishment;

whilst in districts under Muhammadan influence, corporal punishment is adopted in many cases instead of fines.

Parties opposed to each other in civil causes generally stake a certain amount on the issue, and this amount is given to the party who obtains the judgment of the court, besides any fine that the court may choose to impose.

Should a fine be imposed on one not able at the time to pay it, and he has any friends of influence, they sometimes "buy the palaver," or really assume the responsibility of the guilty one.

Should anyone be guilty of contempt of court, or breach of some local custom, or of insulting any person of influence, it is customary to give him *kassi,* that is, to fine him, and upon anyone being apprised by the paramount or sub-chief or principal man that he has been so "kassied," he has to acknowledge his offence and pay the fine imposed before any further steps are taken in any cause in which such person may be engaged.

There is a right of appeal from the decision of a sub-chief to the paramount chief of the country, but the costs attending these appeals generally make them impossible to any except wealthy litigants.

Where the decision of the court is not carried out by the party against whom an adverse decision has been given, his property—and very often, if there is not sufficient property, his family, and sometimes himself—is taken to satisfy the judgment given.

The most frequent palavers which occur in the native States are "women-palavers"—really "criminal connection" cases—in which the fines are imposed in proportion to the position of the petitioner and the co-respondent.

One more word regarding these courts. It may be and has been said by some critics that, as the kings or chiefs who control these courts hold their office by the sanction of the British Government, they will, to retain their position, usually carry out the wishes of the Governors and officials; thus the native court may become an instrument of cruelty and oppression to any native whom the officials would punish. A word in private or a message to the president of the native court may settle the fate of any man. Sometimes the official goes to the court himself, sits with the chief and influences its decisions.

This interference has been known in different parts of British West Africa, but it does not appear general in Sierra Leone.

The inhabitants of the Protectorate remain the subjects of their respective chiefs, even when residing in the Colony, as will be noticed from the following order of the British Government :—

All members of the Mendi or Temne tribe resident in Waterloo or other town of the Colony are subject to the tribal ruler of the Mendi or Temne tribe. Every member of these tribes arriving in such town from the Protectorate or elsewhere must within seven days report his arrival to his tribal ruler. The tribal ruler adjudicates upon and settles disputes arising between members of his tribe relating to :—

(a) The indebtedness of one member of the tribe to another member. (b) The pawning of property by one member of the tribe to another member. (c) Personal property and domestic disturbances. (d) All other matters requiring decision in the interest of the peace and well-being of the tribe. The parties in any dispute have to abide by the decision of the tribal ruler and be governed accordingly. No member of these Mendi or Temne tribes may disobey the summons of his ruler.

Every member of these tribes must carry out the instructions of the tribal ruler with respect to keeping his house and compound clean, and he may not interfere with the tribal authority or disturb the meeting convened by the tribal authority. Every Mendi and Temne man pays the sum of 1s. monthly to the tribal authority, which sum is paid to the credit of an account with the Post Office Savings Bank in the names of the tribal ruler and two of the principal headmen. The monies are disbursed by the tribal authority on objects considered to be by such authority for the good of the Mendi or Temne people in the particular town. Such objects include the relief of the poor and sick, burial of the poor having no relatives at time of death, relief of any member of the Mendi or Temne tribe in distress. The tribal ruler does not disburse the monies thus received by him except with the consent of the two headmen to whose joint credit the contributions have been received by the Post Office Savings Bank, and no withdrawal is made without the written authority of the District Commissioner having been first obtained.

Customary fees are paid to the tribal ruler for the settlement of disputes provided that the aggregate amount of fees payable in respect of a dispute does not exceed 20s. If any Mendi or Temne man remain in Waterloo or other town in the Colony without regular employment for more than twenty-one days, or fails to give a satisfactory account of his means of subsistence, he is deemed an idle and disorderly person, and is liable, in addition to or in lieu of any other punishment, to be ordered by the District Commissioner to return to his chiefdom, and if he fail within a reasonable time to comply with such order he is liable on summary conviction to imprisonment, with or without hard labour, for a period not exceeding three calendar months. Any Mendi or Temne man found in any Colony town may be interrogated by the tribal ruler or by a member of the police force as to his means of subsistence, his present place of abode, and the chiefdom to which he belongs, and on his failing to answer, or if his answers are unsatisfactory, he may be taken to the nearest police station, there to be detained with a view to his being charged under the last preceding clause. If a District Commissioner of the Protectorate reports that any Mendi or Temne man has, in contravention of this native law, left the chiefdom to which he belongs without obtaining the consent of the chief or proper authority, such man is liable to be returned by the tribal ruler to his country. No Mendi or Temne man may forfeit or dispose of any article pawned or pledged to him without first reporting the same to the tribal ruler, who will summon the pawner or pledger; should the pawner or pledger fail to do so, then the tribal ruler causes the pawn to be sold and from the proceeds pays the pawnee or pledgee the amount for which the article was pawned or pledged and pay over the balance (if any) to the pawner or pledger.

Every member of the Mendi or Temne tribe has to report within seven days the birth of a child to the tribal ruler, who causes the same to be at once reported to the Registrar of Births and Deaths. The eldest member of the family of any member of the Mendi or Temne tribes and every inmate of the house in which a death occurs must also within three days report the death of the deceased to the tribal ruler, who causes the same to be at once reported to the Registrar of Births and Deaths. Any member of the Mendi or Temne tribe who breaks any of the foregoing regulations has to pay to the tribal ruler such penalty, not exceeding £5, as may be adjudged by the tribal ruler.

Similar orders have been issued regarding members of the Sherbro and other tribes of the Protectorate resident in the Colony.

The following clauses of the Protectorate Amendment Act, 1913, indicate, however, the increased powers given during recent years to Government officials in regard to native courts, laws and customs :—

(1) The District Commissioner shall have power and authority to inquire into and settle any matters within his district, which have their origin in Porro laws, native rites or customs, land disputes, including land disputes arising between paramount chiefs, or any other disputes which, if not promptly settled, might lead to breaches of the peace.

(2) In any such inquiry the District Commissioner may, if he thinks fit, be assisted by one or more native chiefs as assessors to be summoned by him as occasion requires, but the decision shall rest exclusively with the District Commissioner and no settlement shall be deemed invalid if any or all of the assessors so summoned shall not be present throughout the whole of the inquiry.

(3) Any disregard or defiance of a settlement made under this section shall be deemed to be an offence.

The power conferred on the Court of the District Commissioner by Section 3 of the Protectorate Courts Jurisdiction Amendment Ordinance, 1907, of summoning native chiefs as assessors in hearing cases under the provisions of Section 2 of that Ordinance, shall extend to all cases, civil or criminal, arising exclusively between natives which may be heard and determined in a summary way in the Court of the District Commissioner, and all the provisions of Section 3 shall apply to all such cases, with the substitution of the word "decision" for the word "conviction" in the case of civil cases.

Among the amendments, also, to the Human Leopard and Alligator Ordinance, the following are noteworthy :—

(1) Power was given to the Governor to proclaim any chiefdom in which a murder had been committed in connection with an unlawful society, and to the District Commissioner to arrest and detain any person in a proclaimed chiefdom on a warrant under his hand.

(2) It was made an offence to be a member of an unlawful society, or to take part in the operations of any such society, or of any meeting of an unlawful society. The effect of this provision was made retrospective.

(3) Powers of search were given to the police in the Colony, and to court messengers and the West African Frontier Force in the Protectorate.

(4) Power was given to the Governor in Council to order the expulsion of any alien convicted under the Ordinance after his sentence.

*   *   *   *

The custom of electing the Temne tribal ruler or king outside the Protectorate, in the urban areas, is interesting. The author saw such an election at Cline Town.

Serenading parties of the Temne residents of Cline Town informed the townspeople that the preliminary stage of an interesting coronation ceremony had just started. Acting upon instructions received from their Alimamy, the Cline Town Temnes went king-and-queen hunting. This quaint custom consists in invading the premises of the lucky individual (who has, of course, been previously notified of the intended honour), seizing him and, in spite of the pretended resistance, shouldering him along the streets amid songs of rejoicing to a secluded house, where he is detained for about a month, during which time he is indoctrinated in royal duties and customs. At the end of this period he is taken out and solemnly crowned. In all about five persons were " held," two kings (Santigis) and three queens. The fee for the kingship is about £5, and that for the queenship £2 10s., so that the function is not entirely without a commercial aspect, to which, however, the royal designates are by no means averse, in view of the fat fees they soon make over never-ending native palavers. There was, however, one unwilling candidate who, immediately he heard of the unsolicited honour, cut away to the police station and threatened to do grievous bodily harm to the king-catchers if protection were not given him. His request was granted, and now the unambitious man is plying his more peaceful, if more arduous, trade of fisherman.

* * * *

Ordeals and " charms " are, naturally, still prevalent in different parts of the country, though they are more frequent among the Mendis and Yonnis than among the Temnes.

One ordeal some of the tribes favour for testing adultery is to force the accused to drink a " medicine " made from the leaves of the cotton, " sasswood " and other trees. If the suspected persons drink and vomit they are innocent, if guilty they die. Obviously in this case one is entirely at the mercy of the medicine man; for he has only to put a deadly poison in the drink to dispose of the person, the mixture in the ordinary way causing one to vomit.

The taking of " cassia " and " sasswood " to disprove an accusation of witchcraft is a very similar ordeal, but as this has been described frequently by travellers, I merely mention it here.

Another native " ordeal " applied in the case of women who are suspected of having been unfaithful to their men is as follows : The torbehmor, or medicine man, first rubs over the hands of the suspect a decoction of herbs and leaves. A small iron rod, previously made red-hot, is placed in a pot filled with palm oil. The suspected woman has to thrust her hand into the oil and pull out the hot iron. If she be unable to do so without being burnt she is adjudged guilty. If she suffer no burn the charge fails. Needless to say, the proportion convicted in this mode of trial is rather high.

The *Karu-sortor* is another ordeal especially devised for the discovery of petty larceny. A bowl is " dressed " with certain " medicine," and then handed to a little child, usually a girl, who also has a " medicine " applied to her hands and legs. With the bowl held in her hands she goes off spontaneously into a kind of trance, rushing about from place to place until she finally steps before some person, who is at once hauled before the chief for punishment. Punishment usually takes the form of a fine or a flogging. Formerly it was slavery, if the case were a bad one.

The ordeal of the *battu*, or whip, is carried out in the following way : The accused is placed in the middle of a ring of interested spectators. The *torbehmor* is then introduced, carrying his " medicine whip " in his hand. This he hands to a youth, having first applied some native unction to the lash, and rubbed the lad's arm, hands, and wrists with the juice of certain plants.

The boy seems to fall into a sort of hypnotic trance, runs round the ring, flourishing the whip and making the lash coil about the onlookers without touching anybody. Suddenly he singles out the culprit and commences to belabour in real earnest amid the cheers of the spectators. The beating goes on, in fact, until the boy is called off, and is held down by the " medicine man."

The ordeal of the whip is the final method adopted to discover a guilty person. Its decisions are never appealed against, even by the party most nearly concerned.

Marriage customs and ideas have been mentioned in a previous chapter. The cost of celebrating marriages and funerals keeps most of the natives poor.

Funeral rites are always elaborate, especially in the case of a chief. A dismal dirge or lament by the women is heard immediately there is a death, while messengers are despatched with the news to relatives in other villages, the body being kept in the house until they have all arrived. If, however, the man belonged to the " Porro," or if the dead person be a woman who was a member of the " Bondu," the body is kept in the " bush " belonging to either of those secret societies, and, in the former case, no woman may look upon the corpse.

On the burial day the mourners appear plastered with white clay, and a long procession is formed to follow the corpse. Cloths and other personal possessions are frequently buried with the deceased, the quantity varying according to his wealth. After the interment, which usually takes place at or towards sunset, a gun is fired to frighten away evil spirits, while a sacrifice of a fowl, or cattle, according to the locality and the deceased's rank, is usually offered up on the grave to propitiate the dead man's ancestors, who might otherwise torture his soul.

When a man dies and is buried, his sword, or stick, or other article that he was in the habit of carrying about with him, is often buried with him, the idea being that he shall not lack a weapon wherewith to fight and overcome such evil spirits as he may encounter in his journey to *Gewarlahun* (the abode of spirits). Passing natives' graves near a bush village, one notices that they are decorated with bottles, bundles of tied leaves, and other charms, all placed there for the invocation of the good spirits and repelling of the bad.

Among numerous birth customs, it may be mentioned that, although infanticide is punishable, it has not been altogether stamped out, especially in cases of deformity or abnormal births.

In the north and north-west of Sierra Leone, particularly among the Korankos and Limbas, ill-luck is believed to attend the birth of twins—a superstition found in several parts of West Africa and outside Africa. The twins are often killed, and the mother driven out into the bush, for twins are held to be a curse from the gods. Among one tribe the opinion was openly expressed that one of the twins must be illegitimate, and, unless by actual features this one could be detected, it was safer to dispose of the two. Another reason given in other parts of Africa, where one of the twins—usually the first-comer—is spared, is that the strength of the one depends upon the destruction of the other. This superstition regarding twins is by no means confined to Africa. It was prevalent among Aryans, the Teutons in particular regarding one of a twin birth as illegitimate.

In explanation of how death came into the world, the Temnes have a tradition that long, long ago, God was in constant communion with man, and when he thought that anyone had lived long enough on earth, he sent a messenger to invite such a person to come up into the sky and stay with Him. One man, however, who received such a message did not accept the invitation, as he was devoted to his wives and other riches. When the messenger returned without the man, God was angry, and sent down another messenger named Disease; but still the man refused to accept the invitation. So this messenger stayed on earth, and sent word back to God of the man's refusal, and asked for help to bring up the ungrateful being. Then God sent his messenger Death, who, with Disease, seized the man and conveyed him to God. Since then, God has always sent these messengers to fetch men.

Partial circumcision is a custom practised at puberty among some of the tribes. I was privileged to witness such a rite performed upon boys of from 12 to 14 years of age, though some seemed older. After having bathed in the river, the boys to be circumcised seated themselves in a row in a squatting position entirely naked, knees apart, elbows resting on knees, chin on hands, and eyes upturned. Behind each boy stood an old man who acted as a sort of godfather and received a small present from the father for his part in the ceremony.

The operator's knife was shaped like a bay-leaf, and was about 3 in. long, exclusive of its wooden handle.

Made of soft native iron, it takes a very sharp edge. The operator seized the end of the foreskin between finger and thumb and drew it as far forward as possible, cutting off the extreme end in two cuts with the knife. Sometimes also he makes a transverse slit across it just behind the base of the *glans penis*. The shouting and screaming of the assembled company drowned any cries. The whole operation was performed with surprising speed and dexterity. The boys sat quite still, and lost little blood. The operation over, the boys leaped into the air and threw themselves backward into the arms of their godfathers, who rubbed their faces to prevent fainting. After rest, the boys were conducted to the bush. There, I am told, they subsist at first entirely on milk, but after a few days they may eat whatever they wish. Healing takes from a few days to a month, rarely longer.

CHAPTER XVIII.

Through the Protectorate to Boia and Yonnibana.

The Sierra Leone Railway and its Tramway Extensions—Would a Timber Trade Pay?—The Uses of the Savannah Forest—Songo or Prince Alfred's Town—Rotifunk and its Massacres—Boia, Yonnibana, and Messrs. Lever's Concessions—First-class and Fifth-class Roads—Makomp and the Palm Country—Moyamba and its Mission—Susuwuru and its Gum Copal.

The Sierra Leone Railway shows a regular annual profit. The receipts for 1912 were £141,844, against £107,320 in 1911, and the total earnings from January to May, 1913, were £70,422, as compared with £59,320 for the same period in 1912.

Extensions by means of tramways—which are, however, quite as speedy as the train—have been made from Boia through the Yonnibana district to Makomp, on the other side of the Rokelle River, thence to Baga, near the Mabole River, Koinadugu district, and from Baiima at the end of the line to Pendembu, a few miles only from the Liberian frontier.

Still the demand exceeds the supply, and the country is clamouring for more goods vans and an increased number of second and third class compartments, especially on the Boia-Makomp route, where the up branch trams run Mondays, Wednesdays, and Fridays, and the return journey is made on the other week-days.

From Waterloo to Songo, and for some considerable distance, the country is decidedly disappointing.

On the whole the soil is shallow, but the mineral content is of such a character that a heavy growth of timber trees is induced.

Some years back an attempt was made by a native

of Sierra Leone to export timber to England, but owing to mismanagement it was not successful financially. Altogether some 300 trees were felled, but the logs were for the most part left " in the round," and the ends were not properly squared. This kind of timber the market does not want.

This, of course, is not a fair criterion as to the prospective value of the forest, as under proper auspices, I believe the export of the various mahoganies, woods used for furniture making, &c., would probably pay.

In this portion of the country extensive outcrops of laterite rocks are found scattered about. Surrounding them the vegetation is of a scrubby and dwarfed character, yet the soil formed by the weathering of these rocks is fairly rich where it has accumulated to a sufficient depth. Such patches one meets with immediately below the lower level of the " strike " of the outcrops, narrower deposits bordering the channels of streams. Frequently these patches of soil, where they are rich and moist and consequently clothed with evergreen forest, form the actual sources of streams draining the plain, and the course of such streams may be traced by evergreen fringes growing along the banks.

There is a disposition to regard the forests of the savannah type as practically worthless. I noticed, in more than one place, that no inquiry was made into the species or uses of the trees, either by European or native, where space had to be cleared for cacao, rubber, or even ginger and cassava.

The dense evergreen forests are certainly more imposing and strike the imagination in a manner which no savannah forest could; but the proportion of useful species is small, natural regeneration is poor, and age gradations are in a very unsatisfactory condition compared with the more deciduous forest.

Songo Town—known for a time as Prince Alfred's Town, from the visit to Sierra Leone by the late Prince Alfred, Duke of Edinburgh, in 1861—was once a more flourishing place, and formed a centre for wars and rebellions in bygone days. Now there is not even a store or refreshment place for the hapless visitor. Yet from here is the high road through the bush to the Kwaia country. Upon another occasion I explored the bush around Songo for several miles on either side of the railway.

Songo passed, the train enters a territory which is inhabited by a mixture of tribes, Mendis, Temnes, and Yonnis, of which the Mendi is predominant. Roti-funk appears to have been the largest town of this district before the rising of 1898, and possessed a flourishing American mission. In and around this dis-trict occurred some of the most fearful episodes of the war, for, unlike the Temnes, the Mendis gave the white people no opportunity to leave the country, but mas-sacred them in cold blood.

The mission-house here was burned to the ground. All the ladies were stripped naked and outraged, then left in the burning sun for hours to be gaped at by thousands of dancing war-boys, a great number of whom were half mad from drink and capable of any-thing. The youngest lady was kept a close prisoner by the chief. He wished to make her his wife, but she refused him, and was consequently beaten and tortured. She was kept a prisoner for eight days and then handed over to a party of war-boys, who took her into the bush. Then the chief's wives were sent to argue with her, and they treated her very cruelly. After being kept a close prisoner in the bush for three days she was taken back into the town and brought again before the chief and a large crowd of people. A sort of trial took place, the chief himself presiding, and at the con-clusion there was bargaining among the headmen about the girl, several offers being made for her. Still re-fusing to accept the chief or any other man as husband, she was kept a closely guarded prisoner in a small hut on the outskirts of a farm inside the bush, where the chief's second wife looked after her and treated her kindly. At length she was again brought before the chief, and again refusing, she was flogged, tied and outraged, the chief finally ordering the girl to be killed, but not too quickly. She was then led into the bush, stripped naked and bound, nameless atrocities being perpetrated upon her until she expired.

From Boia, the next town of importance, the train accommodation becomes more roomy, the bulk of passengers leaving for Yonnibana and Makomp, a delightful country, scarcely tapped, where the oil palm abounds in profusion. At Yonnibana, Messrs. Lever Brothers have erected a large factory to deal with this raw material, and a special railway siding has been constructed for their convenience.

This granting of a monopoly for twenty-one years to Messrs. Lever Brothers, Ltd., for the extracting of palm oil and the cracking of palm kernels by machinery, within an area of several hundreds of square miles in the district of Yonnibana, is an event of fundamental and far-reaching economic importance, well worthy of every encouragement if machine power is ever to take the place of hand power in doing these kinds of tedious and wasteful work.

There is nothing in the granting of such a monopoly which will prevent the local merchants or traders from buying palm oil and palm kernels from the natives as heretofore, or which will prevent the indigenous Africans from extracting the oil or cracking palm kernels by hand power, as they have been doing from time immemorial.

The original scheme was to have acquired a forest area by purchase, but this was very wisely abandoned.

The establishment by Messrs. Lever Brothers, Ltd., of a great factory, completely equipped with the most modern machinery, for extracting palm oil and cracking palm kernels will, however, release from these two kinds of work tens of thousands of human beings and enable them to be more usefully and profitably employed in increasing, progressively, the area of land under palm, kola, cacao, rubber, rice, and maize, &c., and thereby swell the volume of the supply of these articles and add enormously to the wealth resources of Sierra Leone.

The factory will become also a school of applied mechanics and chemistry, wherein the coming generations of Sierra Leoneans, who will supply the labour force employed therein, may obtain opportunities of learning thoroughly, in a practical and business-like manner, the arts of extracting the oil, cracking the kernels, and of preparing the palm products for export to the market of Europe and the whole world.

Other large firms are following Messrs. Lever's lead, notably the Co-operative Wholesale Society in the Karina district. Personally I am doubtful of the immediate success of such enterprises, although after some years and much money has been spent in perfecting expensive machinery, industry should triumph under exceptional management. Several mechanical contrivances for this particular industry have proved failures; the climate of the West Coast is peculiarly antagonistic to machinery, and the native prejudices die hard, particularly while time, to them, is not money. Yet, of all firms one would wish to see in Sierra Leone, that of Lever Brothers is decidedly the most desirable and the most likely to succeed. Throughout they have acted straightforwardly.

The chiefs were called together by the District Commissioner, who explained the whole matter to them. They expressed their satisfaction with the proposal and agreed to the terms of the agreement.

Certain newspapers alleged that the right of making oil by their crude process was to be taken away from the natives. These allegations were absolutely untrue. Neither the Government nor any concessionaire has the power to interfere with the rights of the natives in any way. The natives can still go on making oil by their own crude methods, and no concessionaire has any right to stop them. The concessionaire has simply the right to put up a mill and lay down mono-rails or

MR. W. H. SEYMOUR FORMERLY OF MESSRS. LEVER BROS., LTD.),
WITH YOUNG CHIMPANZEE.

Face p. 150.

anything which will enable him to bring in his produce to the mill, and facilitate the deal between buyer and seller. The native is as free as he ever was; he can sell his produce to whom he likes, and is under no obligation to go to the firm which erects the mill.

Yonnibana is already showing signs of progress. There is a special shunting yard, constructed by the Government, for which Messrs. Lever Brothers pay a nominal rent.

A fifth-class road runs in a northerly direction to Massimera, near the Rokelle River, another proceeds north-westerly to Robekki, about 12 miles, and yet another to Roghese and Roting. Fifth-class roads are nearly as good as the first-class roads which run north from Bo, Blama, Hangha, and Segbwema, the most important trading stations on the line; but whereas the bridges on the former are " stick " bridges of native construction only, those of the latter are of concrete with steel girders. The first-class roads are about 33 ft. wide, the fifth-class roads about 16 ft. wide. Both kinds of roads are maintained by the Roads Department of the Public Works Office.

" Improved " roads, of which there are many in this part of the country, are constructed and maintained by the paramount chiefs, who receive subsidies of from 10s. to 20s. a mile for upkeep. Paramount Chief Coker, of Jimmy Ghaboh chiefdom, was expecting a sword from the Government when I was there for his services in road-making and sanitation. Certainly his efforts were most praiseworthy. Another enthusiastic and progressive chief—this time a woman—Madam Humonyaha, engaged no fewer than 400 labourers to make up her roads for about eight miles to the Konnoh boundary. She sent presents to the labourers by her consort chief Amara, such as the following : two bullocks, eleven bushels of rice, fifteen cases of trade-gin, several demijohns of rum, £5 10s. sterling, &c.; besides these, she gave some other presents to Keifu, the native engineer, and the five sectional headmen;

she had been regularly sending dashes to the men whilst the work was going on.

The other chiefs have asked Madam Humonyaha for the native engineer to direct the men in their own chiefdoms so as to carry on their roads to the Konnoh district—a country of palm trees.

At Mano, a few miles away, in the Ronietta district, a site of about 1,000 acres in area has been selected as the headquarters of the reorganized Agricultural Department, and experiments with the various native crops have been commenced. One of the objects of the Department is to evolve a practical rotation of crops which will enable the farmer to grow produce on his land for a longer period than has hitherto been possible. The different varieties of rice, the principal food of the natives, are being carefully investigated, and improvements are being made in cultivating ginger, maize, guinea corn, cassava, and ground-nuts. It is further intended to establish experimental stations in each district.

The soya bean having been successfully cultivated in the Koinadugu district, experiments are being made at Mano.

Special attention is also being paid to the cultivation of the castor oil plant and of benni seed, products which may eventually come to be of considerable importance.

Although allowance must always be made for the peculiarities of the soil and the strong conservatism of the native farmer, it may in general be said that a considerable advance may be looked for in the agricultural development of Sierra Leone.

Returning to the main line, the next place of importance is Moyamba, where there is a prison accommodating forty-four culprits. Its walls are built of stone, its floors and ceiling of concrete with a corrugated iron roof.

Moyamba is a flourishing West African village. The chief is of a progressive turn of mind, as were apparently his predecessors. Kola and rubber farms are cultivated here, both by the chief and the Roman Catholic mission stationed at this village.

The rubber plantation of Chief Kangajo was originally laid down by a woman, Madam Yoko, under the superintendence of the Government Agricultural Department. Those who are apt to think that women have no place in the councils of the African races would do well to live out here and find for themselves the many traces of woman's power and prestige.

Pará rubber was planted in this spot seven years ago—200 trees at about 15 ft. apart—but the trees have been much neglected, the soil is poor—chiefly dry, hard laterite—and the growth has been retarded by the dense scrub which has grown around them. Hevea, as previously mentioned, wants full sunlight after the first year, otherwise the tree becomes lank and weak. With considerable surprise, I noticed what a brave fight these Hevea had made against adverse conditions, which demonstrated still further that this species of rubber can and must succeed in Sierra Leone.

The Roman Catholic mission at Moyamba have some good specimens of Pará, four years old, planted alternately with Castilloa rubber and kola.

A bridge was being built over a running stream in the town, but as much inconvenience was being experienced in getting labourers to attend the mechanics, I inquired the reason, and was told that the labourers are not paid for their services and no allowance is given them for food. The Government consider that as the making of roads and bridges in this district in particular is for the improvement of the town, and as the chief and people are to benefit most, the chief should provide men, free of cost, for the Roads and Works Department to do the work; the result is that the labourers supplied by the chief decamp after a couple of days' work without pay, and the chief has to find another set of labourers for the progress of the undertaking. The labour problem in West Africa, as I have elsewhere intimated, requires very careful handling. The black man will not work unless his wage is assured to him and paid regularly. Should at any time, in the remote future, independent native states arise, their standing army would always be a source of weakness in their relations with more civilized nations. No one can imagine the West African enduring prolonged military discipline unpaid, like the Turk.

The gaol and government buildings at Moyamba are supplied with water from a dam in the hills; new quarters are being built upon the high lands for the European officials, and the school for chiefs at Bo is being removed to this progressive place.

Close to Moyamba is a village called Susuwuru, over land on which the old forest has evidently been destroyed during the last thirty years. Large monkey-apple trees are still standing there. These are said to survive fires for a longer period than any other tree.

The town of Susuwuru stands among a belt of gum copal trees, which extends about ten miles north and south, and is about half a mile to two miles broad. As the name indicates, the town was founded by a Susu man, some thirty-five years ago, with the idea of settling there in order to be able to tap gum copal trees, the value of which up to that time was unknown to the local natives. The trees were overtapped, and, consequently, nearly all the old trees are dying. The tapping incisions, having been made too close together, evidently aggravated the overtapping.

The gum copal tree is one of the few gregarious trees of West Africa, and this makes it particularly valuable, as more can be collected in the same time and a larger area can be supervised more easily. I remembered noticing some on the Christineville estate in very good condition and recommended that gum copal should be cultivated by a subsidiary company.

Here, in Susuwuru, are a great number of seedlings, but few medium-sized trees. Probably the majority of the seedlings die before reaching that stage. When the old trees have all died the whole forest will die out.

Part of the gum belt is subject to annual floods, which appear to be getting worse. There has been suggested, I believe as a means of saving gum copal, a co-operative scheme, using the native labour and a Forestry Department's supervision with a division of the final yield of gum copal, a fifth part going to the Government, a fifth to the paramount chief, and three-fifths to the village respectively. A system such as this has been started with regard to rubber planting in the Province of Southern Nigeria, with the result that some 1,000,000 rubber seedlings have been planted. The trees are now growing well. The expense is not very great and the whole community gains.

The people at Susuwuru seem quite keen and ready to undertake the work if the Government will show them how to do it, but they will not do it on their own initiative.

To tap the gum the native uses a miniature hoe with a sharp cutting edge and a handle about 12 in. long. At the beginning of the dry season he visits the gum belt and chops small holes about 1 in. square and $\frac{1}{4}$ in. deep all around the stems, as closely together as possible, and to a height of 20 ft. The gum exudes and hardens, when it is collected.

The average price paid by the local traders appears to be 1s. a pound. No attempt is made by the native to grade his gum or to separate it from dirt and chips of wood. By cleaner preparation and grading, a higher price could be obtained.

CHAPTER XIX.

To the Liberian Frontier.

Bo—Bandajuma—Blaima—Mawfé and Sumbuyah—The Sewa and its Falls—Proposed Electrification of the Railway—The Loma Mountains—The Funtumia and Landolphia Rubber—Koronkos—Konnohs and Kissis—The Source of the Niger and its Superstitions—Crossing the Meli and Moa Rivers—Cotton—The Liberian Frontier—The Red and the White Ants.

Bo is said to be one of the rising towns of the Protectorate. All I remember of it is the discomfort and darkness of the place. When you steam into a semi-terminus late in the evening, after a long and slow railway journey, one is perhaps naturally pessimistic, unless comfort in some shape or other awaits you. And, as I was off again early the following morning, I admit that I could not do justice to the place.

The rest-house built of mud-bricks, with concrete angle pillars and floor, and a thatch over a corrugated iron roof, cost £265. What sort of a place Bo must have been before this was erected I dread to think.

The town is peopled chiefly by Temnes, Susus, Lokkohs, Syrians, and Sierra Leoneans or Creoles; and there were some disputes between these peoples and the Paramount Chief Boymah at the time.

All around this district, down to Bandajuma, and along the beautiful Boom River, waged the fearful rebellion war of 1898; and the towns and villages are only now beginning to reap and to realize the effects of the peace which followed upon rapine and destruction. Here, at Bo, which is another favourite place of the Creole, were ruthlessly massacred all those who were suspected of leaning to the British, among whom was the nephew of Sir Samuel Lewis.

The Boom River is the next feature of beauty. On the other side of the railway it becomes the Sewa, but a trip either way is well worth doing. On the south of the railway one or two towns are particularly attractive. The pretty and picturesque town of Mawfé, in the Boompé country, is situated on the south side of the beautiful Big Boom River, about twenty-eight miles from Bandajuma and nineteen from Kambia. Stores and " factories " surround it on both sides of the river. On the opposite side lies Mobongo, and 200 yards lower down is the trading station of Sumbuyah, now a formidable rival, with a *jopowahun* or market. Mawfé, before the rising, was a very large town in which a number of educated people from Sierra Leone resided. It is now recovering its former importance. A brisk trade is always going at Mawfé and Sumbuyah, for in the rainy season the river is navigable for large craft to Sherbro, and much produce is received here from the interior. The Big Boom River in the " dries " is magnificent. The water runs clear and sparkling over a sandy and rocky bottom. Above the town, huge rocks and boulders stretch from one bank to the other, forming a roaring cataract. The steep banks, 8 ft. to 15 ft. high, are lined on both sides with beautiful tropical vegetation, while here and there, dotted among the noble palms and other giant foliage, peep the conical thatched roofs of the villages. In the rainy season the river is between 350 and 400 yards wide, but during the " dries " half that size, leaving long stretches of sand exposed.

Here in the Bompeh chiefdom is the great centre of the rice trade of the district. Tobandah, about four miles away, was the scene of a large gathering of native chiefs with their followers for the purpose of settling an important boundary dispute between Kapandah chiefdom, in the Northern Sherbro district, and Bompeh chiefdom in the railway district. Assistant

District Commissioner Shaffery, of Gbamgbama, and Assistant District Commissioner Boddam-Whetham, of Kennema, sat as judges over the case; Chief Backie John, of Gbapp, Acting Paramount Chief Abraham Tucker, of Mattru, and Paramount Chief Sehburah, of Tormah, were the assessors. Owing to ill-health, Paramount Chief Lasanah, of Bompeh, was unable to attend; he was represented by his chief speaker, Posowa; whilst Chief George, of Mawfé, an educated chief, defended the rights of the Bompeh chiefdom.

One of the most picturesque chiefs of the Boom district was Chief Kenneh Coker, who was frequently chosen by the District Commissioner as an assessor for various boundary disputes.

There is telegraphic communication between Serabu, Sumbuyah, Bandajuma, and Pujehun.

Between the Boom River and Baiima, the country gradually becomes wilder and more primitive, although, for the real African forest, one has to journey for some distance from the railway track, either on the Panguma side or from Kennema to Beribu.

Three of the most interesting places *en route* are Blama, Kommendi, and Daru. At the last-named town, occupying a very picturesque spot on the Moia River, is the military barracks of the Frontier Force. Kommendi was once considered the dullest place in the district, and it was said that the station was always kept so clean and its fittings so bright because the railway porter had nothing else to do. To-day there are several European firms there with their factories, including, of course, the ubiquitous Société Commercial, Cie. Française, and Paterson Zochonis.

At Blama also are several trading firms. One can journey from here, up the Sewa, to the falls above Dombulu. At the Sewa Falls, Messrs. Norton Griffiths, Ltd., the well-known engineers, hoped to secure their principal means of water power for their scheme of electrification of the Sierra Leone Railway. The scheme, which was to include concessions for oil mills, fell through, though many people believe that electrification is possible under other and cheaper conditions and methods. Certainly, with power at its command, much of the iron and other mineral wealth of the country could be commercialized.

The journey up or along the Sewa towards the Loma and Nimmini mountains is particularly charming. Here a portion of the evergreen forest, which once must have been extensive in Sierra Leone, still exists. The *Funtumia elastica* (*Ireh,* or silk rubber tree, of the Gold Coast, *Bubui* of the Mendis, and *Watia* of the Temnes) is to be found in the forests of the Kagnari, Nimmini, and Loma mountains. To extract this rubber, some natives fell the tree and cover it with dry grass, which they light. The heat is just sufficient to cause a partial coagulation of the latex in the lactiferous vessels. They then bruise off the bark with a stone, and, taking the débris down to the river, wash it thoroughly and separate the bark from the rubber. The separation is seldom complete, and the result is a dirty rubber, fetching 2s. a lb. Properly prepared, this rubber realizes a good price, generally about 9d. less than Pará.

More intelligent natives ascend the trunk by means of a sling passed round it. To one end of the sling is a loop which fits over the right thigh. They keep the left foot on the sling. Thus, by moving the rope up the tree the ascent is quickly accomplished, and, when stationary, both hands are left free.

The climber carries a gouge, or chisel, with which he cuts vertical as well as transverse oblique grooves, forming a rough " herring-bone " pattern, which may be continued for the whole length of the trunk, and even extend on to the main branches. To make the cuts, the tool is sometimes used with one hand only; but some natives hold it in the left, and drive it by blows on the end of the handle, given with the palm of the right hand. The flow of latex commences at once, and comes down the vertical channel into a calabash placed at the base of the tree, into which the latex is guided by a lip of clay or a chip of wood. The quantity of latex procured at one tapping varies from half a quart to two quarts per tree. The tree is not tapped again for several months until the wounds have healed. On the second tapping the same form of cut is made upon the opposite side of the tree, and the transverse channels often intersect those made previously.

Here also abounds the Landolphia vine, with its wonderful festoons. The Landolphia vine yields the native wild rubber. The vine is a parasite found on old lime, coffee, and other trees, forming dense tangled snake-like masses of dark green, bearing in profusion conspicuous sweetly scented jasmine-like flowers which turn to fruit, often brightly coloured and sometimes edible. This is the rubber, the collection of which in the Congo and in Putumayo has been enshrouded by horrible tales of unhealthy conditions and worse atrocities. Of atrocities I cannot speak; there are none in Sierra Leone. But no unprejudiced person who has travelled through a wild rubber forest can acquiesce in the descriptions of " boggy pestiferous land," " dreadful sloughs of despond covered by some curse," or other fanciful pictures drawn for the public by doctrinaires and novelists.

There are several kinds of Landolphia, of which the *owariensis* is the best. In the drier regions *L. owariensis* coagulates upon the wound almost immediately upon exposure to the air, whereas in moister places it runs from the cut in such a manner as to allow it to be collected in a vessel. The acid juices of the lime are added to hasten coagulation when necessary; or the collector smears the fresh latex upon his naked body until enough has been coagulated to form a small ball, which serves as a nucleus for winding on the strings of fresh latex as the new cuts are made.

Some miles away is Foyama, an important town in the Railway district. Here was held a large gathering of native chiefs to decide a boundary dispute between the Marlaine and Jaiama chiefdoms. The District Commissioners were judges, and the assessors were Alimami Kie Kie, of Kpanda and Sowa, John Mannah, of Kpaka, and Sokoh Bongoh, a chief of the Railway district.

The Loma mountains rise to a considerable height above the surrounding plain and are clothed with forest, except where outcrops of rock occur or where the slope is too steep to support ligneous vegetation. These mountains are situated in the south-east of the Koina-dugu district, some twenty-five miles from the English, French and Liberian boundary. The foot-hills and lower slopes are being farmed, but the forest on the upper slopes is virgin. Here and there the forests come down into the foot-hills, following the course of a river or clothing the steep sides of a valley. The River Bagbe, which, after being joined by the Bafi, forms the Sewa, flows round the north-east, north-west, and south-west of the Loma mountains, and relies on the small and large streams that rise in the forest of the mountains for the maintenance of its water supply. The Inyni River, a confluent of the Bafi, rises on the eastern slopes; thus three-quarters of the water of the Sewa River, at the junction, rises in the Loma mountains.

Travelling is very arduous here owing to the complete absence of villages, and consequently the difficulty of obtaining food for carriers. The paths are for the most part mere rubber-hunters' trails, so that it takes four days to get through the forests and cross the range.

The forests are in good condition, and there is an absence of tangled undergrowth, which is an indication that no farming has been done—that it is virgin forest and not re-growth.

In places on the top and highest slopes the ground is precipitous, and here and there the syenite outcrops in great masses. This is a typical feature of the country, and the bold outlines of these peaks may be seen at great distances. The districts of Kondondu and

Kundema are swampy and covered with a thick cutting grass exceedingly unpleasant to travel through. Some miles farther along, in the Koranko country, is the source of the Niger, or Joliba, as the Susus call it. "Joliba" means "He who can run faster than any other man." The Susus' language is much spoken in this part of the country, although comparatively few Susus seem to live there.

The natives have a legend that a devil lurks inside the rock where the Niger rises. Any man who is bold enough to approach the rock and gaze upon it will be killed by the demon. If the local savage can be induced to show a stranger the spot, he will, on leaving the rock, turn round and walk backwards towards it, covering his eyes with one hand, so that he may not see the haunted place, while with the other hand he points to where the river rises.

This rock forms one of the boundary marks on the Anglo-French frontier, separating Sierra Leone from French Guinea. The stone has inscribed on both sides the names of the members of the Boundary Delimitation Commission. The country is exceedingly rocky and precipitous, and the sides of the mountains are covered with thick grassy bush, which grows to a height of 12 ft. Descending south, one crosses the River Meli on rafts of rough logs bound together by a ropy creeper called "tie-tie," and manœuvred by a long pole. This brings us to Kissiland. The country and people here are very primitive. An old chief offered us hospitality, but we were not sorry to leave these uncivilized spots. The town he inhabited consisted of about forty or fifty huts, irregularly placed, and interspersed with palm, banana, plaintain, orange, lime, paw-paw, and kola trees, which in a great measure supply the natives with food. The houses are built in a circular form and have a pyramidal roof; the outer stakes which form them are wattled together with small turgs, and afterwards plastered inside with mud. The roof or eave of the house projected about 2 ft. or 3 ft. beyond the sides, forming a pleasant shade under which the natives sit without being exposed to the scorching heat of the sun. To each of these houses are two doors, which are placed exactly opposite to each other. The space inside is rarely, if ever, divided into compartments.

The usual dress of the natives is a small piece of cloth, fastened round the waist and brought between the legs. The natives seemed a cross between Kissis and Konnohs.

Descending south again, we gradually approached the railway terminus, still keeping along the Liberian frontier. The Moa River, which has to be crossed by dug-out canoes worked by a single paddle, is very picturesque here, but the forests are being rapidly cut down by the natives.

Mafindo, a very typical town of this part of Sierra Leone, is a very dirty cattle town, with houses like pig-styes, but it is interesting because it is half in British and half in Liberian territory. The centre street divides one country from the other. Each portion has its own chief with its own set of laws. There cotton is grown and spun in small clearings close to the villages. It is picked by the women. The cotton-pod is rolled between two smooth stones in order to crush out the cotton seeds, then spun on to wooden spindles and rubbed with bone dust to harden it.

Cotton has not hitherto been a success in Sierra Leone. The imported plant has been badly attacked by the red cotton stainer bug (*Dystercus superititiosus*). This red bug lives on the cotton seed, and it excretes a yellow fluid which stains the cotton. The cotton stainer bug is very common in this country, and there will be difficulty in checking it because the native farmer leaves his cotton growing on the farm till the bush eventually kills it, the result being that the cotton plant is flowering nearly all the year, and, consequently, the cotton stainer keeps on breeding the whole year round. If the farmer would destroy the cotton plant after the crop has been harvested, this would check a continuous supply of food for the insect and in that way diminish the number of this pest.

Speaking of pests, a few words as to red and white ants may not be out of place.

The red ant is an interesting but dangerous little creature. Larger than the so-called white ant, his particular hobby is to bite, and he is fond of blood. Hence, the Temne natives far up the Rokelle River place " medicine," in the form of chicken or cow blood, under the trees infected by these creatures, to entice them down. Once gorged with blood, they can be killed in thousands by kerosene. Their only sphere of usefulness is to destroy other ants or similar insects. Hence, one branch of their family is called the " driver " ant, because they drive almost every animal before their myriads. Another is called the " Amazon " because, sallying forth in large number in military array, they proceed to a neighbouring ant-hill and plunder it of the larvæ of its neuters (the working portion of the community), which, when hatched by their foster-mothers, become a kind of pariah or slave caste.

The red ant is an unpleasant pest to meet at any time, for he has a sharp sting, and will attack anybody. He attacks men camping out as well as animals. One former pagan method of killing a man was to strip the victim, tie him up, and leave him to be devoured by red ants.

The only way to check the march of the red ant is to light a fire and spread kerosene around.

The white ant, to call it by its popular name, although it is a misnomer, is a fearful pest to the planter. It attacks any kind of wood except the mature coconut palm, the dum palm, and the oroko (the *Sime* of the Mendis), which are believed to be impervious to its attacks. Considering the durability and the plentifulness of the oroko tree and this special quality of resisting white ants, it is astounding that more use is not made of it for erecting bungalows and stores.

If the white ants attack the uprights of your dwell-

PENDEMBU (NEAR THE LIBERIAN FRONTIER) WHERE THE RAILWAY ENDS.

Face p. 164.

ing, its sudden collapse may mean personal injury, not to speak of serious inconvenience and damage. The white ants work so secretly that unless you constantly examine woodwork its collapse is the first intimation of anything wrong. The minute creatures travel along in thousands, either in single file or two abreast, in a little channel which they excavate themselves and which shelters them while they work. This channel consists of a narrow streak of earth, which directly it appears upon a tree or any kind of wood should be instantly removed.

Saucers of water are placed under wooden boxes which, ordinarily, would rest on the ground. This prevents the ants from climbing up. Coal tar is used both as a preservative and a protection.

For some time rubber planters believed that the white ants did not attack green wood, but now careful attention is given to rubber infected. In young plantations the trees are examined regularly; if they appear infected then search is made for the nest and it is destroyed. Not only the queen, but the whole nest must be destroyed. In older plantations of more than six years old these pests can be destroyed by an oil from one of the fruit trees, which I found on a Sierra Leone estate. Experiments with the oil proved it to be exceptionally efficacious upon the woodwork infested by these pests.

* * * *

A few more miles, but a long day's journey down the Moa River or by hammock, brings one to Pendembu, the railway terminus. Here one would almost expect to find civilization once more. But the chiefs in this district and across the Liberian frontier are often more cruel and exacting than many of those in the remoter districts through which I passed. At the time of my visit, the native court of Pendembu was inflicting a fine of £150 on headman Davoah and £127 on a native called Banyba, of Kanrelahun, for cutting roads to farms, the fines apparently being proportioned so that the victims could not pay without forfeiting some, if not all, of their wives and children. The District Commissioner, I believe, afterwards caused these fines to be readjusted.

There was also in exile here a Liberian chief who was " wanted " across the border for more than one offence.

CHAPTER XX.

THROUGH MENDILAND.

The Malema Country—The Morro and the Maho—Taiama, Lalehun, Beribu and Bulma—Yanduhun—Elephant Hunting—
The Gola Forest—The new Frontier—Habits and Charms of
the Mendis—Enforcing an Oath—Influence of Juju—The
Author as " Medicine Man."

PERHAPS the most beautiful part of Sierra Leone is
to be found in the south-east portion, known as the
Malema country, in Upper Mendiland, lying along the
borderland of Liberia, and watered by the Morro and
Maho Rivers with their many tributaries. Around
Taiama, Lalehun, Beribu, and Bulma the scenery is
exquisite, with its fairylands of palms amid ferny
foliage, and its forests, grand in their immense and
stately beauty. Most of the little towns in this district
have recovered from the wars of rebellion in which they
took part. Bulma was once a strongly stockaded town
and was subject to repeated attacks from the wild Gola
tribe, who continually warred upon the Mendis to obtain
slaves.

A few years ago these beautiful lands were filled with
fetishes, saturated with superstition, groaning under
civil war and slavery, and dominated by dark secrets
and darker deeds. As late as 1894, when Sir Frederic
Cardew visited the hinterland, he found civil wars and
slave traffic rampant. These were suppressed by the
vigour of British government. Then came the rebellion
of 1898, and again the forest reeked with bloodshed.
As I traversed this delectable district, all seemed peaceful and tranquil, but, even as I write, there comes
news of recrudescence of petty troubles, jealousy between rival chiefs, and the removal of one by the British

Government to preserve the peace; while the Liberian Government has been obliged to act likewise on the other side of the forest.

Both the Morro and Maho are large rivers in the wet season, which was now upon us. In the dry season rocks and rapids appear, but even then the Morro, with a minimum width of 50 yards near Goli, and about a hundred yards at Yanduhun, is an impressive sight. During May, after a tornado or two, it rises from 3 ft. to 4 ft., and later as much as 20 ft. to 25 ft. At the beginning of the wet season transport by boat quickens many a journey which otherwise has to be made by road or forest track; but in the "dries" the rocks, rapids and mud are prohibitive; and, in the middle of the rainy season, few Europeans would care to trust themselves on the native boats with such rapid currents.

Tributary creeks open on either side, narrow, dark, and full of mystery or romance. Gliding silently from among the shadows of such a stream small black canoes would suddenly appear and disappear. Some would contain men and merchandise, others dusky maidens clad only in wristlets and anklets. And the forest here is of the evergreen rain forest type, untouched in many places by the hand of man.

Underneath it is dark; the foliage of the trees intercepts the light. The quiet of death reigns there, and nothing is seen of the animal world up in the tops of the trees. The plants grow up slender and tall, longing for light and air. Creepers climb upwards, winding themselves round the trunks of the trees, making the woods almost impenetrable for those who do not carry a knife. Beautiful orchids live on those trunks, but, wanting their share of the sunshine, grow so high that their flowers are not easily seen. Where the fall of a tree has made a gap in the roof of leaves, through which light and air are again able to reach the soil, small brushwood at once begins to shoot up, struggling to keep the spot thus acquired. Yet, however thick the forest, the Mendi finds his way with ease, wriggling under creepers, avoiding entangled vines, twisting between branches, imperceptibly, and without causing a crack or snap to betray his whereabouts; while from the practice of years he can do it with extraordinary rapidity. Children are taught when young how to go quickly and quietly through the bush, and those not so taught are bound to learn from having to go into it nearly every day of their lives from their earliest years, following the elder boys who go hunting, wood-cutting, or farm-making. Even were it possible to follow a native into his forest, it would still be extremely difficult to keep him in view. For here Nature comes to his aid. The human inhabitant of the forest, with his naked and thick-skinned body, harmonizes closely with his surroundings, and the long grass, which, in the dry season, cuts the European if he push it aside carelessly with his bare hand, seems to have no effect upon the black-skinned races.

The land falls going from the northern to the southern part of the forest. The lowest point, just below Yandahun, is 400 ft. above the sea-level, and the highest near the boundary stone, marked 2,347 ft.

These hills and mountains are very steep, and the valleys between are extremely narrow, usually with a rapid stream coursing between rocks at the bottom and without any level land at all.

The land in the northern half of the forest is almost entirely of this character, but the southern part is much more undulating, the rock only cropping out here and there with swamps between. The underlying rocks vary a great deal, from soft laterite to very hard serpentine. Granite occurs in some places with a considerable admixture of hornblende. This weathers into a good soil, which is not seen on the hills, owing to its being washed away into the swamps and streams; with the exception of the swamps there is very little real soil.

The rainfall does not exceed 100 in. a year in the higher portion, but is far greater in the south.

Between Pendembu and Gohru, through the Mandoo

country, the land is fairly level, the rise being only
about 20 ft. There are many streams and one river,
the Mauwa. Farther along are the Kehya and Lan-
gura Rivers, then numerous small streams, especially
towards the Tungea and Goura countries. In that part
of the country, Pujehoon is the chief town. There is
a large amount of iron ore in that neighbourhood.

At this end of Sierra Leone, the tracks of elephants
are seen in every direction. I have heard that officials
frequently make valuation surveys by following such
tracks instead of cutting the bush. Far in the distance
I saw a herd of elephants, but it was impossible to come
up with them. Even had we done so we should have
been in a dilemma. For I had not a " full " licence.

As elephants are so scarce now in this country no
European thinks it worth while, I am told, to pay the
price. He waits until he can get his elephant, and
takes the risks. If he can secure an elephant, he applies
at once for the licence. If he miss—well!—that's
another matter. But even with a full licence you may
not hunt a cow or calf elephant, nor kill nor capture
more than two full-grown elephants, rhinoceroses, or
hippopotami.

I doubt whether elephants are so scarce in this
quarter as they are supposed to be. The paramount
chiefs of Manina and Fiama derive a large source of
revenue from ivory, and I came across a " chief hunter "
who had at least twenty apprentices.

The animals which I saw did not strike me as being
very large, and they all seemed to have rather small
tusks. The females' tusks are usually shorter and
thicker than those of the male, but all of these could
not have been females. Even among the human species
females seldom herd together. I am told that there is
both a bigger and a smaller species than the one I saw,
the smaller coming from over the Liberian frontier and
being only about 4 ft. high.

The native hunter will shoot at all seasons of the year
without regard to sex or age, and this is the only forest

PROSPECTING FOR IRON (FOUND IN ABUNDANCE IN SIERRA LEONE).

Face p. 170.

portion of Sierra Leone where the elephant is to be found in any numbers.

African elephants might surely be trained for transport work, when the human carriers are required for more productive work as the country is opened up.

The forest on the Sierra Leone side of the Morro is frequently called the Gola forest, but, strictly speaking, the Gola lies on the left bank only, " Gola " being the name of a distinct tribe, said to be addicted to cannibalism. These people originally inhabited the land on the left bank of the Gola, and from there to the Mano and Liberia. Many years ago the Mendis attacked the Gola people and drove them back across the Mano, so that now only the old foundations of the houses and the kola trees they planted mark the sites of their many towns or villages.

However, by a treaty with Liberia, signed on January 21, 1911, this south-eastern district of Sierra Leone, lying south of the Morro River, was ceded to the Republic in exchange for the district of Kanre Lahun. Immediately north of the Anglo-Liberian frontier the Anglo-French boundary underwent a modification, resulting in the transference to Sierra Leone from French Guinea of a narrow strip of territory with an area of 125 square miles.

But Sierra Leone can well afford to lose the whole of the uninhabited Gola to Liberia as long as she retains the magnificent land and scenery from Malema to Bulma. Even from there through Dara, Damawuru and Gorahun to Bandasuma, through which one has to travel patiently and slowly to reach the Sherbro country, the scenery could not be described as tame.

The following is a list of some of the more important chiefs in the districts around the last portion of the railway line and Upper Mendiland. It will be noticed that four of them are women, including the famous Madam Humonyaha, already mentioned : —

Manyeh, of Deah ; Lamin, of Manowa (Pejeh East) ; Bondoe, of Leppyama ; Perenyamu, of Small Bo ;

Madam Margow, of Lubu; Borri, of Baoma; Soko, of Bongor; Boyma, of Big Bo; Boyma Dorwi, of Wainday; Pokawa, of Jaiama; Madam Mabaja, of Bagbeh; Pokie, of Badja; Keketay, of Yarwoy; Sumbo, of Konjo; A. Bai Comber, of Mando; Madam Humonyaha, of Nongowa; Kutubu, of Pendembu; Farma, of Bambara; Bundeh, of Luawa; Comey, of Koya; Saio, of Gowra; Ammara, of Tunkiah; Foray, of Jwai; Samawova, of Jalluahun; Bondowa, of Damma; Baion, of Bongray; Farma Gevow, of Mallema; Bonboto, of Jahn; Manna, of Hurohun; Kerjono, of Pejeh West; Madam Jungar, of Nomor.

A little farther away is the chiefdom of Bolum, over which reigns the distinguished Tucker dynasty.

*   *   *   *

The Mendiman has a high sense of hospitality and expects you to have the same. When he honours you with a visit one of the first things you have to do is to " pull " his " how-do." If he finds you too tardy about it, he coolly reminds you of your obligation by asking if you won't " pull " his " how-do." The only successful answer to this is to give him a drink. Uncommon, is it not?

Of all the tribes in Sierra Leone none is more superstitious than the Mendi, excepting perhaps the Sherbro tribe, which is closely allied to and much intermarried with the Mendiman.

A new arrival needs to be careful how he meddles with things in this country. Everything "catches." Toiling along once with my Mendi boy, I noticed he was looking indisposed. Asking him what was the matter, he replied, "Water catch me, massa."

Yes! animals, trees, stones, sand, fire, even the chair you sit on "catches." And so strong is the people's belief in this sympathetic magic that many of those who have settled there for a long time are afraid to go into territory outside Mendiland for fear that the antidote might not be to hand, should any of those numerous objects "catch" them away from this particular district.

The Mendis hold two particular charms in great respect. One is called "suk," and is said to bring the lucky possessor good fortune. The other is called "hoare" and is used to protect the owner from evil influences. The latter is made of a plant fairly common in the hinterland, which is boiled into a thick greenish substance. This is then eaten, and has the property of increasing the drinking powers of the consumer. This property enhances the prestige of the individual, as the Mendi is much given to drinking.

Among other special medicines favoured by the Mendis are "Marfanga," "Kaikumba," "Tehlang," and "Borfima." Only by the aid of one of these "medicines" can one frequently elicit truth or secure fidelity from the natives here. "Kaikumba" in particular is used to enforce an oath. On the "Kaikumba," which is really an ancient stone, you place one of the other medicines—red pepper or a kola nut for preference. Addressing the Kaikumba, the Mendi man swears to do his duty or not to steal; if he fail the medicine will enter his stomach and swell it till it bursts. The words *nya voteh* are then repeated three times, and then *en Gewar*, equivalent to "So help me God." Medicine, magic, juju, call it how you will, is profoundly settled at the back of the black man's mind.

Here is another instance of the powerful belief, even of educated natives, in magic and "medicine," and of the profound influence of mind over body. After settling a boundary dispute, the natives against whom I had decided, threatened reprisals on the friendly old Creole who had, by his knowledge of the place and previous owners, greatly assisted me in my judgment. He was accustomed to sleep for five nights in the week on the plantation, spending the week-ends with his family at a village on the other side of the antagonistic native village, necessitating his passing through or

near it. To attack him openly would have brought
swift punishment upon the whole community. They
therefore threatened that they would spread "medicine" across his path, so that he should gradually
wither and die. The acting manager, noticing that the
old fellow seemed greatly upset as the week-end
approached, suggested that the Creole should stay on
the plantation instead of going home as usual. Perceiving, however, that the man was obsessed with the
"medicine" idea, and realizing that for him to stop
over one week-end was simply to postpone the evil for
a week, an idea occurred to me. Getting a bottle, and
gathering various fruits and herbs in the near vicinity
without arousing attention, I concocted a drink or
"medicine" chiefly consisting of cashew, paw-paw,
lime, pepper, some spices and spirits. Then, summoning the Creole, and giving him the bottle, I told him I
had heard that the neighbouring villagers had threatened
him with "medicine," but that I had a medicine and
charm which was more powerful than any over here,
and of which a drop could counteract the effects of these
villagers' "medicine." The result was electrical.

His face beamed, and he hugged the bottle. He
passed through the antagonistic village next day without a fear, and I have heard since that he is still doing
so, and remains hale and hearty.

Possibly my ruse might not have been so successful
but for the fact that the natives had noticed that I had
come back from the interior without any ill-effects from
the abnormal heat and never seemed indisposed. This
they attributed to my possession of some "medicine"
or some occult influence. Upon several other occasions
I acted the part of a medicine man, as many of the
blacks seem to feel the effects of heat and fatigue quite
as much as the white man, and they appeared to value
and use the contents of my medicine chest in proportion
as I disused them. But upon this particular occasion
it was a case more of faith than of pharmacy.

(Prime Minister.)   CHIEF BAI SHERBRO.   (Son.)
(Chief Medicine Man.)   (Children.)

(Chief Wife.)

Face p. 174

CHAPTER XXI.

THE SHERBRO COUNTRY.

The two Districts of Sherbro—Gbangbama and the Trial of Can-
nibals—Secret Societies and Private Marks under Thumb-
nails—The Kittam—Malaria, Blackwater, and Mosquitoes—
Superstitions of the Black Rivers—Daimah and Bamba—
Bonthe—Back to Freetown.

THE Sherbro country, owing to its many waterways
and islands—thus affording exceptional opportunities
for trade—is better known to Europeans than any other
part of Sierra Leone. For purposes of government it
is divided into two districts. Northern Sherbro is under
the Senior District Commissioner, Major Fairclough,
D.S.O., the genial and capable officer who played so
prominent a part in the 1898 rebellion. Sherbro Island
is under a separate District Commissioner.

The journey between the two districts is mostly
through swamps of dark vegetation and murderous life;
but in Northern Sherbro one has not altogether left
behind the unutterable loneliness, the unspeakable loveliness of forests festooned with fantastic tendrils, and
fireflies flitting through the gloom with their fitful light.

The town Gbangbama, a sub-district of Pujehun, the
headquarters of the Northern Sherbro district, was, a
short time ago, the centre of attraction where visitors,
friends, and relatives of prisoners assembled to hear
the trial of those accused of cannibalism in the Human
Leopard Society.

The importance of the occasion, the novelty of a
court composed of three European judges, of whom
Sir William Brandford Griffiths, specially commis-
sioned from England for this important inquiry, was
President—created intense interest and anxiety in the

minds of the people. The trial of the prisoners committed for murder and cannibal practices was delayed for an unusually long time, and there were great suspense and tension during the interval.

Gbangbama, the town in which the court sat, and which thereby acquires historical and traditional importance, is situated among lovely and beautiful country, and, from a sanitary point of view, is healthy. Comparatively recently the sub-district was removed from Victoria to this place. Both towns, Victoria and Gbangbama, are in the Imperri chiefdom, a country fertile and with luxuriant vegetation, but, unfortunately, with a bad reputation for cannibal practices. The quarters of the District Commissioner and the officers are built on a hill commanding a picturesque and beautiful landscape of the surrounding and adjacent towns and "fakkies." The soldiers' barracks are built at the foot of the District Commissioner's quarters, on a level piece of ground; the new structure—specially built as the court-house for this occasion—stands on the roadway leading to the neighbouring town of Gamgamah, which is about an hour's journey from Gbangbama. The site at which the court stands marks the position of the old barracks, where, before an outbreak of small-pox, the prisoners committed for trial were confined. The old huts were demolished and the site burnt before the new *barrai,* the court-house, was built. On the west of the court, at about a distance of 100 yards, are the newer huts constructed for a gaol; a long shed of about 60 ft., with partitions, serves as quarters for the officers in charge of the Frontier Force. The populated portion of the town is about 200 yards from the court-house and on the roadway leading to Victoria. Owing to the large influx of people arriving daily from all parts of the Protectorate and Bonthe, Sherbro accommodation was scarce, and many persons had to travel every day to and from Victoria, which is about two hours' journey. The court-house is small, and when a large number of prisoners, as upon this occasion, is admitted, there is no standing room for the public within its precincts.

About a dozen rustic seats are provided for prisoners and persons other than court officers and attendants.

The black man dearly loves litigation, and the arguments heard in this court on the occasion in question were dexterously bewildering. The evidence against those prisoners connected with the secret societies appeared to rest principally upon certain marks and disfigurements, the cutting of nails to the quick, and secretion of marks underneath the nails. Paramount Chief Bunting Williams, among others, was deported in connection with this trial. (This chief possessed quite a palatial residence, built and furnished in European style.)

There has been a system of assuming that if some native has some mark or scar on his body, that person belongs to an unlawful society; an idea which has resulted in numerous influential persons being arrested and kept in custody. Because, however, certain information has been furnished to some District Commissioner, that a scar is on someone's body, it is no indication at all that such person is a member of an unlawful society. Yet the theory appears to have been that a mark of any kind found upon the body when searched involves membership; and this idea has been carried out in operation, not only in places like Imperri, the hot-bed of unlawful societies, but in places like Pujehun, Kittim, and numerous other places peopled by Moslems of respectability who are averse to the things for which the Human Leopard and Alligator Societies exist.

The Kittam district, to the south of Gbangbama, is perhaps the most unhealthy part of Sierra Leone.

The Kittam River is dreary and monotonous, and the surrounding country is swampy and depressing. The water is inky black, the inlets thickly fringed with reeds where crocodiles abound. The open grass field on the banks, though densely populated, is low-lying and unhealthy. No other part, perhaps, of Sierra Leone is so infested with mosquitoes; water-deer, pig, and hippopotami are abundant.

Small-pox, both here and in other parts of Sierra Leone, is the most dreaded disease affecting the natives. The afflicted person is taken out to the bush to live or die. I remember seeing some natives with their faces chalked, and was told they had or had had small-pox.

A trip in this portion of Sierra Leone suggests an answer to the question, " Why has not tropical Africa become civilized long ago? "

Africa is near to Europe. Even in the times of the ancients there was a high civilization in Egypt which, one would have thought, could easily have spread into Central Africa. There have been plenty of routes of communication, both across the desert and by sea, down the west and east sides of the continent; and yet civilization never took a hold, but was repulsed at every step. Surely this phenomenon was due, partly, to the great tropical diseases of Africa? For these diseases affect not only immigrant Europeans; they are disastrous also to the natives, tending to keep down their numbers to such a low figure that the survivors can subsist only in a barbaric state. To believe this, one has to see a village in Africa full of malaria or sleeping sickness, or a town under the pestilence of cholera or plague.

Malaria amongst indigenous populations often affects every one of the children, killing a large proportion of the new-born infants and rendering the survivors ill for years; only a partial immunity in adult life relieves them of the incessant sickness.

In Europe, it is true, nearly all children suffer from certain diseases—measles, scarlatina, and the like—but these maladies are short and slight compared with the enduring infection of malaria. Nor is this all!

Malaria and yellow fever are only some of the more important tropical diseases. Dysentery, blackwater, elephantiasis, and sleeping sickness are fearful complaints. Apart from these more general or fatal maladies, life tends to be rendered unhealthy by other parasites and by innumerable small illnesses, such as dengue and sand-fly fever, filariasis, and other tropical skin diseases.

To describe or prescribe for all these complaints were impossible in this book, and, indeed, as far as prescriptions go, my experience inclines me to regard them as useless, each person having to find the cure which best suits him. A few words concerning a malady which I have not, I think, mentioned elsewhere may not, however, be amiss here. Blackwater fever is a disease from which many a European has died. At one time it was considered incurable, and no one was expected to live after an attack. To-day there are many survivors, but I doubt that it ever leaves their system.

The symptoms of blackwater are : pains in the loins, calves, and forehead; in several cases diminished temperature; tongue covered with an ash-coloured fur, or preternaturally red; eyes watery and suffused; the skin assuming a dusky yellow tinge on the fourth or fifth day, with great irritability of the stomach. As the fever advances, black vomit—like decomposed blood serum—ensues. Just before death, delusive ideas of feeling better, comfort the sufferer.

Many tropical doctors now attribute "blackwater" to excessive doses of quinine after several minor attacks of malaria. I am inclined to agree with them. A habit of drug-taking is like a habit of alcohol, exhilarating for a time, then causing depression until another dose is taken. Presently there comes a time when the exhilaration fails altogether to take place. But blackwater fever is falling off, I believe. As for malaria itself, much has been done to minimize it, thanks to the efforts of the School of Tropical Medicine, though their discoveries can scarcely be called new.

The connection of malarial fever with stagnant water was known to the Greeks. Five hundred years before

Christ, Empedocles, of Sicily, delivered Selinus from a plague by draining its marshes or turning two rivers into them, after which he became so disgusted with the world's ingratitude that he flung himself into the crater of Etna, to be immortalized in a later age by Matthew Arnold.

The Government also has taken elaborate precautions and laid down valuable rules for reduction of malaria to a minimum of danger. One of these is sequestration, already noticed. Possibly this might be extended further. A Creole sarcastically pointed out to me that " If the mosquito does not bite the European before it has bitten and extracted some poisonous germs off the native, which it then carries off to and deposits by its bite in the white man, then the logical inference is that it is the native who then must come in for the greater share of protection from the mosquito, if, as it has been found, he cannot be exterminated from the surface of his own zone."

" But the poor native clerk," said he, " has no share in all these governmental precautions and indulgence."

A German proverb has it that the best and safest way to avoid loss in a game of cards is not to play at all. If mosquitoes, fever, and the native be the drawbacks to Europeans in the Tropics, and as medical research has demonstrated that none can be entirely annihilated, then the best and only way is to stay at home. At least, thus reasons the average man. Fortunately for Britain, her colonial pioneers have been better than the average man. Ever may they remain so !

*   *   *   *

There is a sort of enchantment about the little township of Bonthe. Once there you want to go there again; and if you lengthen your stay there for two or three days, it is an effort to shake its dust from your feet. The town proper is, perhaps, a little larger than Kline Town; but as proper roads are being laid out, Bonthe is becoming quite a large place. There are extensive fields awaiting cultivation, yet few people make use of the opportunity.

To see Bonthe at its best you take a walk along Heddle Road (the commercial quarter), which gives you a splendid view of the channel, or along the Victoria Road. The canal by the Jehu Jones Bridge, at the upper part of this street, presents a delightful sight in the reflection of the moonlight. As for the people, Creoles, Sherbros, and Mendis are here in one grand process of amalgamation.

In two or three decades more there will be hardly one pure-blooded native of Bonthe. As in Freetown, Saturday is the market day. If you want to have a pleasant time you must wake up early and go for a stroll along the Mokolo Road, a splendid promenade, about three miles long, lined on either side by a thick mangrove forest, and ending in a 310 ft. concrete-floor bridge, which connects it with the once-famous town of Mokolo. This bridge, with the large sweep of water flowing calmly under it, and the thick dark forest around, leaves a lasting impression upon the onlooker. All along this route until you reach Mokolo Town— which, by the way, is a far more healthy place—there is a brisk business of all kinds, extremely interesting to watch, but scarcely profitable to the stranger who participates.

Bomp Lake, the popular name for the island opening on to the stream of that name, may one day be considered of importance as a shipping and trading centre. There are excellent landing facilities here. The water is deep, and if a pier were erected steamers could go alongside and cargo could be landed without that risk of loss which the present craft system involves. Another use that could be made of this island is as a signalling station. As, from its situation, ships can be seen at an incredibly great distance, their arrival can be announced hours before they come into port, so that business people would have time enough to make their arrangements. Of course, all this will entail some expenditure in the felling of the taller mangrove trees and the filling up of swamps; but the benefits derivable are surely worth the expense. I may add that as a trading centre, Bomp Lake is a point of vantage. From there one could easily corner a great deal of the trade from Bompetuk, Shenge, Jamaica Timdale, and several other towns. The French company used to do good business there once, the remnants of their old pier testifying to the former importance of the island. Whichever site our shipping friends may choose, there is one thing for which the public would be grateful to them, and that is the institution of a bi-weekly mail service between Freetown and Sherbro.

An important and interesting native family in the Sherbro district is that of the Margai. Mr. M. E. S. Margai was quite the merchant prince of Bonthe, and his brother Samuel was the Paramount Chief of Banta. Both had great plans for the betterment of their race and country, and Samuel was also a keen sportsman.

Superstitions, however, are still exceedingly strong in the Bonthe country. One or two of these are worthy of notice.

In the Black Rivers district there is a famous cotton tree, the roots of which shoot out across the road. Woe betide the luckless wight who stubs his toe against one of these roots. Next morning he finds himself a victim of incurable elephantiasis. This fearful cutaneous disease, which is very prevalent here, derives its name from the transformation it effects in its victims, the size of their legs and the texture of their skins resembling those of elephants. The causes of the disease are unknown. But it is useless to argue with the native that the disease is found elsewhere where cotton trees do not grow. Equally futile is it to stub your own toe against the roots of this famous tree. Either you have not done it badly enough, or you have discovered beforehand and used the charm or antidote.

Then there is the famous Diamah, about which a disappointed visitor may not express any dissatisfaction.

SIERRA LEONE POLICE WITH COMMISSIONERS HOOKER AND HOLLAND.

(*Photo by W. H. Seymour.*)

SHERBRO BEACH.

Face p. 182.

A casual remark uttered in a disappointed way, *e.g.*, " Is this the Diamah? " has doomed more than one such speaker never to see his home again.

Equally weird are the superstitions concerning Bamba, a place notorious for skill in black magic and upon whose soil no one may go shod. Whoever you may be, you have to walk there barefooted or you are a dead man by the morrow.

* * * *

From Sherbro the quickest if, perhaps, the least interesting route back to Freetown is by the steamer. In the wet season it is practically the only way. Rain in West Africa is something never to be forgotten after one or two drenches; and one welcomes the comforts of a steamer after the discomfort of a swamp.

Once back in Freetown, however, all the discomforts seemed to vanish. The sudden realization that the time had come for me to leave this much-maligned country reawakened all the pleasant memories of the months past. The chirping of the crickets, the roar of the buffalo, the dances of the Temnes, the superstitions of the Mendis, and the call of the bush re-echoed in my ears, and I would fain have returned to the Rokelle River, the Loma Mountains, or the Malema forest.

CHAPTER XXII.

CONCLUSION.

Causes of Recent Failures in Commercial Enterprise—The Wealth of Sierra Leone—The Decrease in Death-rate of Europeans—The Decline of the Creole—The Europeanized African.

WHAT, then, one may ask, is my general impression of Sierra Leone and its people? Is it a country for the white or the black man to live in? And which should rule? Are the people becoming Europeanized in habits and religion? Is it a place for commerce and capital?

To take the last first! The recent records of capital and enterprise in West Africa are nothing short of lamentable. The mahogany boom, and subsequent slump, the gold fever, and the depression of mining dividends, were bad enough, but the débâcle of the rubber companies has been worse, and the ordinary capitalist has become shy of investment in this quarter of the globe. West Africa in general, and Sierra Leone in particular, is being left to those big capitalists who wish to secure the raw material needed for their greater enterprises. Firms like Lever Brothers, Brunner Mond, Lipton, and the Co-operative Whole-sale Society have already secured, or are securing, concessions for the monopoly, within certain areas, for treating palm kernels by machinery. Yet West Africa—particularly Sierra Leone and Liberia—is full of possibilities for the smaller capitalists and companies; and tropical produce and minerals still await exploitation.

A recent Annual Report of the Colony concludes with this most significant paragraph : " It cannot be too strongly impressed upon capitalists and companies starting new ventures in a country like this that it is absolutely necessary to send out men who thoroughly know their business, as, probably, more promising schemes have been wrecked through incapacity than by any other cause."

Unfortunately, capitalists rarely read, and their secretaries seldom secure such reports, while the agents for the Crown Colonies will help nobody to secure statistics or other information.

The paragraph just mentioned undoubtedly touches the weak spot. The difficulties hitherto have been due chiefly, not to the climate, the people, or even the transport facilities, but to falsified reports written by untrustworthy men—who, in many cases, had not been near the place—to incompetent management, to the ignorance of the country on the part of the directorate at home, and, in the case of plantations, the absence of any residential visiting agency, as in the Federated Malay States, to check and advise the local management.

I have met a man who suddenly blossomed from a steward on the steamer to a mahogany expert, several bank clerks who suddenly became assistant managers of plantations, and various other freaks, appointed to managerships by "a friend on the board" or by the vendor. Given your planter, manager, or trader who knows his work, there is still the question of character. As long as the Coast has to put up with those whose habits preclude them from employment elsewhere, so long will enterprise in this Colony remain unattractive. But capital is becoming alive to these previous failures. The directors of Messrs. Lever Brothers and of the Co-operative Wholesale Society have visited Sierra Leone personally. If other leaders of enterprise follow their example, West Africa will no longer be recognized as a place to which many are called but few are "chosen."

As for the climate, Sierra Leone is much maligned.

Government and other officials and employés have frequently overrated its deadliness, and now that science has reclaimed the swamps the white man should, in the near future, be able to contemplate a more prolonged stay, perhaps one day even come to it as a health resort for certain complaints.

Every year the Government spends large sums upon the improvement of drainage and road construction in and about Freetown. But, strangely enough, while the death-rate of Europeans decreases yearly, that of the black man, at any rate in Freetown, is increasing. A committee was recently appointed to inquire into the infant mortality. The Sierra Leonean or Creole is distinctly declining in numbers. The quarterly returns published by the Registrar-General of the Colony regularly discloses an excess in the death-rate over the birth-rate. Compare the number of Sierra Leoneans with that of Syrians—or even Europeans—engaged in trade during the last few years. Here, again, is a constant diminution. Yet the number which leaves the Colony for education or trade abroad is not large, and comparatively few take up permanent residence in a foreign country. Nor, despite the efforts of the Government to induce them to take up agriculture, do they return to the land. Perhaps, if some of them sought to work lands in the interior which they seek to secure as concessions for sale, an improvement in this state of affairs might happen. For—if I may venture a kindly word of advice, tempered with criticism, to the Creole, who will, I know, read this book with avidity—I would say that it is to the town life, the adoption of extravagant European dress, drinks, food, and methods that much of the decline is traceable.

Apart from this, Freetown itself cannot be described as a healthy place, even for Creoles, though it is improving yearly. One day, perhaps, Waterloo will be made a more popular and permanent centre.

From the preceding remarks let it not be thought

that I echo a prejudice, very popular among Europeans, concerning the Creoles and the black races.

Much has been written on the necessity of Africans keeping to their native customs and developing along their own racial lines. A school of thought has grown up on the question, and this school has been very loud in preaching that the African must go back to Nature; that it is criminal for him to abandon any of his customs, that it is suicidal to the interest of his race for him to wear European clothes, marry according to the rites of the Christian Church, or the forms of the Christian State; that he must move, live, and die in the atmosphere of social customs created for him by his ancestors, and however stagnant the air, however insufficient and cramped the space for his present needs, the African must not struggle for a change, for the introduction of fresh air, the enlargement of space; the struggle for change must end for him in racial extinction and death.

I do not support this theory in its entirety, and I believe it has very little effect upon the African. In Freetown the primitive native huts have given way to fine, elegant and commodious buildings, built and owned by natives. Go inside these modern native houses, and you will find good furniture and everything in them kept neat, clean and orderly—the neatness and cleanliness varying almost directly with the enlightenment of the African occupant and the training he has received at the hands of European or European-trained teachers. These are signs of progress resulting from the inter-action of the European and Sierra Leonean, and he who would tell the African that it is against his native customs, and inimical to his racial interests, to live in good, comfortable houses, is not a friend of the African. As Europeans, with their enlightened ideas, have affected the Africans in the matter of building houses, even so must they affect, and are affecting and modifying, their social and political customs.

But while the African is partaking of the beneficial civilization of the European, let him not adopt it *in toto*. Let him eschew those luxuries and habits which may be pardonable in a temperate clime, but are quite unsuitable for the Tropics. Let him wear rational European dress if he will, but discard its dilettantism. Let him move freely among Europeans without relinquishing his religion.

From Wellington to Songo Town, and from Lumley to York and Kent, with the exception of Wilberforce, there is a marked deterioration in the village population that is sapping away at the pith and marrow of rural life. Some say the establishment of the railway up-country destroyed the prospects of the villages of the Colony that are in the direct route, but the western villages, from Lumley to York, are not affected by the railway, yet are fast reaching an equally parlous state as those on the railway route. Streets that formerly teemed with life and markets that were daily visited are now unused, except by stray persons. Farm and garden cultivation, which formed the bones and sinews of the districts in times past, have all but languished; due partly to the gradual but sure appropriation of lands for public purposes, the redemption of Crown lands, and the increasing desire of the inhabitants for trade, town life, and European luxuries in preference to agriculture and the simpler African life.

Much has been said of the laziness, untruthfulness, and dishonesty of the aboriginal tribes. My experience was the reverse. Perhaps I was more fortunate than other travellers. Perhaps I humoured the natives or adapted myself more to the conditions. An unreasonable master always gets a bad servant.

The black man will only respect the rule of the white man as long as the latter can prove his superiority, and, consequently, reasonableness. The European cannot be too careful as to his habits when in West Africa, both for the sake of himself and for the reputation of his country. The native is as imitative as a child and quick to perceive innate weaknesses, even if he does not immediately trade upon them. For example, both the servant and the soldier notice at once if their masters or officers take " liquor " on the march or on the plantation during the day. They feel that if you do so, why should not they? And when I speak of liquor, I may as well include liquid of any kind. The native is tempted to quench his thirst whenever he sees water of any kind, and bush water is often very poisonous. The European also is inclined to satisfy the same inclination as long as there is any palatable liquid near him. Now it must be confessed that out on the water, or tramping through the bush—but particularly the former—with a temperature of over 90° F. in the shade, the temptation is often very strong. But nowhere more than in the Tropics is self-control so essential to secure powers of endurance; and I am quite sure that those who control their thirst and only quench it at certain regular intervals are more immune from tropical complaints.

The same remarks apply to other habits of speech and manner. Self-control, justice and mercy are essential qualities for those who rule, and the black man soon recognizes these possessions. He may love display and ostentation, but he is not wholly deceived by them, especially as he becomes more educated, or learns the tricks of trade. He may bow the knee and doff the cap to the representative of British authority, but if he be expected to do this to every Tom, Dick, and Harry who happens to be white, the acts lose their significance and the Government is weakened thereby. Now, in parts of Nigeria every white man claims the deference due to the ruler.

This same unfortunate tendency has been recently manifested in other parts of the West Coast. I say " unfortunate," because I believe strongly in British supremacy in this part of the globe. West Africa must be worked by the African, but guided and ruled by the European. There are too many differences between the various tribes, in customs, traditions, beliefs, habits, and ideas for any one tribe to accept the sovereignty of another, or to form—at any rate for many centuries—a homogeneous self-governing community. In Sierra Leone, for example, the Temne would not recognize the rule of the Mendi or the Susu, still less would any one of the three acknowledge the authority of the Creole.

But all of them have a keen sense of justice, and are not blinded by hypocrisy. Neither the white man nor his religion must rule because they *are* white and not blacks. They must not rule for themselves but as representatives only. It is Britain that must rule— Britain which has one law for all, and administers it not for white or black, but for all people who own her sway whatever their colour, race, or religion. And Britain must choose her representatives well. For, if the various tribes have too many differences for political unity against her, there is one subtle influence always to be reckoned with—Muhammadanism. This religion, by its simplicity and remarkable adaptivity to the African races and their customs, has been making remarkable strides, and it must be confessed that the Muhammadan native is frequently preferable to the Christian native.

But Muhammadanism can never play other than a religious part as long as British administration maintains its best traditions and policy, and carefully selects its representatives among those who understand the black man's mind. This has been forcibly illustrated since the author first wrote these words by the attitude of Moslems and Africans in a recent crisis. When Britain was forced to declare war upon Turkey at the end of 1914, a mass meeting of Muslims of Sierra Leone, at which Alfa Muhammad Alghali, Sheikh-ul-Islam, presided, was held to consider the position of Turkey in the War. The Muslims of the Protectorate and of French Guinea and Algeria were represented.

The Secretary for Muhammadan Education delivered

an address which lasted an hour, in the course of which he referred to the hostile attitude of Turkey towards Great Britain, and the patience of that nation, previous to being forced to take up arms against the unprovoked aggression of the Porte. He dwelt on the total absence of any connection between the war Turkey commenced and the religion of Islam; spoke of the freedom which Muslims exercised under British rule, freedom they could never expect under any other Power, Turkey not excepted; a situation that should make every serious Muslim consider which ought to be trustee of Islam, Great Britain or Turkey?

Speeches followed by some of the principal Alfas, all in strong condemnation of the action of Turkey as unjustified and un-Islamic.

The Chairman cited from the Koran and the Traditions of the Prophet, explaining the circumstances under which a Muslim State might take up arms against another, none of which applied to Turkey in that case.

The meeting was unanimous in support of Great Britain.

Some of the natives of the West Coast of Africa are natural philosophers. The aborigine is not a genius, as a few admirers have pictured him, but he has a memory upon which centuries of habits and experiences have left their impression. He trusts to impulse and instinct, and believes things which we cannot believe until we have proved them to our own, if no one else's, satisfaction. When he acts upon his primary instincts he is very often right. Many of his customs are evil and bad because they are not founded on primary but on secondary instincts, which are the result of ignorance and perverted desires.

Some people find these the most interesting part about him, and a great injustice has, in consequence, in many cases been done to him. He is credited with all the wickedness common in reality to all mankind, and the good in him is not sought. If any kind of a higher religion or philosophy is discovered, it is at once assumed that it must have been imported, in spite of the anthropological recognition that people at the same stage of civilization often think and act in the same way.

Everywhere is to be seen a little stick, bone, monkey-skull, piece of wood, or other fetish hung over or in the native hut and canoe to keep the occupant from misfortune. These are often smiled at by Europeans, who forget that it was quite a common practice in England and Europe a short time ago—and not altogether obsolete now—to keep a horseshoe over the door for "luck." Even regiments have their "mascots," and many Europeans will not walk under a ladder or sit down to dinner if their number be thirteen.

Perhaps the most amusing illustration of this prejudice and self-illusion was afforded me by a European who prided himself upon his freedom from superstition, and even religious dogma. Upon my return to Freetown he commented upon the gross superstitions of the African. He concluded by asking how I had stood the climate. I remarked that it had had no ill-effect upon me and that I never felt better in my life. To my amazement he exclaimed, "Touch wood!"

The truth is that superstition dies hard in the minds of men. Christianity, Muhammadanism, or any other religion, science, or doctrine, only superimposes others upon more primeval beliefs. The new faith or ideal may last for a time, but with the majority of men, be they African, Asiatic, American, or European, old traditions seldom die. This is being recognized by the educated African after centuries of missionary effort.

The Lagos *Standard* says: "The Christian religion is at its ebb in the Protestant churches in Lagos. The Bible has not its usual place in the schools. There is no time now for Catechism among the infants, and ignorance of Bible history is most alarming. The churches are now only fully attended when some new dress is to be displayed, as when a newly married couple or a bereaved family have to attend the service in procession. The rising generations subscribe more to clubs and secret societies than to the support of their ministers." The true African, whatever his creed, never wholly abandons his aboriginal faith. I know of a native African clergyman, educated in the schools of Europe—such a character, perhaps, as Mr. Grant Allen has immortalized in his " Rev. John Creedy "— who, in his dying moments, exclaimed : " I die in the faith of the Lord Jesus Christ, and of the fetish of my fathers." That man died in peace, satisfied, as Naaman was, when, with the prophetic benediction, he bowed down in the house of the god Rimmon.

Probably West Africa will always remain a land of romance, mystery, and imagination. Science may reclaim the swamp. The iron railroad may open up tracks for the engineer and planter to exploit its vast resources. But Nature, unchecked by man, has been allowed too long to run riot there among its impenetrable forests. Never, perhaps, will it be entirely subdued. As with the primeval forest, so with the people. Muhammadanism, Christianity, modern education, have all tried their civilizing influences upon the West African, and nowhere, perhaps, with more success than in Sierra Leone. But the old Adam dies slowly. Civilization is too tame, too quiet for those who love noise and mystery. And this feeling is infectious.

As I sit by a comfortable fire in England and pen these concluding pages, I seem to see again the dark blue tropical sky, the mystic rite and the forest fire, while there reverberates in my ears the cry of the leopard, the croak of the frog, the hum of the insects, the drum, drum, drum of the Temnes' tom-toms, and the call of the bush. And I know I shall see and hear them all again. Kismet !

H. O. NEWLAND.

POSTSCRIPT.

PRACTICAL PLANTING NOTES FOR SIERRA LEONE AND WEST AFRICA.

Contributed by H. HAMEL SMITH.

———————————

I.—SIERRA LEONE AS A PLANTING CENTRE.

THERE are many who hold up their hands and raise their eyebrows in horror, or at least in doubt, when anyone suggests the West Coast as a suitable planting centre for investment and development by financiers and others on this side and elsewhere in the Empire. Twenty years ago perhaps there would have been some reason for such objections, but to-day I cannot agree with the determined opposition that one hears raised to such a proposition and to the lengthy arguments against any white men (outside the present *clique*) taking an interest in the Coast, especially as a planting centre, if the land is owned or the undertakings financed and managed by men from this side.

To such anti-Coasters I would point out that in a recent letter (dated March 2, 1916) I received from one of the leading agricultural authorities—if not *the* leading authority in Sierra Leone—the writer told me :—

" I shall be glad to give you any help with reference to the book you are publishing with reference to Sierra Leone, of which centre, as you say, very little is known at home. Unfortunately, the planter and the investor fall shy of this Colony, as it seems to have a bad name on your side. The chief cause of this is due, I believe, to those who came out, or were sent out in the past, knowing nothing of the conditions and the people before they started, and proving a failure whilst here.

" Let us, however, sum up the advantages of the place. To begin with, there are 4,000 square miles in the Colony proper, and 27,000 miles in the Protectorate area. In the former case the land available is limited in extent, but in the Protectorate, although the land, since it belongs to the tribes inhabiting those regions, cannot be purchased, it can be leased for periods up to 99 years, which is long enough to prove remunerative if managed by capable hands. Where large areas of land are required, an application must be first made to the Governor, as such (large) areas can only be leased by approval of the Secretary of State of the Colonies at home, but with small areas it is only necessary to obtain the sanction of the Governor.

" Meanwhile, it will be a good thing for the revenues of the Colony if you can make it known that there are large areas on the coast where coconut planting would be a paying proposition, whilst in certain localities cacao thrives well, and a native industry is being worked up in the south-eastern portion of the Protectorate in connection with this article that has done so well in the Gold Coast.

" Then, again, I wish you could make it known that limes thrive wonderfully here; so much so that I feel sure it would pay one of the big lime-juice producing firms to start in a small way in Sierra Leone by opening up a factory to deal with the limes that are, at present, running to waste. I have seen better limes here than I saw in Dominica, which claims to be (and rightly so) the premier lime-growing centre in the West Indies; this being so, well-organized lime plantations and exploitation industries should do well in the Colony. To show how the trees develop on this side, I can state that those on the lime plantation on the Government Farm averaged 7 ft. 2 in. in height at two and a half years old, as the trees have been properly cultivated; whilst elsewhere, when grown under ' orchard conditions,' which means that they get but scant attention, they average 5 ft. 10 in. high.

" Sierra Leone is also a good country for coffee. I wonder how many of the ' old folks at home ' know that this is the case, or, if they have heard that it is so, how many will agree that such a statement is true ?

" With regard to the cultivation of *Hevea brasiliensis* in Sierra Leone, the trees that have been planted are too young at present for me to be able to say definitely whether they will prove a commercial success; all I can say is that they are growing well. A fair amount of labour can be obtained in the Protectorate at 6d. to 8d. per diem, and everything has to be done by ' humans ' because of the tsetse belt, for, so far, steam or oil power have not been given a trial. As times goes on, however, especially with the help of such a book as I understand you are proposing to publish, I hope that all these drawbacks will become things of the past."

The receipt of this letter confirmed the decision I had already arrived at to devote the following chapters to a short chat on :—

(1) Estate Planning and Management.

(2) Mulching and the Conservation of Moisture during Periods of Drought or Insufficient Rainfall.

(3) The Cultivation of Cacao.

(4) Ground-nuts.

Other crops such as coconuts, tobacco, coffee, oil-palms and limes would have been included, but lack of space prevented this being done.

II.—ON THE LAYING OUT OF AN ESTATE.

IT is essential, before laying out an estate, Pape tells us*—and he is an authority who, having spent the greater part of his life wandering through the tropical zone studying estate management, is well worth listening to—to decide definitely upon the location of the factory and storehouse, as well as of the dwelling-house. The sites for these, for vegetable and flower gardens, for paddocks, and any ornamental or other spaces, must be chosen and pegged out before any planting is started, at least in the locality where the buildings are to be. Then, if the estate is near the sea or on the banks of a big river needing a wharf for shipping from, the site for this must also be marked out, care being taken that all roads, light railways, &c., are so arranged as to lead radially without interruption to the central spot where the administrative and transport buildings, the factories, &c., are to be erected, so that the produce can be moved about the place, either from the trees to the factory, or from the factory to the despatching centre, with the least expenditure of time, labour and money. It goes without saying, therefore, that all such roads, &c., must be arranged for and clearly marked out on the plan before anything else is done.

Do not grudge space for your roads, the wider they are the better for several reasons, and also round-ridge them well so that the rain, &c., will run off the centre as much as possible and not lie there to spoil your work and everything that passes over it. A wide road is the best preventative against both fire and pests. Even squirrels, monkeys, or rats do not care to cross a clear space if they can possibly help it, and the

---

* See "Coco-nuts : The Consols of the East."

tendency, therefore, is, if trouble does arise in any particular patch or section, that the vacant belt round often confines it to that spot until help is forthcoming to stifle it altogether.

If it is unwise to grudge money (when you have it) on making your road wide and wisely, it is trebly so not to spend sufficient on building yourself a really weather-proof house that will protect you, no matter how the wind may blow or the rains pelt down, as they can only do in the Tropics. Let in plenty of air, but avoid draughts; raise your living floor at least 3 ft. from the ground, and even then, if you are wiser than many men, you will build your sleeping room above this dwelling room. Again quoting Pape, I would tell you that to live in comfort and amidst healthy surroundings is more than half the battle in the struggle against the blacker side of Nature in the Tropics; that is, if there is a black side to Dame Nature, which I am not willing to own, provided the man does his share to keep her *au naturel*.

Keep your out-houses, *i.e.*, the lavatories, bathrooms, kitchen, servants' room, stables, &c., at a suitable distance from the house, and as soon as you possibly can erect a galvanized covered way from the house to them. Take care that every drop of drainage and moisture runs away *from* the residence, which should be built on higher ground than the surroundings, even if you have to make an artificial mound on which to raise the foundations of the house in order to do as suggested.

On no account build a dwelling-house directly on the ground without some ventilation being provided underneath it. In the Tropics everything must have light and air, or trouble through unhealthy conditions will arise.

Those who have read what Mr. Pape has to say on this matter and on " Health in the Tropics " in general in his introduction to the Coco-nut book already referred to, will also have acquired many useful hints, first on how to take care of themselves and then of their estates. Some men are stupidly careless of themselves; I knew

one good but foolish Quixote who gave up the best
room in his house to his horse, *i.e.,* the only room that
did not let in the wet. This being so, it was not to
be wondered at that he had chronic malaria. Why
he ever let his house get into such a state was a puzzle,
but since he did so, why he should sacrifice his own
health for that of his horse is beyond comprehension.

The West Indies are extremely healthy, taken as a
whole, but tuberculosis prevails there to a serious, but
perfectly needless, extent, owing to the lack of ventilation and the overcrowding of the negroes. Those who
are now busily engaged in protesting against the
Government's decision to terminate the system whereby
indentured coolies have for many years past been sent
from India to the West Indies to work on the sugar
and other estates, point with pride to their claim that
the better housing in the Indian coolie " lines " or
barracks, whereby the immigrants get more light and
air than the negroes in their " shacks," has caused
the East Indians during their residence on the estates
to be notably free from tubercular complaints. Whether
this claim holds good or not on investigation does not
alter the fact that those who have to do with large
bodies of natives find that it pays to house them
properly and to see that their rooms are as spacious,
airy and light as it is possible to make them.

In his chapter (No. VI) on clearing the estate before
planting cocoa, van Hall has much to say on the
pros and *cons* of burning off the growth when clearing the land that merits attention whether it is cacao
or any other crop that has to be planted. A little further on (p. 101) his advice on drainage should also be
carefully studied, especially where the lands are inclined to be flat and the rainfall is a heavy one; whilst
his plan and diagrams for planting out, if compared
with those that I include in " Notes on Soil and Plant
Sanitation," p. 14, will give the prospective planter
a glimpse at the more modern ideas of how to lay out
an estate to the best advantage under the conditions
there described.

Truer economy can be secured by taking care of the
health of one's self, as well as of the labourers, than
by trying to save on the cost of the buildings, so be
sure to clear and drain the ground around them in order
to render everything as healthy as possible. Dr. Mal-
colm Watson makes a very practical comment on this
point in the opening chapter of his excellent book,
" Rural Sanitation in the Tropics," when he tells us
that " the waste of only a single cent a coolie a day
(through illness) on a labour force of 40,000, means a
direct loss of $126,000 (Straits dollar = about 2s. 4d.),
almost £15,000 sterling per annum, and to increase
the efficiency of the labour by a cent a day means a
corresponding gain."

Since this is so, tend your labour force as you would
the trees, *i.e.*, house them and give them satisfactory
sanitary arrangements, although they neither appreciate nor wish for them. All the same, provide these
so far as you can, for it will pay you to do so. Do
not go slack because you are in a hill district. Dr.
Watson shows only too clearly how many estates have
been caught and had to pay the price on that account.
The general freedom of our West Indian island of
Barbados from malaria is claimed by this authority,
after a most careful investigation, to be due to a practical absence of surface water owing to the geological
structure of the island, and also to the high state of
cultivation in the island, the absence of jungle and
other, at present unknown, conditions governing mosquito life. To properly drain and aerate your lands,
therefore, means a healthier and far more efficient staff,
and larger profits for the owner of the estate.

Keep your tanks covered, and also raise them well
above the ground, and if it is necessary to allow them
to overflow one into the other, let the water pass
through a piece of piping. Do not let all the birds of
the air spoil your supplies, and see that the tanks are
fairly often run dry and cleaned out.

Having placed your buildings, roads, nurseries, &c.,
then look out for suitable places for your manure and

compost heaps, which are by no means a negligible quantity on a well-managed estate, for they increase the output and save money, whilst at the same time they often, and in fact always, help to remove nuisances in the shape of decomposed vegetable matter and even dead animals when not too large. I have written so much on the collection and utilization of all classes of waste on an estate* that I do not think that there can be any need to repeat what I said here beyond reminding my readers that the heap should be erected on a concrete floor grooved to run off any drainage to a small hole or pit (also concreted), and built in such a way as to facilitate the moisture as it collects being ladled out and thrown back on the heap. Such drainage contains the essence of the heap very often and must not be wasted, which it is, as a rule; meanwhile, whereas the accumulations that can and should find their way to the heaps is astonishing. Dr. Alford Nicholls, in his invaluable "Text-book on Tropical Agriculture," pays great attention to this matter when he tells us that waste products of towns and villages form excellent manure, and a good planter should be very glad to obtain them for his land; blood and bones, refuse from the estate slaughterings or elsewhere, decayed fish, hair, rags, sweepings, night soil, ashes, &c., stable refuse, all should go on the heap together with any green stuff, weeds, road-drift, dead animals, kitchen waste. . . . Its value may be increased by pouring some of the liquid manure over it and by turning it sometimes so as to assist the fermentation by allowing air to enter. Lime often improves it. Sometimes an odour of ammonia is easily discovered, and this shows that the heap is too dry and needs some water to be thrown on it. Heavy rains should not be allowed to fall directly on the heap, for that will wash out much of the goodness, which is often shown by the draining away

---

* See *Tropical Life's* series of articles on "The Utilization of Manure Waste, &c., for Tropical Crops," in 1915, p. 26, and in 1914, pp. 183, 203, 233, &c.

of the black liquid from the heap. Such drainage should
be collected and poured back on to the heap.

In concluding these notes on laying out an estate,
which could be extended to any length, as I am so often
asked about the placing and cutting of roads, it may
perhaps be as well to conclude with a few lines on the
subject.

In their work on " Planting in Uganda," Dr. Hunter
and Mr. Brown suggest in their chapter (No. VII) on
laying out a plantation that the plan to be adopted with
land that is fairly level is to cut it up into square blocks
by main and secondary roads, leaving each block of a
given acreage. " If this be the plan," they go on to
say, " a main road should first be made from the site
of permanent water—where a factory can be erected—
right up to the farthest portion of the estate, so as to
cut the whole field into halves. This main road should
be at least 30 ft. in width. On large estates more
than one road may be necessary, but in all cases it is
advisable to consider well beforehand the plan to be
adopted, as once the roads are made and the planting
done, no alteration can be carried out without much
labour and the destruction of many trees." These
authors then go on to discuss the question of hill roads,
and wisely suggest that the factories should, as much
as possible, be so placed that the loaded carts or carriers
go downhill to them and return empty for the uphill
pull. Hill lands when planted are, of course, subject
to heavy soil erosion, which must be counteracted as
much as possible by contour drains or by other means,
such as holes dug on the lower sides of the trees to
catch the silt which can, when the rains are over, be
dug out and placed on the upper side of the trees. It
has even been suggested that cheap earthen pipes and
bamboo lengths be buried in the lower portion of the
hole so that the water can escape through them at the
base down the side of the hill, and thus leave the silt
behind. Whether this is worth the cost or not I cannot
say, but if I made the experiment I would at least try

some with the spout rather at the top of the mound
or embankment, so as to run off the water when the
hole is overfull and leave the earth to settle and drain
in the pit. If the water does not reach the spout that
would be all the better, for if the water does not run
away over-ground the surface soil will not go either.

In 1903, Emmanuel Olivieri, in 'rinidad, British
West Indies, published a very practical treatise on
"The Cultivation of Cacao," which if not illustrated,
"put together," or printed in the finished style of Dr.
van Hall's book, or Hart's latest edition, was written
by an actual estate manager and planter, who has jotted
down the results of his experiences and ideas in a way
that can only benefit the reader. One day I hope this
book, like Mr. Hart's, will be republished in London
and brought up to date as it deserves to be, since, even
if there are any copies left for sale, the work is thirteen
or fourteen years old. The fundamental principles,
however, that it sets forth will hold good for all time,
especially in Chapter (or Part) X, where he discusses
"Flat and Hilly Lands—Drainage and Roads."

Often, he tells us, when planting on flat lands,
if natural streams or sufficient water outlets are absent,
large or main drains are dug as substitutes soon after
the land has been prepared for planting (and hence
after the roads have been cut or mapped out), so as to
avoid any risk of damaging the trees or their roots
later on.

In hilly or highly undulating cacao (or other) lands,
the same authority goes on to say, drains are only dug
and formed to free and open out embarrassed ravines
or water-courses and to assist in the emptying of surface
pools or swampy springs. This is on the principle
that I have just suggested might be tried on steep hillsides to avoid excessive soil erosion, the effect of both
being the same, viz., to let the water escape with the
minimum disturbance of the surface soil. Olivieri then
goes on to warn the hill planter against excessive drainage, especially where a moist and friable subsoil exists,

otherwise, as can be realized, more soil goes down in
the drain than would be the case if no drainage system
existed. In such cases pits or holes on the down side
of the trees might be preferable to catch the moisture
and earth, giving the latter time to settle in the hole
until the water, when rising, meets the overflow spout
and is thereby induced to continue its way along a small
surface drain down the side of the hill and leave the
soil behind.

I am sorry that I cannot reproduce here all that Mr.
Olivieri has to say about the cutting of roads on a
hilly estate with flat lands down below. Being well
acquainted with the lay of the land where he planted
for many years, I can easily understand his descriptions
and instructions, especially where he tells us that it is
only by a permanent and judicious distribution of roads
that the reaping of produce can be done economically.
Unfortunately, having made your mouths water for the
information he gives, I can only offer it to you in very
concentrated form as follows. Slopes and declivities,
he reminds us, play an important part in the gathering
of cacao pods, &c., which can easily roll down and be
lost or else take a long time and fatiguing labour to
discover, whilst on a well-arranged estate they can be
induced to roll down and often heap themselves along
easily accessible spots and so save time and money.
In every case roads and levellings must be considered
the arteries of a well-formed and established estate, and
the most hilly and steep lands can be made to enjoy
the benefit of fairly level, crooking (on donkeys) roads,
which, besides facilitating transport and supervision,
help to drain the land of surplus water and moisture
and lend considerable assistance in the gathering of the
crop. But to possess such roads the owner must make,
or cause to be made, a careful and minute study of the
slopes and hills, taking into account all depressions and
declivities which often constitute the starting points of
better and more extended levels.

III.—MOISTURE CONSERVATION IN THE TROPICS.

THE following notes are based on the paper that I contributed to the Dry-farming Congress held at Tulsa, U.S.A., in order to show planters in those districts in the Tropics that are either liable to droughts or where the rainfall is below the requirements of the crops, how they can improve the climatic conditions and secure more regular and larger crops. Many people seem to imagine that the Tropics are not only daily blessed with copious showers, but are also affected in quite the opposite direction by the tropical torrents that we hear so much about. On this account, therefore, I have been told, any steps taken to conserve the moisture in the soil lest the dry season should last too long or the rains fail to come when expected, must be quite superfluous. Those who think so, however, are quite wrong, and there are very few places that I know of in the Tropics where the ordinary Englishman can live in health and comfort on account of the absence of an excessive rainfall, that do not require at times, the methods, in a modified form maybe, adopted in the American or Canadian dry zones by the farmers to increase their crops.

Again, with planters in the full Tropics as well as those in semi-tropical areas, whilst the total rainfall during the twelve months may be excessive, it can also be, and often is, uncertain and capricious, so that whilst the trees or plants may be washed out of the ground at one time, on other occasions they suffer so severely from insufficient moisture that both the quantity and quality of their crops are reduced, or the trees are hopelessly spoiled if not killed outright through lack of water—the water, that is, without which the plant can neither eat nor drink. In such a case, if the usual fat annual profit is only rendered a very lean one, the planter is a fortunate man, for very often the loss of trees or plants is quite serious, especially when the irregularity or insufficiency of the rainfall continues year after year, as has lately been the case in some of the best-known cacao-producing centres.*

Tropical planters in many districts must, therefore, if they wish to minimize this loss through drought, study dry-farming or moisture-conserving methods in order to utilize them on their estates. These methods include mulching, cross-ploughing, rotation of crops, wind-breaks, reforestation, subsoiling by means of explosives, and the use of moisture-attracting fertilizers, as nitrate of soda beneath the surface with a mulch to cover it, so that no waste shall occur. This will encourage the roots of the trees or plants to remain down in the cool away from the *heat* and drought, and in the midst of whatever moisture there is, restricted though it may be, instead of coming to the surface to be exposed and starved, and often stumbled over and broken when they are left projecting through the ground as the wind blows the loose soil, now turned into dust, over the land and down the hills. Thanks to the dry-farming methods above mentioned, however, the surface soil can be kept cool and retained in its place by means of a mulch, even if only a dust mulch that remains stationary on account of the cultivation it receives; and many a cacao estate during the past few years would have increased their output and benefited their trees had

---

* Bahia, on the other hand, had at that time an excess of moisture, with the result that the floods did great damage to the estates and also to the railways and roads, thereby preventing the cacao from going to the port of shipment. Jamaica in one place was flooded out, and elsewhere (at a later period) wanted more rain. Trinidad (B.W.I.) has suffered from drought for several years in succession, whilst Grenada could often do with a more even supply of rain than she has received.

they adopted one or more of such moisture-conserving schemes.

Like a good many others, I probably use the term " dry-farming " in a somewhat haphazard and not always, perhaps, a very correct fashion. I do so, however, for brevity, and would excuse myself for this by various sentences in Dr. Widtsoe's well-known book,* as, for instance, on the statement that (p. 95) " the fundamental operations of dry-farming include a soil treatment which enables the largest possible proportion of the annual precipitation to be stored in the soil." This is exactly what many of my cacao-planting friends in the Tropics need to remember, so that they may be able to lay up a store of moisture whilst it is still there, for a " rainless " day when it is absent. Reliable experts have long urged, and are still urging, members of the various agricultural societies and others to adopt mulching by means of leaves, cover crops, or even by cultivating the surface so as to " break " that capillary attraction in the soil which brings the moisture to the surface and causes it to be lost. By such means that most-to-be-dreaded result of drought, viz., cracking of the soil (a serious matter that can lead to the death of the trees), can at least be avoided, and the water beneath the surface conserved and kept below to be diverted to, and almost entirely taken up by, the rootlets of the trees, cacao, rubber, coconuts, tea, &c., to feed and nourish them instead of escaping to the surface and being lost by evaporation.

Such methods would lessen the " change of leaf," which discourages, if it does not actually prevent, cacao and other trees from forming their fruit, as it saps their energy, which is (quite needlessly, I would claim) diverted to throw out fresh leaves. This causes the

---

* " Dry Farming, a System of Agriculture for Countries under a Low Rainfall," by John A. Widtsoe, President of Agricultural College, Utah.   Crown 8vo.   7s. 6d. post free.   *Tropical Life* Publishing Department.

crop of fruit to be reduced, and what does come along is of inferior quality, being less nourished.

Manuring also ameliorates drought conditions, and in this term I include the use of estate refuse, stable and pen manure, mulching, &c.; but in all cases precautions must be taken to prevent pests breeding in the compost and spreading trouble around. This can be avoided by mixing a little kainit, when available, with the manure, since this fertilizer acts as an insecticide as well as a plant food.

Taking for granted that you have the moisture safely tucked away under the top soil, you may still want to apply fertilizers to feed the tree and help it fight the drought. In this case apply it as much as possible in such a manner as to still keep the roots well down in the deeper, cooler, moister subsoil away from the dryness and heat of the surface. I have, on more than one occasion, discussed the possibilities of " drilling in " the fertilizer, especially nitrate of soda, which attracts moisture and gives almost immediate results, by means of rather deeply set drills following a cultivating hoe, and being followed, perhaps, in their turn by disc harrows or clod rollers, or other cultivating implement to form an even dust mulch to cover in the holes, and at the same time pressing this home to the desired firmness.* To do so you must have the land free of roots and plant the trees fairly wide apart.

As discussed elsewhere, there always has been, and still is, a tendency in the Tropics to plant too closely, whilst you want to plant wide—that is, remember, as wide as you can, so long as you do not expose your soil to the scorching sun and cause it to crack and the trees to wither and so give no crop, if indeed they do not die. To-day, thanks to the training and publications of the various agricultural departments that both

---

* Since I made this suggestion I have been glad to see that several of my contemporaries have supported me in recommending it, especially the idea of applying the fertilizer by means of drills to get it safely tucked away underground.

the United States and Great Britain have "dotted" about their Colonies, and thanks especially to what the "dry-farmers" have taught us, we have learnt many wrinkles of how to plant wide and still keep the ground moist, cool, and well aerated so as to give the trees those three necessities of life, water, food, air, without which they can no more live than the planter. The result is that, instead of talking of planting up estates at 6 × 6, 9 × 9, 12 × 12, 15 × 15, and so on, we have, with the latest books to guide us, already reached 30 × 30, or forty-eight to the acre, and the sooner that such distances are generally adopted—that is, on the flat lands—the better for the trees and the pockets of the planter as well as for the manufacturer, since the less strenuous struggle for existence gives the latter a better article with a lower percentage of shell and waste. It is only by such means, i.e., by scientific drainage (to divert surplus rains and water) and dry-farming methods (to conserve the moisture in times of scarcity) that we can expect regular outputs independent of the elements, or of whether the sun is shining or the rain raining.

"I submit," Mr. H. A. Wickham, the "father of the Plantation Rubber Industry," told us at the 1911 London Rubber Congress, "that the Hevea rubber tree has been, and still is being, too closely planted for a tree of its natural order and habit. Powers of growth must be arrested under such spacing, and the setting up of a struggle for existence in consequence of deficient root space in a way that constitutes a serious menace for the future." Cultivating and manuring improves the growth and vitality of the roots, and they, in their turn, invigorate the tree and increase its yield. Securing this invigoration and increased and sustained energy is particularly important for crops growing in the drier zones or land subject to drought or irregular rainfalls, for, as already stated, the deeper and more widely distributed the root system is induced to become, the greater is the amount of water and of nourishment taken up, hence the smaller are the chances of the trees being affected, much less of their being seriously injured by drought, and therefore the larger the crop and the more regular its output.

All this refers to planters in the full Tropics, where "dry-farming" is an unknown and even unthought-of science to many. Those who refuse to listen to the invitation or to study what this science has to teach us will, however, find before long that they were wrong, for most planters, often with some reason, since they have not trained their roots to go down, are strongly averse to cultivating the soil, as by doing so they are fearful of damaging and breaking the roots which, if not bad of itself, enables root pests and other troubles to harm the tree. I would maintain, however, that on the whole, even with trees whose roots have been allowed to become surface-feeders, the remedy is not worse than the disease, or that even if it might be at the start, it is often better to disturb them, as by doing so you can with care force them to go downwards in safety instead of continuing up at the surface, to die when the earth gets dry and hot winds and a scorching sun get access to them through being exposed.

If, however, you start right from the beginning all this trouble and loss is avoided. Lay out your nurseries or seed-beds in such a way that the roots start to go down, and when planted out in the open, see that they still continue in this, the way you mean them to go for all time.

The tropical planter may be glad to know that he is not alone in his objection to disturb and break the roots of his trees, for Dr. Widtsoe tells us that "a good deal has been said and written of the danger of deep cultivation, because it tends to injure the roots that feed near the surface. True, deep cultivation, especially when performed near the plant or tree, destroys the surface-feeding roots, but this only compels the deeper-lying roots to make better use of the subsoil. . . . When, as in arid regions, the subsoil is fertile and furnishes a sufficient amount of water, destroying the surface roots is no handicap whatever. On the contrary, in times of drought the deep-lying roots feed and drink at their leisure, far from the hot sun or withering winds, and the plants survive and arrive at a rich maturity, while the plants with shallow roots wither and die, or are so seriously injured as to produce an inferior crop."

I mentioned seed-beds and advised that these should be so arranged as to cause the seedlings to send their roots down, and not spread them out near the surface. Dr. Widtsoe also has excellent advice on this point as well, when he tells us (on p. 93) that " One of the chief attempts of the dry-farmer must be to see to it that the plants root deeply. This can be done only by preparing the right kind of seed-bed and by having the soil in its lower depths well stored with moisture so that the plants may be invited to descend. For this reason an excess of moisture in the upper soil when the young plants are rooting is really an injury to them." It has been argued that in many of the irrigated sections the roots do not penetrate the soil to great depths. This is true, because by the present wasteful methods of irrigation the plant receives so much water at such untimely seasons that the roots acquire the habit of feeding near the surface where the water is. Surface cultivation, therefore, must be resorted to, both to break the capillary extraction and so prevent evaporation, and also to drive the roots down and to keep them from running along close to the surface.

So much, therefore, for the advantages of utilizing dry-farming methods in tropical agriculture, even when the annual rainfall is heavy, if the weekly precipitation is irregular. India, we are constantly being told, would secure large crops if she manured more freely, especially her tea estates, as is done in Ceylon. To this the Indian tea-planter answers, " We would do so if our rainfall was more regular and certain. As it is we get too much at one time, and too little at another ; for these reasons it does not pay us to manure as our fellow-planters do in Ceylon." Could not such cases also be met by adopting dry-farming methods, modified, of course, to suit local requirements?

In conclusion, let me recapitulate where I propose that planters in the Tropics can take leaves out of the handbook of the dry-farmer and adapt and adopt them to their own requirements, say :—

(1) Lay out your seed-beds or nurseries to secure deep and not shallow-rooted seedlings.

(2) Cultivate between the crops to aerate the subsoil and keep it cool, and to prevent evaporation from the surface. Doing so will, at the same time, drive the roots downwards to get their supply of moisture and food.

(3) Plant your crops wide, even up to 30 × 30, to encourage big healthy trees above ground and vigorous and deep-seated roots down below.

(4) Grow leguminous and other cover-crops between your (wide-planted) trees to help nourish the soil, to keep it moist and sheltered from the sun, and to improve its texture and condition by ploughing in such crops when they have served their purpose above ground if grown for a crop, or when they are just past their full if grown as a green manure.

(5) When it is not convenient to grow cover-crops, mulch with leaves, pen manure, even with a dust mulch; anything, in fact, to keep the subsoil as cool and moist as possible, taking care always to mix some insecticide, including kainit, in the mulch to kill any undesirable insect or other life.

(6) In opening up your land to plant, see that the hilltops and promontories, the exposed uplands or wind-swept valleys are not cleared of their timber and growth, but that this is left standing to keep off the hot dry winds, and to catch and break up the rain-clouds. Also, when the rain falls, to divert the moisture down the foliage and trunks *into* and under the soil, instead of allowing it to run to waste over the surface of the ground, taking your valuable humus with it.

IV.—CACAO.

As with all crops, the first thing to be done when arranging to lay out a cacao estate is to see that the soil and locality are suitable. To be successful the trees must have sufficient water. On a gently sloping ground, such as cacao prefers to anything else, provided always that the estate is sheltered from cold, drying winds, the rainfall can be a very high one, provided it runs off and does not remain about to cause the trees to have wet feet. Too much wet is far better than too little, for in the latter case the trees can never flourish, much less yield remunerative crops, whilst if the rain does fall in superabundance, a few carefully constructed drains cut at right angles to the slope of the land should soon run off the surplus water, and still leave enough to penetrate the soil and feed the trees.

Since, however, mistakes will happen on the best-managed estates, planters should study the general principles of what is popularly known as "dry-farming," so as to understand how to check evaporation and by means of a covering of leaves, or even with a dust mulch, to keep the ground as cool and moist as possible, as is described in the section on moisture conservation, which I hope will lead my readers on to go to the fountain-head for full particulars.

The cacao tree is very sensitive to wind.* If, therefore, the soil and position are otherwise suitable, but exposed to stiff and especially to cold winds (I have seen the fresh young leaves curled up by a cold early morning wind just as if seared by a bonfire), the planter must either leave a stretch of the original forest trees

* See " Cocoa," by Dr. C. J. J. van Hall, p. 97.

to act as a wind-break, or else plant suitable trees (if bearers of crops, as the mango, all the better) to protect the main crop from its worst enemy. If a stretch of the original forest is left, this must not be too shallow, for, as is well known, the struggle for existence between forest trees tends to cause them to become surface rooters, and very liable, therefore, when exposed to the wind to be blown down. When this happens it causes more damage than all the winds put together, short of a Jamaica tornado.

Hart discusses natural wind-breaks fairly in detail (p. 26), and then goes on to discuss planted belts, mahogany, balata, mangoes, &c., giving up a fairly long paragraph to the last named. He concludes by telling us that "An ideal spot on which to found a cacao estate is a well-sheltered vale, protected by mountain spurs from the prevailing winds, where the land is well watered and yet well drained, with a good depth of alluvial soil on which rests a thick deposit of decayed vegetable matter, easy of access, and in a district distant from lagoons or marshes for the sake of the proprietor's health. The elevation above sea-level has also to be considered."

van Hall should also be carefully studied (pp. 99-100) on the question of wind-breaks, for he not only supports Hart, but includes several trees that the Trinidad authority (no longer with us, unfortunately, to discuss the matter) does not mention, including, it will be noticed, the *Hevea brasiliensis*. van Hall, quoting Fauchère, the French authority, says that natural forest belts left to break the winds should be at least 10 metres, or 32½ ft., wide, otherwise the trees are not only inclined to fall down, but to wither and die. The objection in some places, on the other hand, to these natural belts is that they are inclined to harbour squirrels and other pests. Johnson, again, devotes nearly two pages to wind-belts, and adds fresh names to the list of suitable trees. Such an experienced authority on cacao planting on the West Coast can well be taken as a guide. He, it is interesting to note, also discusses *Hevea brasiliensis* as a wind-break which, we are told (p. 23), at once suggests itself as a suitable tree to employ as a wind-belt, since it is not seriously affected by the wind when the trees are planted closely together.

Where the West Coast should score over other centres as a cacao-producing centre lies in the fact that it probably contains a much larger area available for planting, below an altitude of 1,000 ft.; for, although I am one of those who claim that the rainfall in most, if not all, hilly districts is more even and dependable than that over flat lands, the trees themselves do better below 600 ft. or 700 ft.

Hart very properly urges great caution on the part of prospective planters, when selecting the site for the estate, to first ascertain that the aspect, altitude, and water supply are satisfactory, and then to see that the soil is suitable throughout and not only here and there. As most men, especially at the start, are not competent to judge such a thing themselves, the aid of an independent, reliable expert should be called in and consulted, preferably someone connected with the Agricultural Department, if such an official is available. Whilst on this point I would like to add a warning, which is this: Do not be afraid to call in the plant or soil doctor. When going to a new locality ascertain at once whence the best advice is available, and do not hesitate to make use of it, any more than you would in the case of a medical man for yourself, and, when you do employ either of these good friends, do not be too close in your remuneration. We all have to live, and it puts money in your pocket in the end to pay your doctors adequately and quickly, whether for attending to yourself or to your stock or the trees.

Taking it for granted, therefore, that we have chosen the locality and are satisfied with the soil, we will then go one step further and discuss the variety of cacao to be planted, and then the nurseries, the moisture in the soil, and the final planting out at stake.

As regards the variety to be sown, I always claim that the best course to pursue is to choose a kind, whether cacao, coconut, or other crop, that has proved successful on land situated amidst conditions as closely resembling your own as possible and similar to it in quality, &c., taking it for granted that what pays best in one place will do so in another. The seed coming also, as will generally be the case, from a neighbouring estate or district, the variety will be acclimatized, which is a great advantage at all times and often indispensable. This being so, the prospective planters need only ascertain what well-managed estates have seed-cacao for sale, and then visit those that have, and take good care to see that the trees from which the pods are taken are vigorous, healthy, free yielders, and, in a word, those which in every way can give cacao just as one wants.

No one—or, at any rate, no new hand—should start to plant any fancy cacao along the Coast. The same type that has done so well in San Thomé and in the Cameroons, and is coming along so well in the Gold Coast Colony, should be the one to plant in Sierra Leone or elsewhere up and down the Coast. Once planted, it remains only for the planter to adequately nourish it with a manure (*i.e.*, food), cultivation (*i.e.*, to give it air both above and below ground), and water (*i.e.*, to see that the water supplied is available for the trees). Water is necessary in all ways, as I have pointed out elsewhere.*

van Hall, I see, also suggests choosing your seed from the best among the local supplies available : " The safest plan for the planter who establishes an estate," he tells us, " in a country where cacao is already grown, is to study the local variety and try to find its best and most profitable types." Any man planting in an English colony will, I am certain, always find the Agricultural Department for the district ready and

---

* See " Coco-nuts—the Consols of the East."

anxious either to supply seed-cacao, as well as the seeds or seedlings of other economic plants, or else they will gladly tell the planters where they can be obtained elsewhere.

We can take it, therefore, that arrangements have been made to secure supplies of seed, and, this done, the best pods must be chosen. When perfectly ripe, these have to be opened and the biggest and plumpest seeds only used. Those at the top and bottom of the pods must be discarded, and only the large, plump, and well-matured ones in the centre used, otherwise the results will be disappointing. Extra large beans are perhaps best left alone, freaks being uncertain in all cases.

Cacao, rubber, coconuts, &c., should, like well-trained children, be brought up in a nursery, where they can be better looked after and protected from the pests and troubles that beset their elders. Elsewhere I discuss the necessity of training the plants from the start to throw down their roots and go deep into the soil for their food and water, instead of running along near the surface, where the soil gets dried and blown or washed away and the sun scorches, so that the tree suffers and perhaps dies either by being blown down or from lack of moisture.

Where bamboos are available, the best way to propagate seedlings is to plant the seeds in bamboo pots made by cutting up bamboos just below each of the nodules or joints. If a hole is made through the bottom the roots can then penetrate, and when the time comes for planting, all that is necessary is to roughly split the bamboo in three places and bury it with the seedling out in the open, thereby avoiding any disturbance to the roots. By doing so it is not necessary to cut off the tap-root, as has often to be done, although many experts appear to think otherwise. I attach importance to retaining the tap-root, for not only does it give the tree a surer hold in the ground, but by penetrating lower down it enables the tree to continue to draw supplies of water, and therefore of food, from sources which are inacessible to those trees whose tap-roots have been cut short. On the West Coast it may not be so necessary to protect the trees against periods of drought; but in the West Indies, especially in Trinidad, I am quite certain that the trees would be healthier and more vigorous, and therefore would yield better and withstand disease more effectually, were adequate precautions taken to conserve the moisture around the roots and to guide the water to the rootlets of the trees instead of allowing it to escape through the soil and be lost by evaporation.

If the seeds are to be planted in the ground, choose a place well shaded from the sun, but not shut in in such a manner as to check the free circulation of air, or to cause a moisture-laden atmosphere to hang over the little plants. Such a place should always be available; it is often to be found on an estate that is already established, otherwise a suitable patch with a good quality soil of sufficient depth can be utilized if bananas are planted around to shade it, and cassava cuttings planted at intervals to throw out a leaf or two, just sufficient, that is, to shade the cacao seedling when it first comes out of the ground. In such a plot the seeds could, I imagine, be planted 6 in. apart, or if not to be removed too quickly, perhaps 9 in. would be better, especially when it comes to remove the seedlings for the final planting out, as the plants take up a fair amount of room once they begin to throw out leaves, and it is not good to allow them to touch each other.

Hart has a very good chapter on " Nurseries " in his book, in which he gives much good advice, but the bulk of what he says need not be mentioned here, as only those with an estate in the making need to study them, and I am only discussing the forming of a plantation with prospective planters. A point, however, which it is good to seize hold of from the very beginning is that it pays you well to rear up trees as uniform in character as possible, for the variations are many, and so are the disadvantages of having them.

Planters will soon realize the benefits, when choosing their seeds or seedlings, of aiming at uniformity throughout the estate as much as possible, and this, of course, does not apply to cacao only. Hart proposed to secure this evenness of output by grafting one variety of cacao on to another, and he reasons out very sensibly why such a scheme deserves attention. For anyone, however, on the Coast such a course is not applicable—at any rate, just now. What is wanted, however, is to secure trees right across your property that will give large beans, of even quality and size throughout, so far as the arts and attentions of man on Nature can induce her to give, and it is wonderful how careful and skilful cultivation of the soil and knowledge of how to tend and prune your trees will benefit and increase the quantity and quality of the crop you gather. Those, therefore, who are about to lay out their nurseries and start an estate should carefully note what I have said, and then see that the seeds they plant are as uniform in character as possible. Choose the best trees on an estate, and the best pods on those trees, and, when the pods are opened, see for yourself that only the larger beans towards the centre are taken. With such a process of selection much can be done to equalize the quality of the output of the estate, which in its turn advantageously affects both the curing of the beans previous to shipment and the roasting of them by the manufacturer previous to being made up for consumption.

In laying out the estate proper there are, as a rule, the forest lands to be cleared off by felling and burning, unless, of course, the plantation is to be formed by taking over a number of smaller properties already started. In any case, before you do a thing, go over the property and choose the site of your future residence, of the outhouses, stables, sweating-boxes, and drying sheds, &c., as everything else is of minor importance to the choice of the most suitable spot for these, and especially your own house. Taking it for granted that

a stream runs through the estate, then try and place
the house on an elevation as near the stream as possible,
so as to enable all water and waste to drain from the
buildings towards the spot where the water leaves your
property. Doing so leaves you free to have the water
to bathe in, to use for your stock, and even at times to
use in the house, as free from pollution as possible; and
always remember that, in the same way as you want
the water to come to you as clear as possible, do all you
can to let it flow on to others in the same state.
Remembering the joys and sorrows of estates I have
had to do with elsewhere than on the Coast, I would
tell you that the choice of a piece of land on which the
water comes out of the earth is often a veritable acquisi-
tion. On such a site I have known the owner to tap
the clear, cool water at the source and bring it to his
house, not in expensive iron pipes, but across the cacao,
the fruit, vegetable, and flower garden to the back door
tanks by means of bamboos, and when these overflowed
or leaked, the beds *en route* had the advantage of the
water, or it could be " tapped " on the way when it was
necessary to water the gardens. Unfortunately, bamboos do not seem to grow everywhere, but where they
do, a little patience and forethought will, with their
help, make life much healthier and happier on any
estate. After catching water for use in the house, my
friend then put a low concrete wall as a dam, and thus,
by holding up the river, had one of the coolest and
pleasantest baths imaginable, at no cost beyond that of
the wall and an occasional clean up to remove the slime,
&c., that congregate in such places on account of the
barricade. Below this was the bathing-place for the
stock, and then the river entered the cacao, and got
filtered before it emerged on the next plantation. I was
told that this was one of the last places to be planted
up; when I saw it, however, with its house, garden,
sheltered hills and valleys, &c., I should have thought
it would have been the very first one to be chosen, and
so did most people. If there is any truth in the saying

that it takes a wise child to know his own father, there is double truth in the fact that it takes a very wise man to always know how to pick out the most suitable spot for his estate when buying land.

The question of clearing the land must vary according to local habits, costs, &c. When possible, however —and negroes take very kindly to it, as a rule—the American " bee " system has its advantages. By such means the men swarm on to one place, and clear that in the rough, spasmodic way in which the negro shows to best advantage as a worker, then take a rest previous to swarming elsewhere to do the same thing. Negroes do not always seem able to work continuously, but they can work very hard indeed for short spells, and therefore when the "bee" system can be introduced for clearing the land it often works well, as it falls in with the temperament and moods of the workers. Before starting to clear, draw up details of what wood, &c., you are likely to require on the place for your buildings, bridges, fencing, &c.—and you generally want all your land can yield, and much more—and, having done this, go with the more intelligent men into the bush and mark any trees that it will pay them (and you) to fell and drag out previous to burning off, if the land is to be burnt. By doing so you save much time and money just when both are at a premium.

––––––

Now we have come to the stage when the land is at your disposal to plant up, whether it is virgin land that has been cleared, or smaller estates to be developed. The plants now have to be taken from the nurseries and planted out in their final positions. At once, therefore, the question arises, At what distance apart shall the trees be planted? A query that it is far more easy to raise than to answer. In the old days the stock distance in the West Indies was 12 ft. by 12 ft., equal to 302 trees to the acre. In hilly lands in Grenada, I believe that the spaces can be and are reduced because there is less danger of cramping the crowns as the trees develop, each row being, of course, slightly raised above the other. The whole tendency of the modern planter, however, is to increase the spaces between the trees, especially now that the theory and practice of green manuring is so much better understood and followed out. This is a great advantage, because in times of irregular rainfalls, which at some producing centres almost amount to drought, the ground can still be kept covered, whilst the leguminous crops planted both nourish and aerate the soil. I am calling attention to this because one of the things that must never be allowed to happen is to permit the sun to get at the bare ground. If it does so, not only is a serious depletion of the subsoil water brought about, but the ground soon starts to crack and that can be, and often is, fatal to many of the trees. Two of the principal *leguminosæ* recommended for planting as green manure, viz., ground-nuts (*Arachis hypogæa*) and cowpeas (*Vigna Catjang*), are often spoken of by the unthinking as being capable of supplying crops of economic value, as well as being a green manure; but this is a fallacy, or, to use a milder term, it is expecting too much, for green manure crops, if they are to give the best results possible to the soil, must be turned in whilst still green and before the crops have had time to mature. In a separate chapter I discuss at length the broad outlines of the planting of these useful adjuncts to a well-organized estate and the beneficial results they yield, for not only do they feed and aerate the soil, but also, with care, they keep weeds out of the way and thereby considerably reduce the labour bills. Many weeds are not only no advantage, but positively harmful, whilst they are difficult to eradicate when this must be done. Mr. Johnson, in his book, calls particular attention (p. 47) to the necessity of immediately removing the common nut-grass (*Cyperus bulbosus*), which, he tells us, frequently sends down its roots some three or four feet below the surface.

The best time for planting cacao, according to this authority, whose experience in connection with cacao planting on the Coast is unique, is at the commencement of the rainy season, as this gives the young plants sufficient time to become thoroughly established before the dry weather appears. We do not, however, seem to be told in his book at what distance it is best to plant; perhaps the author does not think it much good to discuss this point with the West Coast native planters, because, as in Samoa and elsewhere, it is notorious how very much too close the trees are planted; in fact, it often seems, by the photographs, as if they are really crowded together.

Hart, however, gives a useful paragraph in his book when he tells us that " the distance apart at which the cacao trees should be put into the ground will be determined by the planter in accordance with the character of the soil, the elevation above the sea-level, and the slope of the ground. The higher the estate is above the sea-level, and the poorer the soil, the closer the trees may be placed, and *vice versâ*. A distance ranging from 12 ft. to 15 ft. apart each way will probably meet all requirements, *i.e.*, 12 ft. in poor soil and 15 ft. in richer soil, whilst some have planted them even 18 ft. apart in extremely rich soil."

The saying that Providence helps those who help themselves is particularly true when a man is laying out an estate, cacao, rubber, coconut, or otherwise, and on no point can a man help himself when planting in the Tropics as in taking nothing for granted and carrying out experimental work on his own account. In urging this, I do not, of course, mean that the newcomer is to at once go contrary to all the accepted axioms of the district in which he means to settle, especially when they are based on native methods, which are the outcome of long and often painful experience, being truly a case, in many instances, of the survival of the fittest, and therefore worthy of the closest attention. Listen to all the Director of Agri-

culture has to tell you in the first place, then go and
see what the (so-called) ignorant native does in the
next, and after that, if you are of an observant nature,
you will possibly have picked up some facts well worth
knowing. All this, however, does not alter the one
fact, that if you want to get on, first see what others
do and then learn to teach yourself, and one of the
first things to practise on is the best distance apart at
which your trees should be planted, according to the
climatic conditions around you and the peculiarities of
the particular plots of land on which the various cacao
patches are to be set out. In some spots, as Mr. Hart
said, extra rich soil may cause you to plant the trees
18 ft. by 18 ft., or 18 ft. by 15 ft., whilst elsewhere,
for one reason or another, you may find it best to place
them in 15 ft. by 15 ft., 15 ft. by 12 ft., or here and
there, on rising ground with a poorer soil, at, perhaps,
12 ft. by 12 ft.; but I do not recommend them being
put closer unless the ground rises very suddenly, as
up the side of a steep hill.

I urge this because I take it that the land, by
adequate cultivation and manuring, will become richer
year by year, and even the leaves from the trees and
the weeds on the ground all help towards its becoming
so. Therefore, even if, as Hart says, you can plant 12 ft.
by 12 ft. on poor soil, but wider apart on richer lands;
one should not be in a hurry to adopt the closer planting, as anyone who has seen a cacao tree grow will
at once realize how easily the branches can cover the
six feet on either side of the trunk, and begin to grow
into its neighbours around, a thing that must not be
allowed. To economize room and to get in a few more
trees to the acre, quincunx or triangular planting has
been suggested, but it does not seem to have become
popular. Meanwhile, plant your trees as you like so
long as you do not allow them to become too densely
intergrown in the crowns. Too much sun on the soil is
very bad, but too little sun and air is scarcely any
better, and so the planter must make a close study at

all times of the ways of his crop when young, middle-aged, or elderly, and ascertain what will be the best distance apart to plant his trees according to the lay of his lands, the quality of the soil, the altitude, &c. Readers of Hart's book (Chapter V) will see that (speaking for the West Indies) he does not seem to consider that nurseries are so advantageous as I do. I believe in them because out in the open it is much more difficult and expensive to shade the young and very young plants and to keep pests away. It is everything to start with a vigorous young plant with a good root and well nourished, and those that are not so you should discard. This reminds me that you must always plant more seed than you want of seedlings, because some will not be vigorous enough to make you wish to transplant them, and others will die after being planted out. At least 30 per cent., I am sure, will go astray, and so, as you want to have plenty to pick out the best from, it is best to plant 40 per cent. and even 50 per cent. more seeds than you want plants to place out in the field.

When planting out there is the tap-root to consider, which if planted whole must go straight down, otherwise you will never get a perfect tree; if this root gets damaged at the tip and you do not want to throw the seedling away, then cut off the damaged end before planting.

The planter, therefore, must decide whether he will plant out from a nursery or direct in the field. In the latter case I recommend using the West Indian method of placing three seeds at a time around the stake (hence the reason of terming this method " planting at stake ") in triangular form, and then immediately plant three cuttings of cassava (*Manihot utilissima*), one over each seed, or similar plants, that throw out leaves before the young cacao first shows out of the ground, taking care when doing so to slope the sticks towards the centre of the triangle, so that they can yield the largest amount of shade to the cacao under them.

Whether planting in this way or from a nursery, the land must first be marked out and staked throughout. This enables those who put in the seeds to know exactly where to go and so saves much time, whilst you are also certain of getting your rows straight, which is important. It always pays, although it is somewhat costly to do so, to turn up the ground where each stake is to go, and to remove any big stones and other impediments that may be there which would interfere with the roots of the seedlings; doing so is beneficial also, because it enables the roots to make easier and therefore better and quicker progress through the ground. This is why, when young trees are to be planted, the use of explosives is recommended, for they, by the explosion underground, crack and break up the ground and so give abundant chances for the rootlets to develop and also to get supplies of moisture and plant food.

Having planted out your cacao pieces or fields, you now have to consider the best means of keeping the ground shaded from the sun, as otherwise there will soon be an end of the young plants. Under the contract system in the West Indies, the labourers who plant the trees are allowed to cultivate the ground and plant vegetables between the rows until the cacao is about four years old, when their shade prevents the ground crops from being profitable. Doing so, however, causes a certain amount of nourishment to be taken from the ground by the maize, vegetables, &c., and so tends to keep back the cacao, which is not desirable. In many, and perhaps in most estates, this practice is not carried out; but if not carried to excess the cultivation that the crops need goes a good way to counteract the drawback of the double drain for nourishment on the soil.

There is one more point to discuss, and that is the question of shade, a subject of great importance, but the cause of as much discussion as the distance to plant the trees. " To shade or not to shade," that is the question, whilst the general answer is undoubtedly in the affirmative so long as the supply of shade trees is not overdone. Excessive shade has, of course, the same effect as over-close planting, viz., it keeps the air and sun from the soil and the lower portions of the trees where they are most necessary, as cacao, the same as people, does not thrive well in a stuffy, airless atmosphere. The rules that affect the placing of the shade trees are very similar to those that guide the observant planter when arranging the distances for the cacao seedlings. The object to attain is to break the direct force of the sun on the plants, and even on the trees as they grow older. As soon, therefore, as you have cleared your land you must plant out bananas or other temporary shade, and then arrange for the larger trees for the permanent shade. The whole matter is too important to discuss here in a few lines, but all the authorities call attention to the need of caution, and it requires as much care not to overdo the shade as to see that all parts get a share. I recommend everyone, especially at the start, to be out just before sunrise and carefully watch the sun break across the field to be planted up and note as the day goes on how it spreads round, roughly marking the ground as you do so; during midday and in the early afternoon it is particularly beneficial to watch carefully as it is then that the heat, both from the sun itself as well as from the heated earth, is strongest. Having done this, then peg out how you wish to plant the cacao, 12 ft. by 15 ft., 15 ft. by 18 ft., or however you have arranged it shall be done, and then taking note of where your shade tallies of the previous day had been put, plant your bananas, not straight, but sloping towards the centre of the field on either side, east and west. In windy centres bananas are, at times, liable to blow down and damage the cacao, but this must be provided against, and possibly many planters on the West Coast will not wish to use them at all. At the same time, it is just as well to know what "tools" are required to lay out the estate, and then leave each man to choose the shape that he fancies, or which the requirements of the district seem to demand.

As the trees grow up they will need to be trained and pruned, and especially must they be trained to *horquet* or spread out so as to expose their main branches to the air, for it is on these and on the trunk that the pods come. Needless branches and suckers have to be cut away, and the careful planter or manager is kept constantly busy seeing that this is done, for if neglected the crop goes back and the profits are soon reduced. It is not at all bad to remember that every shilling allowed to run to waste on an estate comes out of the *net* profits finally, and therefore is a direct loss to the owner. When riding through an estate it is often surprising to see what a number of pods, coconuts, pieces of sugar-cane, &c., are left on the ground to rot and waste, it being apparently no one's business to pick them up. But all this is so much loss to the final profit of the owner, who should see that such waste is not permitted. Therefore, as the trees develop they require to be constantly inspected, and whenever any branch or sucker wants to be removed or pruned it must be done as soon as possible.

Always watch the leaf growth on your trees, for to keep that healthy means a great deal. When they wilt and fall out of season try to prevent it, and even when they must part company with the tree, it need not be done in too much of a hurry, otherwise the shock causes a set-back and your crop suffers, as the energy and life that should go into the pods are needed for the fresh leaf growth. Heavy rains following a drought cause much loss to planters, and the great remedy is to keep the ground round the trunks as cool and moist as possible in the dry weather by means of a leaf or even a dust mulch and so minimize the effect of the drought on the trees. Again, watch for any insect or other pest that may attack the leaves or the tree and have the spraying machine always at hand and in working order to rid yourself of any such visitors, for in such things a squirt in time not only saves nine, but ninety per cent. of the losses that some estates suffer through pests.

The books quoted in the Bibliography given deal fully with the important part that the leaves, and through them the roots (and *vice versâ*), play in the life of the trees and the output of the crops, but I cannot do more than just mention the matter here; at the same time, I again urge those in charge of an estate to tend their trees and keep the leaves fresh and clean, and if they do this, then, as a rule, all will go well with them.

Such matters as the picking and curing of the crop must be studied elsewhere, for I have not space at my disposal here to go into such details. By the time, however, the crop is ready to be picked the planter will have secured the best advice on the subject either through the books mentioned, from his fellow-planters, or the travelling instructors or other officials attached to his Department of Agriculture. The only warning I have to give is this: Do not let the trees yield too young, five years old is young enough, though you may let a few pods come to maturity at the fourth year just for you to practise on and get your hand in for the first real picking when the field is five years old. If you allow the pods to form before this you will only lose in the end, for the trees, like animals which breed too young, get old at an earlier age, and just when they should be at their best they give out.

Since writing the above I re-read the following paragraph on p. 95 in van Hall's excellent book on "Cacao," and cannot refrain from quoting it in conclusion, as it goes such a long way to confirm what I have said about listening to everyone and then trying for yourself.

"While it stands to reason," says Dr. van Hall, "that the experience gained in other countries should give the practical man hints for the improvement of his methods in some way or other, still too much reliance on such experience is a fruitful source of mistake, and a good dose of conservatism is the first thing needed for every grower of cocoa. In establishing and running a plantation, the newcomer would do well to follow the methods locally adopted. These methods may contain faults, but the latter can be found out only in the course of years by close observation of the home plantation and those around it.

" An enormous amount of money has been lost, and is still being lost, by men without local experience who want to improve on the old-fashioned way at once, or who adopt in the Tropics, without thorough experiments, methods used in temperate climates. In reading this chapter, therefore [*i.e.*, Chapter VI, on ' The Cultivation of Cacao '], the reader should remember the final exhortation of an old teacher of agriculture after he had delivered his last lecture to his students, ' And now, gentlemen, go into the field and see how others do.' "

V.—GROUND-NUTS (*ARACHIS HYPOGÆA*).

As regards the planting of ground-nuts, which in this year of grace and war—1916—seems likely to rival the coconut and oil-palm in importance as a raw material for margarine and other manufactured articles needing vegetable oils as their foundation, I do not consider that I can do better than quote from the instructions issued by Mr. J. Stewart McCall, Director of Agriculture, in his leaflet No. 4 of 1915, on the cultivation of the ground-nut (*Arachis hypogæa*) in the Nyasaland Protectorate.

Ground-nut, earth-nut, monkey-nut, or pea-nut, he tells us, is the fruit of a yellow-flowered herbaceous plant belonging to the Nat. Ord. *Leguminosæ* which is cultivated extensively throughout the Tropics. The value of the ground-nut largely depends on its oil content, which in a good sample will average 40 per cent. of the seed by weight. At the same time, the leaves and branches of the plant form an excellent fodder for cattle and sheep and should always be utilized after harvest. The origin of the plant is not very clear, but it is generally accepted as being indigenous to Brazil and also to certain parts of Tropical Africa, although never recorded as being actually found in a wild state. In a memorandum on the subject Professor Dunstan, of the Imperial Institute, directed attention to the fact that India, Gambia and Nigeria produce over seven million cwts. per annum, valued at nearly £4,000,000.

The flower characters are peculiar and worthy of consideration as they have a considerable bearing on the successful cultivation of the crop. After fertilization the torus or seed stalk of the flower becomes elongated, rigid and deflexed, and under the influence of gravity

(geotropism) forces itself into the ground, where the
ovary at its extremity begins to enlarge and develop
into a yellow wrinkled one to three-seeded pod. If the
ground is so hard as to prevent the seed stalk from
burying the developing ovary the whole part withers
and no fruit is formed, hence the necessity of keeping
the soil in a friable condition until the flowers are set.
The natives of Nyasaland seem to recognize the
necessity for this special cultivation and always give
more attention to the preparation of the seed-bed for
ground-nuts than any other food crop, and, for this
reason alone, the average results under native garden
cultivation are frequently better than in the case of
European estates where larger areas are planted under
ordinary field conditions and especially where the soil
is inclined to be heavy.

With regard to the soil suitable for ground-nut cultivation, any soil that can be kept in a friable condition
is suitable if it contains sufficient lime and humus; the
highest percentage of marketable nuts are produced in
sandy loams; soils deficient in lime if rich in nitrogen
will produce luxuriant vines but little fruit, and clay
soils are always unsuitable, producing small pods of low
quality.

In ordinary field conditions the soil should not be
cultivated to a greater depth than 6 in., but it is essential to see that the tilth is thorough; deep cultivation
adds considerably to the cost of harvesting.

If the soil be carefully selected, little after-cultivation
is necessary; three hoeings before the crop covers the
ground are generally sufficient.

It is all-important to have the plants so close as to
completely cover the ground when full grown and protect the soil and roots from direct sun; 15 in. by 15 in.
is a suitable distance.

Flooding is detrimental to the crop in Nyasaland, but
it requires bright sunshine and large quantities of water
at frequent intervals and gives excellent results in
Egypt under well-controlled irrigation.

Manuring the crop needs care and attention, for the high percentage of nitrogen and phosphoric acid contained in ground-nuts makes it an exhaustive crop in spite of the fact that the nitrogen is largely collected from the atmosphere, and the crop therefore responds freely to liming and manuring, although in Nyasaland it is generally raised without manure. In any case, care must be taken to see that sufficient lime is present in the soil before applying heavy dressings of farmyard manure, otherwise the crop may become too luxuriant to produce flowers freely and result in a diminished instead of an increased yield.

Since ground-nuts take from six to seven months to mature the crop should be planted (in Nyasaland) in December or January; early planting is recommended. The quantity of shelled seed required per acre depends on the system of planting, but 30 to 35 lb. per acre is ample with a planting distance of 15 in. by 15 in.

Harvesting the crop is by far the most expensive operation and no system yet devised can do away with the large amount of hand labour necessary for gathering the crop. In Nyasaland it is dug and gathered in a manner very similar to that employed for the Irish potato crop.

White ants greatly increase the cost of this operation by eating away the dead and drying vines and leaving the earth-nuts more or less isolated in the soil, thus necessitating an increased amount of gathering. The nuts themselves are seldom devoured by this pest, although the withered pod is frequently attacked; in fact, during the growing season the crop is specially free from insect attack but suffers to some extent from rust fungus.

After harvesting, expose the nuts to the sun for a week or more until perfectly dry, and do not shell until required for shipment as they keep better in an unshelled condition. Many inquiries have been sent out of late for a machine to artificially dry the nuts, which should be quite easy to do.

In the experiments at Namiwawa Government Farm it was found that the average percentage of exportable kernels was only 55 per cent. of the weight of the unshelled nuts, and at least 5 per cent. would be accounted for by the depredations of harvesters and shellers.

The yield of ground-nuts per acre varies greatly, and in experimental planting of the last six years, on several soils at various elevations, it has ranged between 200 lb. and 1,532 lb. per acre. It might be pointed out that the crop, being less sensitive to climatic variations than cotton and much freer from disease, is worthy of the attention of the larger land companies, who could, if interested, encourage their tenants by distributing selected seed and guaranteeing to purchase the crop at one halfpenny per pound after deducting the weight of the seed issued.

Under ordinary field conditions four acres to the ton of shelled nuts would be an average for Nyasaland, and the following figures taken from a 6½ acre block grown at Namiwawa on unmanured land in 1915 show the cost of production and value of the crop, the figures being based on actual working expenses.

COST OF PRODUCTION PER ACRE AND VALUE OF CROP.

	s.	d.
One ploughing	2	8
One cultivation	0	8
One harrowing	0	4
Three hand hoeings at 7½d.	1	10½
Harvesting and shelling	12	8
	18	2½

The total crop from six and a half acres was 7,318 lb. of unshelled nuts, which on shelling gave 4,024 lb. of sound shelled nuts, or a yield of 619 lb. of exportable kernels per acre, and at £13 10s.* per ton represents a value per acre of £3 14s. 6d.

---

* Average price on home market 1914.

From other sources we learn that various pests are liable to attack ground-nuts, so that although one need not be dismayed by the news, it will be just as well to keep your weather eye open so as to be able to check any signs of trouble before it grows serious. In the Gold Coast Colony, where the Hong Kong as well as the native variety is cultivated, at least in some of the centres, crows and rodents seem able at times to secure more than their fair share of the crop in spite of its being underground. The Agricultural Department in Nyasaland reports that a severe infestation of Pyralid larvæ occurred in one district. This pest, however, has an enemy in the shape of a parasite, *i.e.,* a small *braconid,* eight of which, in two laboratory experiments, were able, we are told, to account for over 200 of the Pyralid larvæ.

The sandy plains in Bida or Kano in Northern Nigeria, according to Mr. Lamb, its able Director of Agriculture, offer the ideal soil for ground-nut production. A yield of over a ton of freshly harvested nuts per acre was being generally obtained at Kano, and at Bida at least 1,400 lb. of kernels per acre were obtained in the 1912-13 season. A superior variety of ground-nut is grown in the neighbourhood of Pategi, Ilorin Province, which might be useful to draw upon for seed elsewhere. These nuts were valued at £19 per ton in Liverpool (March, 1913).*

The proportion of shell to kernels varies, some varieties of nuts give 66 per cent. kernel and 34 per cent. shell, and others up to 80 per cent. kernel and 20 per cent. only of shell. What the extreme proportions work out at I cannot say. A well-grown nut should give, apparently, 48 per cent. to 50 per cent. of oil in the kernels. The following table of yields

---

* With this and my subsequent remarks I am quoting from the *Bulletin of the Imperial Institute,* October-December, 1913, p. 577. Here the reader will find much information on the subject.

of dried nuts per acre was included on p. 579 of the *Imperial Institute Bulletin* already referred to :—

Crop			1910 lb.		1911 lb.
Carolina running	...	...	... 1,706	...	2,438
,, ,, (selected)	...	...	... 1,548	...	—
Gambia	...	...	... 1,479	...	2,041
Gambia (three-seeded)...	...	...	... 1,254	...	2,027
Local variety	...	...	... 1,670	...	1,789
Red Tenessee...	..	...	... 765	...	1,846
Virginia running	...	...	... —	...	1,836

Properly prepared oil, of pale tint, and cleared so as to remove the opalescent appearance, should realize, we were told in September, 1913, £37 or more per ton as an edible oil. In that month soya-bean oil was worth at Hull between £26 and £27. Cochin coconut oil £60 and Ceylon £50 per ton, against £44 10s. for palm-kernel oil and £37 for Lagos palm oil.

In Gambia, ground-nuts, which form by far the most important article of cultivation in that colony, alternated with the staple food crops of the country, viz., guinea corn, maize, millet and cassava, offers a fairly useful form of rotation according to Mr. Gerald Dudgeon, who was formerly Inspector of Agriculture for British West Africa.* The same authority shows that during the eight years 1900-1907 the Gambia exported nearly 300,000 tons of ground-nuts, valued at £1,800,000. A good crop of nuts in this colony is estimated at about 44 bushels, equivalent to over ½ ton per acre, but larger yields are frequently obtained. My readers should study pp. 5-8 in Mr. Dudgeon's book to see how the Gambia crop is produced and handled for export. This useful work also discusses all the crops likely to interest readers. Speaking of ground-nuts in Sierra Leone, the same authority tells us that in 1910-1911 practically no trade existed in ground-nuts, but efforts were then being made to reintroduce the cultivation into Bullom, where at one time a large

---

* See " The Agricultural and Forest Products of British West Africa," by Gerald C. Dudgeon.

quantity was sold for export. The cultivation of this crop is not carried on by means of the ridge system of planting in vogue in the Gambia, for in Sierra Leone the stalks are removed without the nuts attached to them, the nuts being left in the ground, a great mistake in all ways.

Regarding the outlook for the future demand for this article, there is nothing to fear from the supply outstripping the demand for some years after the War is over; in fact, it may be that the demand will far outstrip the receipts. The *London Chamber of Commerce Journal* had a very good article on this at the beginning of the year, when it told us that it is fairly safe to predict that the ground-nut is destined to become of far greater importance than it is at present as a source of table food products; this, too, in spite of the fact that the exports from India and British West Africa in 1913 amounted in value to nearly £4,000,000, about three-fourths of which went to France, whilst large quantities are also consumed in America. In the northern parts of the United States there is hardly a town of 30,000 inhabitants or over which has not one or more pea-nut (as they are called there) butter factories, so popular has the article become as a regular addition to the table, and it should be possible to use much larger quantities in the United Kingdom, where the consumption compared with that on the Continent is insignificant. As high quality ground-nut butter is reported to retain its sweet flavour for many months when packed in air-tight receptacles, it certainly should be a welcome addition to many households and prove well able to hold its own against any rival and perhaps to oust some of them. Those interested in the conversion of vegetable oils into edible products will find an excellent article to start on in the *Bulletin of the Imperial Institute* already referred to (October-December, 1913), on pp. 660-666.

BIBLIOGRAPHY.

In recommending prospective investors to study one or other of the following books on the crops and subjects of which they treat, it is not pretended that the list is complete; lack of space prevents a complete list being drawn up. New books also are constantly being added, and again, as it is impossible to study books in every language, and as no book has been included that we do not know personally, many have been left out that should be included. This is especially the case with the Dutch publications on tropical agricultural industries, especially those issued by Messrs. J. H. Debussy and Co., at Rokin 60, Amsterdam, which firm can supply any book published under the Dutch flag.

CACAO.

Cacao, by Dr. C. J. J. van Hall, Director of the Institute for Plant Diseases and Culture, Buitenzorg, Java; formerly Chief-in-Charge of investigations concerning the Witch-broom Disease in Surinam. With illustrations and map. 8vo. Price 15s. 6d. post free.

Cacao, by (the late) J. Hinchley Hart, F.L.S., formerly head of the Department of Agriculture in Trinidad. Pp. 307. 65 illustrations. Price 8s. post free.

Cacao: Its Cultivation and Preparation, by W. H. Johnson. New edition. Pp. 186. 12 plates. Price 5s. 6d. post free.

The Fermentation of Cacao, edited by H. Hamel Smith. Crown 8vo. Pp. 318. 35 illustrations. Price 11s. post free.

The Future of Cacao Planting in the West Indies, with contributions by leading planters in the West Indies, West Africa, &c. Price 1s. 2d. post free.

The Agricultural and Forest Products of British West Africa, by Gerald C. Dudgeon, formerly Inspector of Agriculture for British West Africa. Price 5s. 6d. post free.

Some Notes on Soil and Plant Sanitation on Cacao and Rubber Estates. Pp. 700. 108 illustrations. Price 11s. post free.

A Text-book of Tropical Agriculture, by Dr. H. A. Alford Nicholls, F.L.S. Crown 8vo. (Includes chief crops.) **Price** 9s. 6d. post free.

COCONUTS.

The Coco-nut, by Edwin Bingham Copeland, Dean of the College of Agriculture, Los Banos, Philippine Isles. 19 full-page illustrations. 8vo. Price 11s. 6d. post free.

Coco-nuts—the Consols of the East, with special sections on their Diseases, and on the Utilization of the By- and Waste-products and the Development of Cattle and subsidiary industries. By F. A. G. Pape and Hamel Smith. **New** and enlarged edition. Price 13s 6d. post free.

Practical Guide to Coco-nut Planting, by L. C. Brown, Ex-Government Inspector of Coco-nut Estates, F.M.S., and R. W. Munro. Crown 8vo. Pp. 150. Price 8s. net post free.

Spices, by Henry W. Ridley, M.A., C.M.G., F.R.S., formerly Director of Agriculture, Straits Settlements. **Vanilla,** Peppers, Cardamoms, Cloves, Nutmegs, &c. Price 9s. 6d. post free.

Maize: Its History, Cultivation, and Uses, by J. Burt-Davy, F.L.S. Price 27s. 6d. post free.

AGRICULTURE GENERALLY.

The Soil: Its Nature, Relations, and Management, by Professor F. H. King. Crown 8vo. Price 7s. 6d. post free.

Irrigation and Drainage, by Professor F. H. King. **Crown 8vo.** Price 7s. 9d. post free.

Fertilizers: Their Source, Character and Composition, &c., by Edward B. Voorhees, A.M. Price 6s. 6d. post free.

Dry Farming (or the Conservation of Moisture in the Soil), by John A. Widtsoe, Ph.D. Crown 8vo. Illustrated. **Price** 7s. 6d. post free.

Agriculture in the Tropics, by J. C. Willis, M.A., Sc.D., formerly Director of Agriculture at Ceylon. Demy 8vo. 25 plates. Price 10s. post free.

Tropical Gardening and Planting, by H. F. Macmillan, F.L.S., Superintendent of the Botanic Gardens, Ceylon. About 300 illustrations. (Includes practically all vegetables, fruits, and flowers in general use.) Demy 8vo. 32 chapters. **Price** 15s. post free.

In the Press.

Green Manures and Manuring in the Tropics, by P. de Sornay.
Translated by F. W. Flattely. Royal 8vo. Illustrated.
Pp. 436 + xvi. Price 16s. net post free.

Many books on manuring have been published and
should be studied, including those of Mr. A. D. Hall,
the Director of the Experimental Station at Rothamsted,
including his " Fertilizers and Manures," " The Soil,"
" The Feeding of Crop and Stock," &c., &c.

RUBBER.

The African Rubber Industry, by Cuthbert Christy, M.B. Pro-
fusely illustrated. Pp. 250. Demy 8vo. Price 13s. 6d.
post free.

There is a long list of books on the cultivation of the
rubber tree, especially the *Hevea brasiliensis,* which
cannot be included here.

The Banana : Its Cultivation, Distribution, and Commercial Uses,
by Wm. Fawcett, B.Sc., F.L.S., ex-Director of Plantations,
Jamaica. Pp. 287. Many illustrations. Price 8s. 6d. post
free.

Tobacco : Its Culture and Cure, by Killebrew and Myrick. Many
illustrations. Price 11s. 6d. post free.

*Industrial Alcohol (for by-products of all crops) : Its Manufac-
ture and Uses,* by John Brachvogel, M.E. Pp. 530. Illustrated. Price 17s. 6d. post free.

HISTORICAL AND TOPOGRAPHICAL.

Life, Scenery, and Customs in Sierra Leone, by T. G. Poole.
London. 1850.

Human Leopards, by K. J. Beatty. London. 1915.

APPENDIX I.

LIST OF JUSTICES OF THE PEACE IN THE COLONY.

Name	Profession or Occupation	Date of Commission	Jurisdiction of Commission	Residence
M. L. Jarrett	Medical Practitioner	Aug. 4, 1878	Sherbro District	Freetown
Simeon O. Lardner	Merchant	Jan. 31, 1889	F'town Police District	Freetown
Maj. E. C. D'H. Fairtlough, C.M.G., D.S.O.	District Commissioner	Sept. 17, 1894	Colony	Protectorate
G. L. Brooks	Commissioner of Police	Nov. 3, 1894	Colony	Freetown
W. A. Valantin	Native Asst. District Commissioner	July 3, 1894	Colony	Waterloo
N. H. Sawyerr	Retired Government Officer	Dec. 3, 1894	Colony	Freetown
D. F. Wilbraham	Attorney-General	June 15, 1896	Colony	Freetown
Ebenezer L. Auber	Clerk, Freetown Municipality	Oct. 21, 1896	Waterloo District	Freetown
F. A. Miller	Clerk of Councils	Aug. 6, 1897	Waterloo District	Freetown
C. A. Crowther	Merchant	Aug. 11, 1897	Waterloo District	Waterloo
Lieut.-Colonel H. G. Warren	District Commissioner	Aug. 20, 1897	Colony	Protectorate
S. A. Metzger	Under Sheriff	Sept. 2, 1897	Colony	Freetown
J. A. Williams	Merchant	Feb. 18, 1898	Sherbro District	Bonthe
M. Z. Macauley	Merchant	Mar. 15, 1898	Colony	Bonthe
Rev. J. D. Garrick	Clerk in Holy Orders	April 15, 1898	Waterloo District	Waterloo
Rev. J. P. Coker	Minister of Religion	Feb. 17, 1899	Waterloo District	Freetown
S. A. Macauley	Chief Clerk, Railway Department	Mar. 22, 1899	Sherbro District	Freetown
E. O. Johnson, I.S.O.	Colonial Treasurer	Mar. 28, 1899	Colony	Freetown
J. J. Thomas, C.M.G.	Retired Merchant	June 1, 1900	Colony	Bonthe
G. W. Page	District Commissioner	Nov. 16, 1900	Colony	Freetown
E. E. Evelyn, I.S.O.	Senior Assistant Colonial Secretary	Dec. 12, 1900	Colony	Freetown
A. P. Viret	Comptroller of Customs	Feb. 6, 1901	Colony	Freetown
C. A. Copland	Director of Public Works	Mar. 13, 1901	Colony	Waterloo
C. T. Reaney	District Commissioner	Mar. 27, 1901	Colony	Kent
Rev. J. N. Grant	Clerk in Holy Orders	May 16, 1901	Waterloo District	Hasings
W. V. Coker	Trader	May 16, 1901	Waterloo District	Freetown
J. S. T. Davies	Assistant Postmaster	May 20, 1901	Colony	Freetown
H. C. Solomon	Merchant	July 8, 1901	Colony	Freetown
C. J. G. Barlatt	Merchant	Oct. 29, 1901	Colony	Freetown
J. H. Thomas	Merchant	Dec. 4, 1901	Colony	Freetown
L. A. Fyne	Retired Government Officer	April 4, 1902	Sherbro District	Freetown
E. H. Cummings	Merchant	April 9, 1902	Colony	Freetown
C. May	Editor, Sierra Leone Weekly News	June 26, 1902	Colony	Freetown

Name	Profession or Occupation	Date of Commission	Jurisdiction of Commission	Residence
Rev. T. A. Smith	Minister of Religion	Dec. 13, 1902	Waterloo District	Freetown
Rev. A. E. Williams	Clerk in Holy Orders	Dec. 13, 1902	Waterloo District	Bonthe
S. Renshaw	Chief Accountant, Railway Dept.	April 30, 1903	Colony	Freetown
N. J. Spain	Retired Government Officer	May 14, 1903	Colony	Freetown
Rev. D. J. Coker	Clerk in Holy Orders	May 24, 1903	Sherbro District	Waterloo
T. C. Frazer	Merchant	Nov. 16, 1903	Colony	Freetown
Rev. S. Hughes	Clerk in Holy Orders	June 13, 1904	Waterloo District	Freetown
J. W. Campbell	Merchant	April 1, 1904	Colony	Freetown
Rev. J. B. Nichols	Minister of Religion	June 6, 1904	Waterloo District	Freetown
J. B. Roberts	Tailor	Oct. 4, 1904	Colony	Freetown
Dr. E. W. Wood-Mason	Medical Officer	Nov. 4, 1904	Colony	Freetown
Rev. W. C. Lawrence	Minister of Religion	Jan. 2, 1907	Sherbro District	Freetown
Rev. S. Williams	Minister of Religion	Oct. 3, 1907	Sherbro District	Wellington
Rev. I. S. Wright	Minister of Religion	Oct. 3, 1907	Waterloo District	Protectorate
T. J. Thompson	Barrister-at-Law	April 23, 1908	Waterloo District	York
A. E. Tuboku-Metzger	Native Asst. District Commissioner	May 26, 1908	Colony	Freetown
E. D. Vergette	Crown Prosecutor	July 14, 1908	Colony	Bonthe
M. M. Lumpkin	Retired Merchant	Sept. 4, 1908	Colony	Protectorate
F. A. John	Merchant	Feb. 17, 1909	Colony	Freetown
C. H. S. Vaudrey	Assistant District Commissioner	April 28, 1909	Colony	Freetown
L. F. Campbell	Supervisor of Customs	July 15, 1909	Colony	Protectorate
J. R. Wright	First Grade Clerk, Master's Office	July 31, 1909	Sherbro	Bonthe
A. S. Fraser	Assistant Comptroller of Customs	Sept. 7, 1909	F'town Police District	Freetown
J. Joannides	Mercantile Agent	Sept. 7, 1909	Colony	Freetown
J. B. O. Johnson	Retired Government Officer	Sept. 8, 1909	Colony	Freetown
F. H. Hamilton	Senior Assistant Treasurer	Feb. 23, 1910	Colony	Bananas
M. A. Nicol	Merchant	May 28, 1910	Headquarters District	Freetown
E. A. C. Noah	Mercantile Agent	June 29, 1910	Colony	Waterloo
J. C. Newton	Assistant District Commissioner	Oct. 31, 1910	Colony	Freetown
W. Addison	Assistant Commissioner of Police	Feb. 24, 1911	Colony	Protectorate
Capt. I. Heslip	Merchant	Feb. 27, 1911	Colony	Freetown
J. W. Macauley	Assistant District Commissioner	April 8, 1911	Colony	Kissy
W. A. Noel Davies	Barrister-at-Law	Dec. 14, 1911	Colony	Protectorate
A. J. Shorunket-Sawyerr	Supervisor of Customs, Freetown	Jan. 12, 1912	Colony	Freetown
R. B. Mackie	Assistant Commissioner of Police	Oct. 28, 1912	Colony	Freetown
A. S. Mavrogordato	Assistant Commissioner of Police	Sept. 10, 1913	Colony	Freetown

APPENDIX II.

REFERENCE LIST OF PROFESSIONAL MEN, &C., RECOM-
MENDED TO COMPANIES OR TRADERS IN FREETOWN.

Solicitors.—Mr. T. J. Thompson, Charlotte Street, Freetown;
Mr. Claude Wright.
Councillors.—Hon. J. J. Thomas, C.M.G.; Hon. J. H. Thomas.
Doctors.—Dr. C. F. Easmon; Dr. A. E. Easmon; Dr. Camp-
bell.
Photographers.—Mr. Lisk Carew, East Brook Lane.
Newspapers.—*Colony and Provincial Reporter* (Charlotte
Street); *Weekly News; Guardian.*

APPENDIX III.

LAWS FOR THE GUIDANCE OF TRADERS AND OTHERS.

I.—AN ORDINANCE TO AMEND THE SUMMARY CONVICTION
OFFENCES ORDINANCE, 1906.

Be it enacted by the Governor of the Colony of Sierra Leone,
with the advice and consent of the Legislative Council thereof,
as follows:—
1. This Ordinance may be cited as the Summary Conviction
Offences (Amendment) Ordinance, 1913.
2. Any person who shall be guilty of any riotous, disorderly,
or indecent behaviour in any thoroughfare, or in any public
place or place of public amusement or resort, shall, on conviction
thereof, be liable to a fine not exceeding forty shillings.
3. (1) No person shall sound or play upon any musical instrument or noisy instrument or sing in any street before the hour
of six in the morning or after the hour of ten in the evening.
Any person contravening this section shall, on conviction thereof,
be liable to a fine not exceeding twenty shillings. (2) Any person
who shall wilfully or wantonly, and after being warned to desist,
ring any bell or blow any horn or shell or sound or play upon
any musical or noisy instrument or shout or sing or make any
other loud or unseemly noise to the annoyance or disturbance
of any person shall, on conviction thereof, be liable to a fine not
exceeding twenty shillings: Provided that this section shall not
apply to the ringing of the bell of any church or chapel either

for divine service or for the purpose of making an alarm in case of an outbreak of fire. (3) Any person found committing an offence against this and the preceding section may be taken into custody without warrant by any constable or other peace officer.

4. It shall be unlawful for any band of music to parade the streets of the City without the written permission of the Commissioner of the Police or any officer acting for him first had and obtained, and any person having the charge or control of any such band which parades the streets of the City without such permission, and shall wilfully refuse to desist when called upon to do so by any police constable or other person duly authorized, shall be guilty of an offence and on conviction thereof shall be liable to a penalty not exceeding forty shillings. Provided that nothing in this section shall be deemed to apply to any military band, bugle, fife or drum.

5. This Ordinance shall only apply to the City of Freetown, but may hereafter from time to time be applied by Order of the Governor-in-Council to any other place or places in the Colony.

II.—An Ordinance to make provision for the Grant of Exclusive Rights for the Erection of Mills for the Extraction of Oil from Palm Fruit.

In His Majesty's name I assent to this Ordinance this Twelfth day of March, 1913.

E. M. Merewether, *Governor.*

Be it enacted by the Governor of the Colony of Sierra Leone, with the advice and consent of the Legislative Council thereof, as follows :—

1. This Ordinance may be cited as the Palm Oil Ordinance, 1913.

2. In this Ordinance, unless the context otherwise requires, " Court " means the Circuit Court of the Protectorate.

" Grantee " means any person to whom a grant has been made under this Ordinance and his permitted assigns.

"Protectorate " means the places and territories to and in which the provisions of the Protectorate Ordinance, 1901, apply and are exercised.

" Tribal Authority " has the same meaning as in the Protectorate Native Law Ordinance, 1905.

3. (1) Subject as in this Ordinance provided, it shall be lawful for the Governor, with the concurrence of the Tribal Authority, to grant to any person, within such area in the Protectorate not exceeding a circle with a ten-mile radius and for such period not exceeding twenty-one years from the date of the grant and upon such terms and subject to such conditions as the Governor may

think fit, the exclusive right to construct and work mills, to be operated by mechanical power, for expressing or extracting oil from the pericarp of palm fruit. (2) The Governor may, with the like concurrence at the expiration of any such grant, renew the same for such further period not exceeding twenty-one years from the date of renewal, and upon such terms and subject to such conditions as he may think fit.

4. Whenever it is proposed to grant any exclusive rights or any renewal thereof under the provisions of section 3 hereof, a notice shall be published in the *Gazette* for a period of three consecutive months specifying the rights which it is proposed to grant, the person to whom and the area in respect of which they are to be granted. Any person objecting to any such grant may, within such period, give notice of such objection to the District Commissioner of the district in which the area affected thereby is situated, and shall in such notice specify the grounds of his objection. No such grant shall be made by the Governor until the expiration of such period of three months : Provided always that nothing in this section shall be deemed to apply to any grant of exclusive rights which shall have been approved by the Governor before this Ordinance comes into force.

5. Nothing in this Ordinance shall confer, or authorize the Governor to confer by any grant under this Ordinance, any right, interest, or property in or over any land or the products of the soil of any land.

6. No transfer shall be made of any right granted under this Ordinance without the consent in writing of the Governor.

7. No grant shall be made, and no transfer shall be permitted of any right granted under this Ordinance in respect of any area, to any person who, at the time when such grant or transfer is proposed, is entitled to or has a substantial interest in any rights granted under this Ordinance in respect of any area, any part of which is within fifty miles of any part of such first-mentioned area.

8. From after the date of any grant under this Ordinance, it shall, so long as such grant shall be valid and subsisting, be unlawful for any person, other than the grantee, to do within the area of the grant any act the exclusive right to do which is by the grant vested in the grantee, and any person contravening the provisions of this section shall be liable on summary conviction to a fine of Five hundred pounds for any mill constructed or commenced in contravention of such provisions, and to a fine of Twenty pounds for any day during which any mill shall be worked in contravention of such provisions, and all plant, materials, and things used in the commission of any offence under this section shall be liable to forfeiture.

9. If it shall appear to the Governor at any time after a lapse

of two years from the making of any grant that no satisfactory provision has been made for the treatment of the palm fruit within the area of such grant, or that the treatment of such fruit is not being sufficiently or satisfactorily carried on, it shall be lawful for the Governor to apply to the Court for a declaration that the said grant is forfeited, and the Court, on proof being made to its satisfaction of the failure to make such provision or carry on such treatment as aforesaid, unless it shall be considered that such failure has been caused by reasons beyond the control of the grantee, shall declare such rights to be forfeited, and all rights under such grant shall thereupon cease and determine. For the purposes of this section want of funds shall not be deemed a reason beyond control.

10. Every grantee not ordinarily resident in the Colony or Protectorate shall appoint an attorney to represent him in all matters relating to his grant, and notice in writing of such appointment and of any change in such appointment shall be given to the Colonial Secretary.

11. No officer of the Sierra Leone Government shall acquire or hold any right or interest under any grant during the tenure of his office or for five years thereafter, and any grant purporting to confer any such right or interest upon any such officer shall be void.

12. (1) The Governor-in-Council shall have power to make rules for the following purposes, viz. :—

(a) Prescribing the form of application for a grant under this Ordinance.

(b) Providing for the taking of a survey of any area within which it is proposed to make a grant under this Ordinance and for the payment of the expenses incurred in connection therewith.

(c) Providing for the collection of any duty on profits or other payment to be made by the grantee.

(d) Providing for any returns to be made by the grantee and any inspection of any area by the Government for the purpose of satisfying it that sufficient and satisfactory provision has been made for the treatment of palm fruit within the area of any grant and that the treatment of such fruit is being sufficiently and satisfactorily carried out.

(e) Generally for the more effectual carrying out of the provisions of this Ordinance.

(2) By any rule made under the provisions of this section a penalty may be imposed on summary conviction for the breach of such rules which shall not exceed Fifty pounds for any one offence, or, in the case of a continuing offence, Five pounds for every day during which the offence is continued.

III.—An Ordinance to Amend the Firearms, Ammunition, Gunpowder, and Munitions of War Ordinance, 1908.

In His Majesty's name I assent to this Ordinance this Twelfth day of March, 1913.

E. M. Merewether, *Governor.*

Be it enacted by the Governor of the Colony of Sierra Leone, with the advice and consent of the Legislative Council thereof, as follows :—

1. This Ordinance may be cited as the Firearms, Ammunition, Gunpowder, and Munitions of War (Amendment) Ordinance, 1913.

2. After section 30 of the Firearms, Ammunition, Gunpowder, and Munitions of War Ordinance, 1908, the following shall be added as a separate section, and shall be numbered 30A :—

30A. (1) Whenever it shall appear to be necessary for the preservation of the public peace in any part of the Protectorate, the Governor-in-Council may from time to time make orders prohibiting the sale of common gunpowder in any part of the Protectorate for such period as he may think fit.

(2) Any person selling any common gunpowder in contravention of any such order shall be liable, on summary conviction thereof before a District Commissioner, to a fine not exceeding One hundred pounds or to imprisonment, with or without hard labour, for a period not exceeding twelve months.

(3) Whenever an order shall be made under this section, the Governor may in his discretion refund to the holder of a licence under section 24 of this Ordinance an amount which shall have the like proportion to the amount paid for the licence as the period during which the order continues in force bears to the period for which the licence was granted.

INDEX.